P9-BYK-600

STUDY GUIDE

FOR

EDUCATIONAL PSYCHOLOGY

STUDY GUIDE
FOR
WOOLFOLK

EDUCATIONAL PSYCHOLOGY
SEVENTH EDITION

PREPARED BY
ELIZABETH MOWRER-POPIEL
UNIVERSITY OF IDAHO

ALLYN AND BACON
BOSTON • LONDON • TORONTO • SYDNEY • TOKYO • SINGAPORE

Copyright © 1998, 1995, 1993, 1990, 1987, 1984, 1980 by Allyn & Bacon
A Viacom Company
160 Gould Street
Needham Heights, MA 02194

Internet: www.abacon.com
America Online: keyword: College Online

All rights reserved. No part of the material protected by this copyright notice may be
reproduced or utilized in any form or by any means, electronic or mechanical, including
photocopying, recording, or by any information storage and retrieval system, without written
permission from the copyright owner.

ISBN 0-205-26338-0

Printed in the United States of America

10 9 8 7 6 5 4 3 2 1   02 01 00 99 98 97

Table of Contents

Preface

Whether you are pre-service educators or lifelong learners in another subject area, *Educational Psychology, 7th Edition* by Anita Woolfolk, can provide you with understanding and insights into the human intellectual process and variables that influence the individual quality of that process. Your text and the field of educational psychology in general, encompass a broad spectrum of topics; theories of learning and instruction, personal, social, and intellectual development, classroom management, motivation, intellectual assessment, cognition, multiculturalism, and special populations, to name but a few. Given this vast amount of information, it is helpful to students if their exposure and subsequent comprehension of the research-supported theories and principles, be presented in a well-organized , easily understood format with many concrete, real-life examples.

In an effort to complement your text, I have surveyed my students about which study guide features they believe to be most beneficial. They suggested that a study guide worth purchasing should enhance their learning and performance within the class. Summaries of key chapter information along with exercises designed to inform students about how successfully they comprehend the material, appear to be valuable aids in the test preparation process. All key terms are in bold and wherever possible, practical examples follow the key term definitions. Essay questions frequently address the point/counterpoint topics within the chapter and require knowledge, comprehension, analysis, and synthesis from Bloom's taxonomy from the cognitive domain.

A recommended approach for the most effective studying and learning would be to first read your chapters from the text, highlighting one sentence per paragraph, stopping at the end of each and using metacognitive skills to check your levels of comprehension. Jot down notes, thoughts, etc., in the page margins or in your notebook and transform the information into your own words. Read the corresponding chapters in the study guide and complete the exercises and applications. Where errors occur, return to your text for clarification. Before you begin to read chapter one, you may want to read the section in chapter 8 of your text entitled *Becoming an Expert Student: Learning Strategies and Study Skills*.

Lastly, remember that the development of expert teaching skills will result from your day-to-day interactions with students but that it has its origins in your fundamental understanding of the principles and theories that guide your classroom practice. These principles and theories are generated from ongoing research within the field of Educational Psychology.

Acknowledgements

To the following individuals I'd like to extend my sincerest appreciation and thanks:

- my beautiful daughter, Cali, for her patience and understanding, her willingness to eat frozen pizza, and for the exceptional job she did with every flow chart in the book. Phil and Louise Mowrer (Mom and Dad) for their endless love and encouragement.
- Dean Dale Gentry, Dr. Lowell Jackson, and Dr. Pat White for making this entire process possible and for helping me to achieve my goals.
- Dr. Anita Woolfolk, without whose outstanding, top-notch text and continuing support, this would have never come to fruition. You're my revered mentor!
- Alicia Reilly at Allyn & Bacon, it has been a genuine pleasure, you made it easy.
- my wonderful students who teach me how to be a lifelong learner and the best teacher that I can be.
- my Grandfather, Paul Waters. In loving memory, I dedicate this text.

Quotations

The quotations used at the beginning of every chapter were compiled from a number of sources. G. Lieberman, GOOD QUOTES FOR SPEAKERS. New York, Doubleday, 1983. H.G. Furth, PIAGET AND KNOWLEDGE. Chicago, University of Chicago Press, 1981. Cable News Network, CBS, and sources unknown.

STUDY GUIDE
FOR

EDUCATIONAL PSYCHOLOGY

Chapter One

Teachers, Teaching, and Educational Psychology

"To teach is to learn twice."
Joseph Joubert   (A French moralist and teacher, 1754-1824) .

Novice and Expert Teachers

If you are studying to become a teacher, someday, you may find yourself in a classroom full of eager learners as you begin the very first day of your professional career. Beginning teachers are called **Novice Teachers.**

Novice teachers: Inexperienced teachers just beginning their careers. These teachers have not had the time to develop a repertoire of solutions for common teaching problems or systems of well-organized knowledge about the many aspects of teaching. Novice teachers have many concerns:

- maintaining classroom discipline
- motivating students
- accommodating differences among students
- evaluating student work
- dealing with parents

As a novice teacher, you may rely heavily on the advice and expertise of **Expert Teachers.**

Expert teachers: Experienced, effective teachers who have developed solutions for common classroom problems. Their knowledge of teaching processes and content is extensive and well organized. Much of their success comes only through experience and practice!

Examine the flow chart in Figure 1.1 to acquaint yourself with characteristics possessed by expert teachers.

Teachers, Teaching, and Educational Psychology

Figure 1.1

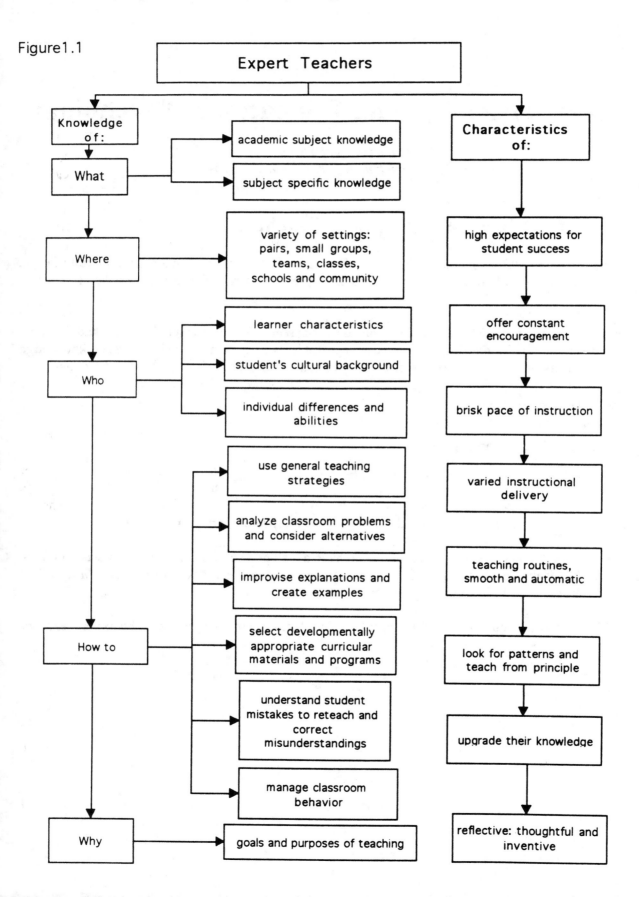

The Role Of Educational Psychology

Educational Psychology is the discipline concerned with teaching and learning processes; it applies the methods and theories of psychology but has its own theories, research methods, problems, and techniques. **Educational Psychology** differs from other fields of psychology because of its emphasis on understanding and improving education and understanding what teachers and students think, do, and feel within the learning environment. Many smart educators believe that teaching is merely a matter of common sense, but research findings from the field of educational psychology teach us that as classroom educators, we must put our "common sense" theories and principles to the test. Excellent teachers are classroom researchers. If findings from the classroom repeatedly point to the same conclusions, we can then develop **principles** about classroom learning, instruction, or behaviors. **Example:** praising the good behaviors while ignoring the negative behaviors is more effective than reprimands for decreasing undesirable behaviors.

Principle: an established relationship between two or more factors.

Given a number of these established principles, educational psychologists combine these principles to form **theories** to explain the relationships among many variables. **Example:** Theories have been developed to explain student motivation based on principles of self-efficacy, past performance, perceived value of the task, intrinsic versus extrinsic rewards, and so on. We know that students who continually fail will have decreased motivation and this relates to whether they perceive their failures are due to lack of native ability, effort, luck, or task difficulty (attribution theory).

Theory: integrated statement of principles that attempts to explain a phenomenon and make predictions.

Many researchers have identified a number of **effective learning techniques** and believe that to be an effective teacher, teachers should be held accountable for their application of these techniques within their classrooms. Equally important, other educators feel that in addition to these techniques, excellent teachers must possess the characteristic of being **reflective**.

Reflective: Thoughtful and inventive. Reflective teachers think back over situations to analyze what they did and why and to consider how they might improve learning for their students. **Reflective Educators** tend to be concerned with:
- how teachers plan
- how to solve problems
- how to create instruction
- how to make decisions
- creative thinking and a commitment to lifelong learning

Beginning teachers need to master some basic techniques and procedures in order to protect their capacity for **reflection**. Many new educators abandon their attempts at analysis and inquiry in their early teaching years to handle the day-to-day problems of motivation and management and just trying to survive (Korthagen, 1985). Reflection is a crucial component of professional development.

An important outcome of reflection is the recognition that some schools need **restructuring** (point/counterpoint). **Restructuring** (National Governors' Association, 1989) should involve:

- modifying curriculum to support higher-order thinking, problem solving, creativity, and cooperation
- bringing together teachers, administrators, and parents at each school to make instructional decisions
- creating new staff roles to make better use of teacher expertise
- holding schools accountable for students' achievement

Using Research to Understand and Improve Teaching

Research is conducted for two reasons:
- to test possible answers
- to combine the results of various studies into theories

Educational research is conducted in a variety of ways. As a classroom researcher, you will employ many of the methods listed below. Acquaint yourself with the following terms and definitions.

Application One: Key Terms and Definitions

Read the following research related key terms. Match the key term to the correct definition. To check your responses, see the answer key at the end of the chapter.

1.	descriptive research	8.	subjects
2.	ethnography	9.	negative correlation
3.	participant observation	10.	random
4.	case study	11.	principle
5.	correlations	12.	statistically significant
6.	positive correlation	13.	theory
7.	experimentation		

Definitions:

1. _5_ Established relationship between factors.

2. _7_ Research method in which variables are manipulated and the effects recorded.

3. _1_ Studies that collect detailed information about specific situations, often using observation, surveys, interviews, recordings, or a combination of these methods.

4. _4_ Intensive study of one person or one situation.

5. _(5)_ Statistical descriptions of how closely two variables are related.

6. ___ Not likely to be a chance occurrence.

4

7. __10__ Without any definite pattern; following no rule.

8. __13__ Integrated statement of principles that attempts to explain a phenomenon and make predictions.

9. __9__ A relationship between two variables in which a high value on one is associated with a low value on the other.

10. __2__ A descriptive approach to research that focuses on life within a group and tries to understand the meaning of events to the people involved.

11. __6__ A relationship between two variables in which the two increase or decrease together.

12. __3__ A method for conducting descriptive research in which the researcher becomes a participant in the situation in order to better understand life in that group.

13. __8__ People or animals studied.

Application Two: Key Terms and Examples

To check your understanding of the following key terms, now see if you can correctly identify practical examples for each key term. Do you think you could generate your own practical example for each term? To check your responses, see the answer key at the end of the chapter.

a. descriptive research
b. ethnography
c. participant observation
d. case study
e. correlations
f. positive correlation
g. experimentation
h. subjects
i. negative correlation
j. random
k. principle
l. statistically significant
m. theory

__(l)__ We feel that the differences in reading achievement for the whole language students versus those who used basals, are in fact due to the reading method employed and not due to chance.

2. __(k)__ Research has established that self concept, perceived value of the task, and anxiety, all relate to motivation to achieve.

3. __i__ As temperature increases, the amount of clothes we wear decreases. As temperature decreases, the amount of clothes we wear increases.

4. __h__ The students in our classes, about whom we will gather data.

5. _d_   I am going to collect data on John's behavior over a two month period to see if I can detect any patterns to his behavioral disruptions.

6. _f_   An increase in time spent studying, predicts an increase in grades. Decreased study time is associated with decreased grades.

7. _c_   I plan to join a nudist colony to better understand the philosophy, morality, and culture of those who prefer no apparel.

8. _j_   I am going to put all of your names into a hat and then select them one-by-one and alternately assign the names to the two soccer teams.

9. _m_   Principles of behavioral management tell us that when we decrease students' behaviors through the use of punishment, we should also provide them with a positive alternative for action. When students demonstrate the positive desirable behavior, we should reinforce that behavior. We then predict that this will increase the occurrence of the positive behavior.

10. _b_   I hope to observe group dynamics and power structure of teachers within their natural habitat, the teachers' lounge.

11. _e_   The amount of food one consumes is related to ones weight.

12. _a_   Through observation, interviews, and videotaping of a class of severely hearing impaired students, I hope to gather detailed information about their learning styles, social interactions, and effective teaching strategies.

13. _h_   I will randomly assign my Intro to Spanish students to two groups. One group will be required to listen to Spanish tapes while sleeping and the other will not, to determine if the tapes influence Spanish fluency.

Application Three: Restructuring

Review the point/counterpoint within your text and discuss the pros and cons of restructuring. What roles might be assumed by expert and novice teachers within the restructuring process? Check your response with the answer key.

A Word About Correlations

To fully understand correlations, you must understand three important factors:

- **Correlation** is just what the name suggests: a co-relation . Correlation **never** implies causation. **Example:** The correlation between the temperature of the sidewalk in the summer and the elderly mortality rate is strong and positive. This is not to suggest that the sidewalk is causing the elderly to keel over. More likely, there is a mediating variable such as the ambient air temperature that causes the sidewalk temperature to heat up and the elderly to suffer from increased heat strokes.

- The size or strength of the relationship between the two variables may range from .00 to $\pm$ 1.00. The closer the correlation is to either positive or negative one, the stronger the relationship between the two factors and the greater the predictive power. **Example:** By predictive power, we mean that if we know that the correlation between hours of study and GPA is .75, and we also know that the correlation between height and weight is .70, given the amount of hours that a student studies and given her height, we are better able to predict her GPA than her weight, because it is a stronger correlation.

- The positive/negative sign has **nothing** to do with the strength of the correlation or relationship. A correlation of -.87 is a stronger relationship than a correlation of +.67. The sign simply tells us the direction of the relationship between the two variables. If the sign is positive, the two variables relate in the same direction. In other words, when one variable increases, the other variable increases. When one variable decreases, the other variable decreases. **Example:** As your college class attendance increases so might your grade. But if your class attendance decreases, so will your grade.

  If the sign is negative, the two variables relate in the opposite direction. As one variable increases, the other variable will decrease and vice-versa. **Example:** As the price of homes increases, the sales of homes will go down. As the price of homes decreases, the sales of homes will increase.

Application Four: Correlations

Now that you have acquainted yourself with correlations, lets see if you can identify the strength and direction of the relationship (correlation) of the following variables. See the answer key at the end of the chapter to check your responses.

For each situation, designate whether you believe it to be a positive or negative correlation and make an educated guess as to whether you feel the correlation is strong, moderate, weak, or difficult to determine.

1. — S   coffee consumption and hours of sleep

2. + S   temperature of the air recorded in Fahrenheit and recorded in Celsius

3. + S   weight lifting and muscle mass

4. — M   hours spent partying in college and hours spent studying in college

5. + S   IQ of identical twins reared in the same environment

6. + W   occurrence of student illness and occurrence of exams

7. — W (+S)   socioeconomic status and academic achievement

8. — W   volume of your stereo and the happiness level of your parents

9. + M   frequency of smiling by your professor and student respect

10. + M +S   your success of responses within this study guide and your self efficacy

---

Application Five: Awareness of Effective Instruction

For this exercise, you should obtain a journal or a notebook. Carry it to all of your classes. Now is the time for you to practice being a **classroom researcher** but from a student perspective. Most of you who will be reading this text will be enrolled in college classes. Practice **descriptive research** and jot down brief notes about your instructors' most effective teaching practices and activities. **Reflect** upon the following as you observe:

    1. Who were your favorite instructors and why?
    2. Which instructors best challenged you and motivated you to learn?
    3. Which teaching methods were most effective relative to your level of achievement and enjoyment of the learning process?
    4. As an educator, what pitfalls, practices, and activities would you avoid?

Reflect upon the type of organizers initially presented by your instructors when beginning a new topic. Do your instructors relate new topics to what you already know? Do they provide numerous examples? Do they frequently stop to summarize and demonstrate the applicability of what you are learning? Are they organized? Do they demonstrate concern for student comprehension? These are just a few examples of what you may observe in your favorite/most expert instructors. Make note of these and your favorite learning activities and you will have a valuable reference tool for when you enter your own classroom as an instructor.

Practice Tests

Essay Question
The author of your book stated that years ago, a wonderful principal told her that teachers are the *professional learners* and students are the *amateurs*. Given what you've read in the first chapter, can you explain what the principal meant by that?

Multiple Choice
1. Expert teachers can best be described as those teachers
    a. whose training has surpassed the undergraduate level
    b. who have taught for many years
    c. who possess elaborate systems of knowledge for understanding problems in teaching
    d. who are born with the natural ability for teaching

2. Which of the following is **NOT** an immediate concern of beginning teachers?
    a. dealing with their students' parents
    b. experimentation with new methods and materials
    c. maintaining classroom discipline
    d. evaluating student work

Teachers, Teaching, and Educational Psychology

3. What method should a teacher use in selecting students to participate in oral reading in the primary-grade reading class?
   a. go around the classroom in order and select every child for participation
   b. call on the volunteers who feel most confident about reading aloud
   c. call on students randomly so they will have to pay attention to the text and what is being read
   d. call on those who never volunteer to provide them with much needed practice

4. When students continually break the classroom rules by getting out of their seats without permission, what should the teacher do?
   a. remind students of the rule to help them remember
   b. reprimand the students to maintain discipline and consistency in the classroom
   c. send the rule breakers out of the classroom to decrease distractions
   d. praise students who are following the rules while ignoring the rule breakers

5. Current thinking regarding acceleration of bright students (skipping grades) suggests
   a. that these students will probably become social misfits
   b. that bright students are more susceptible to "academic burn-out" and should not be pressured to advance
   c. that this choice depends on many specific individual characteristics
   d. that parents are the best judges as to whether this will be beneficial for their child

6. Jane Goodall's exacting research involving ape populations could be characterized as
   a. experimentation
   b. case study
   c. correlational studies
   d. descriptive research

7. Which of the following is the best example of experimentation?
   a. the teacher observes playground behaviors to determine whether first-grade boys or girls engage in more rough and tumble play
   b. the teacher surveys students' parents regarding their children's sports related experiences
   c. the teacher uses a whole language approach with one reading group and basals with the other to determine which approach is more effective
   d. the teacher records the social interactions of one student for a month to explore why the child is a social outcast

8. Which of the following is **NOT** characteristic of correlations?
   a. can indicate cause-and-effect relationships
   b. allow you to predict events
   c. signify that a relationship exists between two variables
   d. is determined by a numerical value that ranges from .00 to ± 1.00

9 Which of the following studies best characterizes descriptive research?
   a. Three groups of hyperactive children receive different methods of behavior modification to determine which method has the most calming effect
   b. Researchers train boys and girls on a series of spatial tasks to determine if training can eliminate gender differences
   c. Researchers examine the classrooms of novice teachers to discover common problem areas for the beginning teachers
   d. Administrators reduce teachers' pay and give them large classes to see if they will continue to teach

10 To be successful, teachers **MUST** be
   a. technically competent and inventive
   b. able to use a range of strategies and invent new strategies
   c. have simple routines for managing classes but flexible and receptive to change when necessary
   d. all of the above

ANSWER KEY

Application One: Key Terms and Definitions

1. k, principle
2. g, experimentation
3. a, descriptive research
4. d, case study
5. e correlations
6. l, statistically significant
7. j, random
8. m, theory
9. I, negative correlation
10. b, ethnography
11. f, positive correlation
12. c, participant observation
13. h, subjects

Application Two: Key Terms and Examples

1. l, statistically significant
2. k, principle
3. I, negative correlation
4. h, subjects
5. d, case study
6. f, positive correlation
7. c, participant observation
8. j, random
9. m, theory
10. b, ethnography
11. e, correlations
12. a, descriptive research
13. g, experimentation

Application Three: Restructuring

Restructuring: Today, more than ever, we are confronted with the increasing challenges of diverse populations, increasing numbers of students and needs that are specific to communities. Every school district cannot follow the same model and hope to effectively educate it's youth. On a positive note, educators, administrators, and communities are realizing that what has worked historically may be outmoded for today's society and culture. Education and school settings are being assessed for areas of weakness and need for change. In overpopulated regions, year-round schooling is becoming a viable alternative. In areas such as parts of California where there is a large Latino population, Spanish is being introduced at the elementary level. What is important is that people are willing to accommodate change to meet the specific needs of the community and the community of learners. Creative innovative thinking on the part of teachers can help a great deal to eradicate specific problems within an educational setting. Teachers are probably more aware than anyone of the problems encountered on a daily basis. Their input in the restructuring process is invaluable.

Conversely, many have suggested that these responsibilities are not within teachers' job descriptions and that teachers rarely have enough time to accomplish their already over-burdened slate of teaching responsibilities without assuming more. There is also "fear of stepping on the toes" of administrators by interfering in school-level decisions. Moreover, novice teachers, who are still trying to successfully establish themselves within their classrooms, may not be as aware of the school-wide problems surrounding them as the expert teachers. They may feel unqualified to speak upon issues of change about which they lack experience.

Application Four: Correlations

1. negative correlation, strong because the more caffeine, the less you sleep
2. positive correlation, perfect because an increment in Fahrenheit is matched by an equal increment in Celsius
3. positive correlation, probably moderate to strong, given differences in body build and size of weights
4. negative correlation, because usually more partying means less studying but it may be a positive correlation for some students who must study more to compensate for excessive partying; or they may have to study more if they have to attend college longer due to excessive partying, difficult to determine
5. positive correlation, strong, as supported by research
6. positive correlation, but probably weak to moderate because the majority of students don't contract illness when facing exams
7. positive correlation, strong, as supported by research
8. negative correlation (unless your parents are die-hard rockers who enjoy your music, and then it's positive); difficult to determine
9. positive correlation (unless your professor constantly smiles causing one to question his/her mental soundness); difficult to determine
10. positive correlation, probably strong, because if you can successfully complete all of these exercises, then your belief in your ability to achieve in this class will probably increase

Essay Question:

Professional learners (teachers) know effective strategies for learning: good organizational skills, memory techniques, process information at deep levels of understanding versus rote memorization, possess good study strategies, and are motivated to be able to apply their learning and seek to improve. Amateur learners (students) must be given time to develop the finer aspects of "how" to learn, in addition to learning "what" or the subject matter. It is suggested that teachers be good guides and learning coaches so that students learn to become expert learners too.

Multiple Choice:

1. c
2. b
3. a
4. d
5. c
6. d
7. c
8. a
9. c
10. d

Chapter Two

Cognitive Development and Language

"The principle goal of education is to create men who are capable of doing new things, not simply of repeating what other generations have done."　　*Jean Piaget*

Development

Crucial to effective learning and instruction, is developmental readiness. This means that students must be developmentally ready to learn in a cognitive sense, there must be progressive changes in their thinking before they are ready to understand certain ideas and concepts.

Development: certain changes that occur in humans or animals between conception and death. These changes appear in orderly ways and remain for a reasonably long period of time.

There are many different aspects to human development:

physical development:	changes in the body
personal development:	changes in an individual's personality
social development:	changes in the way an individual relates to others
cognitive development:	changes in thinking
maturation:	changes that occur naturally and spontaneously and are, to a large extent, genetically programmed

An individual's **physical development** is primarily maturation. **Personal, social, and cognitive development** additionally rely upon interaction with the physical and social environment. All changes cannot be defined as development and many would disagree about "why" and "how" it takes place. There are, however, generally agreed upon developmental principles:

1.　　**People develop at different rates. Example**: Some infants may begin speaking or walking earlier than others. Cognitive development, such as spatial skills, may develop earlier for some individuals than for others. Girls are said to mature earlier than boys in a social sense. These differences in developmental rates contribute to the individual differences of the students in your classrooms.

2.　　**Rate of development is orderly. Example:** Children will realize that a box has a surface before they realize that it has angles. Children will learn to stand before they will walk.

3.　　**Development takes place gradually. Example:** An infant will not walk the first time he/she stands up but will require a progressive development of balance and coordination. A student will not spontaneously multiply without understanding concepts of number and groupings.

The Brain and Cognitive Development

The part of the brain that is primarily responsible for what we accomplish as humans is called the **cerebral cortex.** It constitutes 85% of the brain's weight and covers the greatest number of nerve cells for storing and transmitting information.

Cerebral Cortex: The outer 1/8 inch-thick, wrinkled-looking covering of the brain. It has the following functions:

- receives signals from the sense organs, i.e., visual or auditory signals
- controls voluntary movement
- forms associations

Within the cerebral cortex, different areas have different functions however all of the areas must work together. **Brain Lateralization** also plays an important role in cognitive development.

Brain Lateralization: specialization of the two hemispheres of the brain. The left side of the brain controls the right side of the body and vice-versa.

Application One: Brain Terminology

DO WE NEED TO KNOW?!

Identify the areas of the brain that are responsible for the following functions. Check your responses within the answer key. Some of your responses may be used more than once.

a. left hemisphere   b. right hemisphere   c. Wernicke's area
d. Broca's area   e. auditory cortex   f. visual cortex
g. motor cortex

1. _E_   receiving language/sound

2. _A_   processing language

3. _C_   connecting meaning with particular words

4. _F_   receiving visual signals

5. _D_   setting up grammatically correct ways of expressing an idea

6. _B_   processing spatial-visual information

7. _B_   handling emotions (non-verbal information)

8. _A_   movement on the right side of the body

Piaget's Theory of Cognitive Development

Jean Piaget, known as the *Genetic Epistemologist* (one who is concerned with the study of the nature of knowledge from a genetic or biological perspective) has made substantial contributions to our understanding of cognitive development. According to Piaget, we constantly strive to make sense of the world and master the environment. This is accomplished through four factors:

1. **biological maturation:** genetically programmed biological changes. **Example:** "learning" to walk
2. **activity:** interacting with and upon the environment to learn from it. **Example:** A child may know how to walk but learn a different way of walking by shifting balance when walking down a hill. Interactions with the physical environment alter our thinking processes.
3. **social experiences:** in addition to physical interaction with the environment, Piaget stated that we need social interaction with others. **Example:** Without social discourse, we would never develop our currently spoken language.
4. **equilibration:** maintaining a state of balance between our cognitive structures and the environment. **Example:** Correcting the speech of a child when he says "I runnded all the way home" creates an imbalance within his cognitive structure for the past tense of "run." When he modifies his structure to say "ran" his cognitive structure is now in balance with his environment's conception of proper grammar.

These four factors greatly influence cognitive development. As biological creatures, we demonstrate certain basic tendencies in responding to these factors. Two of these basic tendencies are **organization** and **adaptation.**

Organization: the combining, arranging, recombining, and rearranging of behaviors and thoughts into coherent systems. Simple **structures** of knowing are coordinated and integrated with one another to create a more meaningful system. **Example:** We integrate our **structures** of mathematics with our spatial **structures** which results in **structures** called geometry.

Structures = Schemes

Schemes: organized systems or actions of thought that allow us to mentally represent or "think about" the objects and events in our world. Schemes are frameworks we have constructed for understanding the world. According to Piaget, schemes confer meaning on environmental events and transform them into objects of knowing. We "construct" our schemes of knowing based upon our interactions with the environment so children's schemes differ greatly from adult schemes. An adult's scheme for "fun" is probably different from a five-year-old's and unique to the individual. Schemes can be very simple or very complex.
Example: a simple scheme might be a scheme for strawberries. More complex are our schemes for manners which might change situationally and culturally.

Adaptation: As biological creatures, in order to survive, we must adjust to our environment. Piaget stated that we engage in two forms of adaptation: **assimilation** and **accommodation.**

Assimilation: occurs when we take in or incorporate environmental data into our schemes of knowing. This is inwardly directed; from the environment into our structures. **Example:** If I tell you that equilibration is the mental equivalent of biological equilibrium, you can assimilate (take in) this information into your biological schemes to make sense of the terminology.

Accommodation: occurs when we apply, modify, or adapt our schemes in accordance with whatever environmental reality we are currently experiencing. This is outwardly directed; you apply what you know to match the situation. **Example:** You have a scheme for how to be recognized in class (classroom protocol scheme), you raise your hand and wait to be called upon. Let's say you go to another class and you **assimilate** that everyone else is calling out and NOT raising their hands. You now must accommodate (modify) your scheme for classroom protocol to meet this particular situation or class, in order to survive in this class.

Disequilibrium (disequilibration): This is what occurs when some of our interactions with the environment result in conflict or an awareness that there are gaps in our structures of knowledge. It is an upset to our equilibration or balance between what we know or think we know and what the environment is telling us. If it were not for disequilibrium, our existing structures/schemes would never be challenged and our need to compensate for the gaps in our knowledge would never exist. Disequilibrium generates the need for us to restore cognitive balance by assimilating new information to correct the conflict or gap. This results in improved knowledge and is at the heart of why we experience intellectual growth. **Example:** A small child sees the sun at her friend's house, and then again when she goes home, and yet again when she goes to school. She **assimilates** this and constructs a scheme for the sun that says the sun follows her wherever she goes in addition to being a big yellow ball in the sky. Her mother tells her that the sun does not follow her which causes **disequilibrium.** Now, to compensate for the imbalance and lack of knowledge regarding the sun she must **accommodate** her scheme by **assimilating** new information regarding the sun. This will restore **equilibration** and result in an improved scheme.

One must always remember that what children experience and assimilate when constructing schemes, differs greatly from what adults perceive. Adult perceptions are derived from already existing adult schemes and past experiences. Adult schemes are much richer. **Example:** An adult's scheme for conductor may include electrical conductors, orchestral conductors, and train conductors, but a child's scheme for conductors, based on his/her limited experience, may only consist of the man who collects tickets on the train.

To further demonstrate how schemes confer meaning on the environment, read the following situation as related to me by one of my former students. My student was working part-time in a lingerie store to earn some extra money for Christmas. A father came into the store with his two young children to purchase some nightwear for his wife. While the man was being assisted by my student, the children had discovered some bawdy-gag lingerie, specifically designed to slip over the male anatomy like a knitted red, white, and green nose warmer. Do you get the picture? Giggles erupted, and much to the father's dismay, he saw that his children had tied the woolly appendages onto their faces like festive Christmas colored elephant noses.

To analyze this from a Piagetian point of view, we can surmise that the children had assimilated, (taken in) the featural components of the lingerie (shaped like a nose with strings with which to tie it on like a mask). They accommodated (applied) their scheme for mask to the woolly covering and conferred *their meaning upon it, transforming it into a known object* or something with which they could identify. This operative transformation is the essence of intelligence. This is why Piaget said that "we construct the world" and "the world is as we know it." We uniquely interpret the world through the schemes of knowing that we ourselves have constructed through assimilation and accommodation.

17

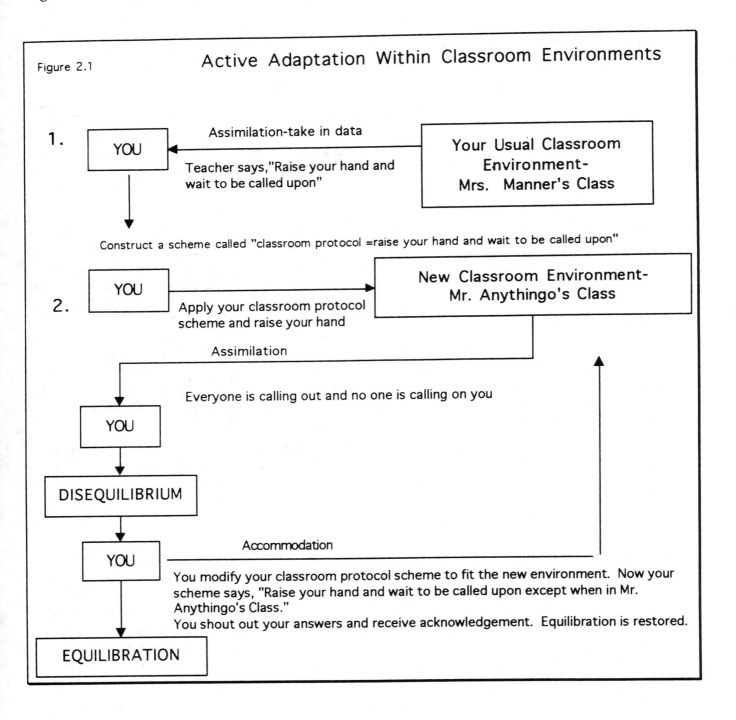

Figure 2.1   Active Adaptation Within Classroom Environments

1. YOU — Assimilation-take in data ← Your Usual Classroom Environment- Mrs. Manner's Class

    Teacher says,"Raise your hand and wait to be called upon"

    Construct a scheme called "classroom protocol =raise your hand and wait to be called upon"

2. YOU → Apply your classroom protocol scheme and raise your hand → New Classroom Environment- Mr. Anythingo's Class

    Assimilation

    Everyone is calling out and no one is calling on you

    YOU

    DISEQUILIBRIUM

    YOU — Accommodation

    You modify your classroom protocol scheme to fit the new environment. Now your scheme says, "Raise your hand and wait to be called upon except when in Mr. Anythingo's Class."
    You shout out your answers and receive acknowledgement. Equilibration is restored.

    EQUILIBRATION

Figure 2.2
Piaget's Biological Perspective on the Development of Knowledge

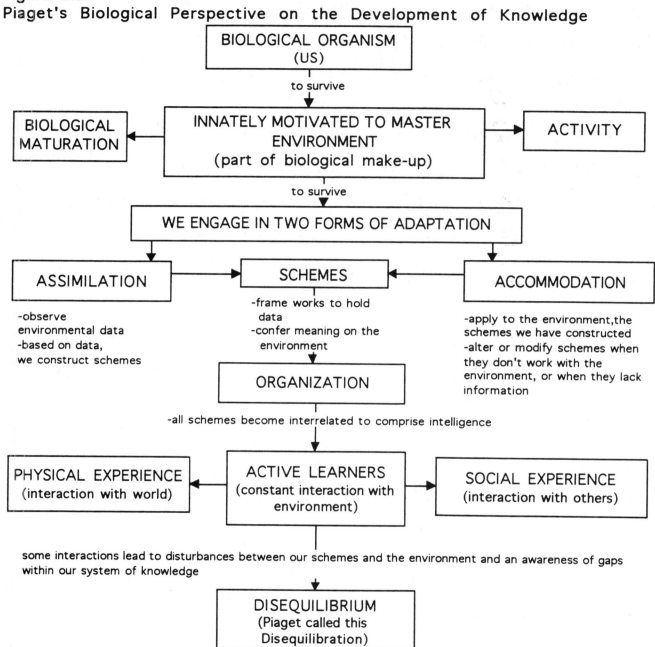

BIOLOGICAL ORGANISM
(US)

to survive

BIOLOGICAL MATURATION ← INNATELY MOTIVATED TO MASTER ENVIRONMENT (part of biological make-up) → ACTIVITY

to survive

WE ENGAGE IN TWO FORMS OF ADAPTATION

ASSIMILATION → SCHEMES ← ACCOMMODATION

-observe environmental data
-based on data, we construct schemes

SCHEMES
-frame works to hold data
-confer meaning on the environment

ACCOMMODATION
-apply to the environment, the schemes we have constructed
-alter or modify schemes when they don't work with the environment, or when they lack information

ORGANIZATION

-all schemes become interrelated to comprise intelligence

PHYSICAL EXPERIENCE (interaction with world) ← ACTIVE LEARNERS (constant interaction with environment) → SOCIAL EXPERIENCE (interaction with others)

some interactions lead to disturbances between our schemes and the environment and an awareness of gaps within our system of knowledge

DISEQUILIBRIUM
(Piaget called this Disequilibration)

-requires further assimilation and accommodation to compensate for lack of information and promote the growth of knowledge

EQUILIBRATION

-balanced state between cognitive cycles and environment
-harmony restored, conflict resolved, improved organization

Cognitive Development and Language

Application Two: Matching Key Terms and Definitions

Select the word from the left column that corresponds to the phrase on the right. Put the number of the matching word in the blank in front of the letters and next to the same letter in the matrix below. If your answers are correct, all numbers across, down, and diagonally, will add up to the same number.

1. Maturation   ___6___ a. When we apply or adapt our schemes in response to the environment _2_

2. Accommodation   ___9___ b. An imbalance between our cognitive cycles and the environment

3. Organization   ___4___ c. When our intellectual structures are in harmony with the environment

4. Equilibration   ___3___ d. When we incorporate environmental data into our structures _7_

5. Schemes   ___5___ e. Mental frameworks of perception and experience

6. Adaptation   ___2___ f. Arranging thinking processes or schemes into larger structures _3_

7. Assimilation   ___7___ g. Adjustment to the environment

8. Development   ___1___ h. Natural, spontaneous, and genetically programmed changes

9. Disequilibrium   ___8___ i. Orderly adaptive changes that occur physically, mentally, and socially

A 6   **B** 9   **C** 4

D 3   **E** 5   **F** 2

G 7   **H** 1   **I** 8

What is the correct number ___15___ *?*

Four Stages of Cognitive Development

Criteria for Stages

- The order of the stages is fixed; the sequence of concept attainment within each stage appears to be universal.
- It is a **stage** theory and not an **age** theory. Piaget is often criticized because the ages at which children attain the concepts associated with each stage, varies somewhat, but we must take into consideration individual differences in maturation and the quality of cognitive experiences.
- Old structures become part of new structures. Old structures are not abandoned but modified and expanded.
- Concept attainment that corresponds with the end of one stage, is the starting point for concept development within the next stage.

Infancy: The Sensorimotor Stage (approx. 0-2 yrs.)

This stage is aptly named because in the initial part of the stage, all of the knowledge that the infant possesses occurs only while the infant is acting upon the environment in some motoric sense. The infant knows the world NOT through mental thought, but through her actions, her sensory motor actions. Therefore, the infant's first schemes are not schemes of thought but rather **sensorimotor schemes.**

Sensorimotor schemes: schemes of knowledge specifically related to motoric action. **Example:** When an infant holds your finger, the infant "knows" your finger as a "graspable" and only while she is grasping it.

In other words, objects in the world exist for example, as "see-ables, or touch-ables, or taste-ables" and so on. The infant knows the world only through her actions upon it and if she is not performing some motoric action upon an object, then that object ceases to exist. We would say that the infant lacks **object permanence.**

Object permanence: knowledge that an object exists apart from any actions upon it. **Example:** If an infant drops some keys in his lap and you cover the keys with a napkin, the infant who has not attained object permanence will not look for the keys, as they only exist when the infant is seeing, touching, grasping, or tasting them, etc.. If the infant looks for them however, then you know that the keys exist for the infant on a mental plane. He knows that the object exists through thought apart from any action. This is object permanence and Piaget stated that it is the first scheme that occurs on a mental plane. This occurs at approximately nine months of age but others have argued that object permanence can occur as early as four months of age.

Object permanence occurs due to the repeated coordination of all of the sensorimotor schemes. The rest of the sensorimotor stage is characterized by (1) further refinement and coordination of these schemes, (2) the internalization of the schemes to a mental plane (once object permanence has occurred), and (3) another primary accomplishment; **logical, goal-directed activity.**

Goal-directed actions: deliberate actions toward a goal. The infant has moved from reflex actions to seeking an end to a means. **Example:** Initially when the infant lies in her crib and hits the mobile suspended there, it is fortuitous or by chance. Now the infant sees the mobile, and as she is developing eye-hand coordination, can reach out, with intention, and touch the mobile *to make it move.*

Cognitive Development and Language

Early Childhood to Early Elementary: Preoperational (approx. 2-7 yrs.)

Thinking in this stage is characterized by the development of a symbol system for communication and the ability to make actions symbolic through words, gestures, signs, and images. The ability to turn a "chair" into a "train" is called the **semiotic function.**

Semiotic function: The ability to use language, symbol, pictures, gestures, etc., to mentally represent objects or actions. **Example:** A towel can become a crusader's cape. Leaves on a plate can be a salad.

Symbol use has a high frequency in play situations. Children at this stage also play with speech with no real intent to communicate but just to hear themselves talk. This is called **collective monologue.**

Collective monologue: Form of speech in which children in a group talk but do not really interact or communicate.

Language emerges as a means for thinking and problem solving. Thinking that corresponds with this stage is still closely associated with actions or performing what one is thinking. It is thinking that is very tied to the "here-and-now." The child's thinking at this stage tends toward but is not yet fully **operational.**

Operations: reversible actions a person can carry out by thinking them through instead of literally performing them. **Example: (a)** When holding an empty basket, if you ask a child who is **fully operational**, how many objects would there be in the basket, if they first put in an apple and then two pears, the child would respond "three" without actually doing it. **(b)** If you asked how many objects would be in the basket if the two pears were removed, the child would respond "one" because he is able to reverse his action (operation) mentally. The **preoperational** child could respond correctly to **(a)** but not to **(b)** because his mental actions lack **reversibility** and have only one-way-logic.

Preoperational: the stage before a child masters logical mental operations characterized by reversibility.

Reversibility: thinking backward from the end to the beginning. **Example:** mentally going from A to B, and then from B to A.

Because **preoperational thinking lacks reversibility**, the child at this stage is markedly different from children in the next stage. Their lack of reversibility makes them:

- **egocentric**
- not able to **conserve matter**
- not able to **decenter**
- not able to comprehend **identity**
- not able to **compensate**
- not able to **classify**
- not able to **seriate**

Egocentric: Assuming that others experience the world the way you do because you cannot reverse your thinking to understand their position. **Example:** Seated across from a preoperational child, if you asked her to touch your right hand, she would touch your *left* hand because that is the hand which corresponds to *her* right hand. It is not that she is self-centered, it is just that she can only understand her perspective.

Cognitive Development and Language

Conservation: The principle that some characteristics of an object remain the same despite changes in appearance. **Example:** A conservation of matter task begins with the child asserting the equivalence of water in two identical containers. The experimenter then pours the water from one of the containers into *a shorter but wider* container. The child now asserts that the wider container has more water for four reasons: (1) because the child is incapable of mentally reversing the pouring process which would take her back to the beginning, canceling out the change that has been made, and (2, 3, & 4) she can't **decenter, understand identity, or compensation.**

Decenter: to focus on more than one aspect at a time. **Example:** The child in the above example is focusing on the *width* of the third container but is not taking into consideration the *height*. She feels that since it is wider, it must be holding more water.

Identity: the principle that a person or object remains the same over time. **Example:** If the child in the above example had a complete mastery of identity, she would have realized that if no water had been added or taken away, the amount of water would have remained the same as it was poured into the third container.

Compensation: the principle that changes in one dimension can be offset by changes in another. **Example:** Again, the child in the above example did not realize that changes in the apparent width of the water (making it seem like more) occurred because the water was also shorter.

Classification: grouping objects into categories. Simple classification depends on a student's abilities to focus on a single characteristic of objects in a set and group the objects according to that characteristic. More advanced classification involves recognizing that one class fits into another. **Example:** The preoperational child can understand that a man can be a father and a man can be a policeman, but not that a man can be both a policeman and a Dad. Reversible thinking is necessary for the child to know that both fathers and policemen are subordinate to the higher class of men in general.

Seriation: Arranging objects in sequential order according to one aspect, such as size, weight, or volume.

Example: The preoperational child cannot seriate a bundle of sticks from smallest to largest because to do so would require reversibility; The child must compare larger stick B to smaller stick A on the right, and then reverse the direction of comparison to compare stick B to larger stick C on the left.

Application Three: The Preoperational Child

Examine the following cartoon to determine which term from the preoperational stage most accurately describes this child's thinking. Check your response in the answer key.

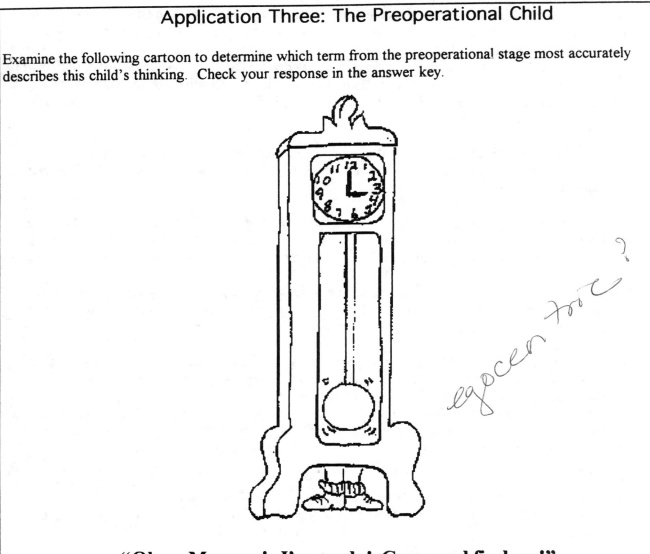

egocentric?

"Okay, Mommy! I'm ready! Come and find me!"

Application Four: Preoperational Resemblance Sorting

The object of this exercise is to group two or more objects together because they are the same on the basis of one common attribute. Fifty % of the four year olds possess this ability as well as about 90% of the six year olds. (Kofsky, 1966, Allen, 1967).

Materials - these should be cut out from construction paper.

1 small diamond - red

2 medium diamonds - 1 orange, 1 blue

1 large diamond - blue

1 small star - yellow

7 medium stars - 2 red, 2 yellow, 2 orange, 1 red

3 large stars - 1 red, 1 blue, 1 yellow

1 small equilateral triangle - orange

2 medium equilateral - 1 yellow, 1 blue

1 large equilateral triangle - red

2 medium rectangles -1 orange, 1 red

Procedure

The experimenter shows three sets of eight objects consecutively to each subject. Each of the sets, the shapes, colors, or sizes of objects is chosen so that the subject is forced to match on the basis of only one attribute.

Set 1

The experimenter places the following objects in front of the subject.

1 large blue diamond and one small red diamond

 2 medium red stars, 2 medium yellow stars, 2 medium orange stars

The experimenter points to the large blue diamond and asks the subject to select from the remaining seven that object which is most like the blue diamond and state the reason for that choice. The subject must ignore color and size and match on the basis of shape.

Set 2

The experimenter places the following objects in front of the subject.

1 small yellow star

1 medium orange diamond, 1 medium blue diamond

1 medium orange rectangle, 1 medium red rectangle

---

1 large red rectangle, 1 medium blue rectangle, 1 medium yellow rectangle

The experimenter points to the small yellow star and asks the subject to select from the remaining seven, those objects that are most like the small yellow star and state the reason for that choice. Here, the subject must ignore shape and size and match on the basis of color.

Set 3

The experimenter places the following objects in front of the subject.

1 small, orange triangle

1 small yellow star, 1 medium yellow star, 1 medium blue star, 1 medium red star, 1 large yellow star, 1 large blue star, 1 large red star.

The experimenter points to the small orange triangle and asks the subject to pick from the remaining seven, those objects that are most like the small orange triangle and explain their reason for their choice. The subject must ignore shape and color and match on the basis of size.

Summary

If correct matches are made for two out of three sets, the subject is probably at or beyond the resemblance sorting level of development. If the subject has difficulty with one set, you might provide guidance and more instructional experiences to help the subject attain understanding of the set's attribute.

Later Elementary to the Middle School Years: The Concrete Operational Stage (approx. 7-11 yrs.)

Concrete operations: Mental tasks tied to concrete objects and situations. At this stage, children's thinking has developed a very complete and logical system of thinking. Children are capable of concrete problem solving and reversibility of operations. They can think through a procedure and mentally reverse the procedure to return to the starting point. Because their thinking is now truly operational and characterized by reversibility, the concrete operational child can conserve matter, seriate, classify, and understands there is a logical stability to the physical world involving principles of identity and compensation. The concrete operational child can also decenter, taking more than one feature into consideration at a time.

Application Five: Concrete Operational Multiple Membership Classifying

By ages 8 to 10, most individuals will understand that something can be a member of more than one group at a time (50% by age eight, and 90% by age 10, Inhelder & Piaget, 1964; Allen, 1967).

Materials - cut these shapes from colored consruction paper

6 small diamonds - 4 blue, 2 orange
4 large diamonds - 2 blue, 2 orange
1 small star - orange
1 small rectangle - blue
1 large rectangle - yellow
4 loops of yarn - 1 blue, 1 orange, 1 back, 1 white

Cognitive Development and Language

Procedure
Place the following eight diamonds in front of the subject.

1 large blue diamond	1 small blue diamond	1 large orange diamond	1 small blue diamond
1 large orange diamond	1 small blue diamond	1 small blue diamond	1 large blue diamond

The experimenter sets the blue loop of yarn on the table and says," Only blue objects can be placed in this blue loop. Do the small objects you see belong in this loop? Explain your reason."

The experimenter sets the black loop of yarn on the table and says, "This loop is only for diamonds. Do the oranges belong in this group? Explain your reason."

Then the experimenter asks, "Do the blues belong in the loop for diamonds? Explain your reason."

The experimenter sets the loop of white yarn on the table and says," This loop is only for small diamonds. Do the oranges belong in it? Explain your reason."

Summary
The subject's explanations should involve an accurate explanation of the attribute that the objects in the loops share. If the subject correctly responds and explains three out of four questions the subject is at the multiple membership classifying level of development.

Junior and Senior High: Formal Operations (approx. 12 yrs.-adulthood)

All individuals do not attain the level of thought that corresponds with the stage of **formal operations. Formal operations:** Mental tasks involving abstract thinking and coordination of a number of variables. Thinking tends toward levels of abstraction , possibility is at the forefront and reality is seen as just one possibility. The child's thinking is not so tied to the concrete world but to the hypothetical. When the individual formulates hypotheses, combines theoretical possibilities through advanced reasoning, and systematically evaluates factors to deduce solutions, this is called **hypothetico-deductive reasoning.**

Problem solving is often approached from an idealistic, "what-if" perspective and adolescents may develop righteous interest in social issues and political causes and dreams of creating "utopias" for future generations.

This stage is also characterized by **adolescent egocentrism:** assumption that everyone else shares one's thoughts, feelings, and concerns. Adolescents perceive themselves as the center of their world, believe their ideas to be better than others', and also believe that "everyone is watching them."

Piaget has stated that not all individuals attain the level of formal operations and that perhaps some people achieve this level only within their fields of expertise. What is important for educators to remember, is that formal operations may in fact be the product of experience, and repeated practice in solving hypothetical problems and using formal scientific reasoning. These abilities may not be taught within all cultures or academic settings. Some students may not be developmentally ready for abstract problems beyond their grasp. To determine if your students are reasoning at the level of formal operations, assess their abilities with the following task.

Application Six: Formal Operational Hierarchical Re-Classification Task

Objects or events may be arranged and rearranged into useful hierarchies of increasingly more inclusive classes. The fewer attributes used to define the class, the more inclusive or general the class. Students from the ages of 14-16 can perform this task (Kofsky, 1966; Allen, 1967).

Materials

1 green triangle, 1 red triangle

1 blue square, 1 green square, 1 yellow square, 1 orange square

1 blue diamond, 1 yellow diamond, 1 orange diamond

5 stars - 1 blue, 1 green, 1 red, 1 yellow, 1 orange

Procedure

The experimenter places all of the objects on the table in four groups: triangles, squares, diamonds, stars.

The experimenter says, "Make 3 groups out of these 4 groups. If you move one object in a group, you must move all of the objects in that group. Explain your reason."

Next the experimenter says, " Now, combine these three groups into two groups and tell me why you made your choice."

Lastly, the experimenter says, " Now make one group and tell me your reason for it."

Summary

By being able to combine four groups to form three and then three to two demonstrates competence in hierarchical reclassification. These groups may be grouped as "four-sided, three-sided, and one-sided sets and then regrouped as those with straight sides and curved sides and finally as all shapes.

Implications of Piaget's Theory

By observing how children problem solve we can make many inferences about the level of their thinking (empathic inference). Understanding their level of developmental readiness will guide the curriculum and instruction. There is a wide range of abilities within the classroom and educators must respond to those differences in ways to make learning optimal for all individuals. Students learn most effectively when given opportunities to experiment and construct their own knowledge. Students should encounter disequilibrium and discrepant events at a level that is not too difficult but just challenging enough to promote further investigation and equilibration leading to improved knowledge. Students need the opportunities to apply their constructions, to test their thinking with feedback, and to observe how others solve problems.

Application Seven: Piagetian Terminology

Fill in the puzzle with the correct terms. Terms with two words will not have a blank in between. Check your responses in the answer key.

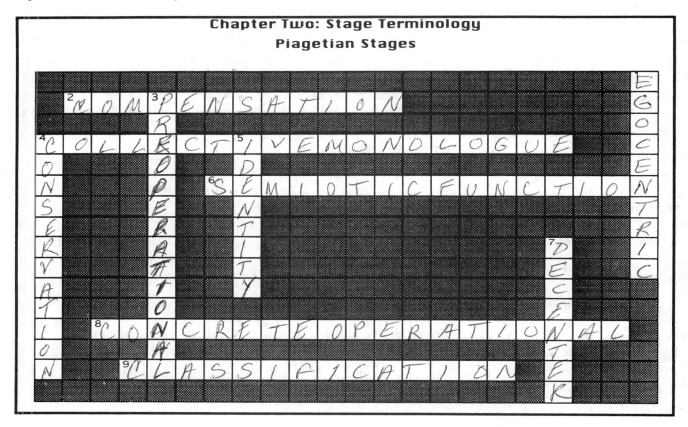

Chapter Two: Stage Terminology
Piagetian Stages

Clues

Down:

1. Assumption that others perceive the world as you do.
3. Stage before a child masters reversible mental operations.
4. Principle that some characteristics of an object remain the same despite changes in appearance.
5. Principle that a person or object remains the same over time.
7. To focus on more than aspect at a time.

Across:

2. Principle that changes in one direction can be offset by changes in another.
4. Speech form where children talk in a group with little interaction.
6. Ability to use a symbol system to mentally represent objects or actions.
8. Children are capable of concrete problem solving and reversibility of operations.
9. Grouping of objects into categories.

Vygotsky's Sociocultural Perspective

The **sociocultural perspective** emphasizes the importance of the individual's culture in shaping cognitive development by determining "how" and "what" the individual learns. Vygotsky subscribed to the sociocultural perspective relegating greater responsibility to the people and tools in the child's world as contributors to cognitive development, contradicting Piaget's emphasis on the individual for constructing her own knowledge. Vygotsky believed that the tools of contemporary culture as well as language play a crucial role in determining the paths of our intellectual development. **Example:** A friend confessed to me that he now thinks differently as a result of becoming a computer expert

Vygotsky believed that language is essential for cognitive development. He placed great emphasis on what Piaget called "egocentric speech." Vygotsky called this **private speech.**

Private Speech: talking to yourself.

Piaget viewed egocentric speech as another indication that children have little interest in the perspectives of others. As they mature they become more verbally interactive with others. They learn to listen and exchange ideas.

Vygotsky suggested that rather than little interest in others, children engage in private speech for the purpose of "thinking out loud," so to speak, to guide their behaviors. Eventually, the self-directed speech loses volume, turning into whispers, and ultimately becoming silent thought. Vygotsky suggested that this linguistic path helps the child to:

solve problems - direct attention - plan - form concepts - gain self-control

Research supports the notion that children engage in more private speech when encountering difficulties and that as adults, many of us use inner speech to regulate our behaviors, i.e., "let's see, the first thing I have to do is......" Because self-talk is used to guide thought, it is suggested that children be allowed to utilize private speech in the classroom in the form of **cognitive self-instruction.**

Cognitive Self-Instruction: a metacognitive process that students use to talk themselves step-by-step through the process of learning.

Vygotsky also believed that language plays another crucial role in that developing children interact with knowledgeable others who serve as guides and providers of feedback to advance their learning. Therefore, children are not alone in their discovery of conservation or classification. The discovery is mediated through family and peers. Bruner calls this process **scaffolding.**

Scaffolding: Through the interaction with the adult, the child will be supported, assisted and challenged by the adult at each rung of the "cognitive ladder."

Vygotsky assumed that "every function in a child's cultural development appears twice: first, on the social level and later on the individual level; first between people (interpsychological) and then inside the child (intrapsychological)" (Vygotsky, 1978).

Implications of Vygotsky's Theory for Teaching

There are three ways that cultural tools can be passed from one individual to another:

1. imitative learning--where one person tries to imitate another

2. instructed learning--where learners internalize teacher instructions and use them to self-regulate
3. collaborative learning--where a group of peers try to understand each other and learning occurs

Assisted learning: guided participation that requires scaffolding—giving information, prompts, reminders, encouragement at appropriate times and amounts, gradually allowing more independent work by students. Listed below are the strategies that teachers could utilize for scaffolding:

1. procedural facilitators--teaching students to use signal words such as "who, what, where, when, why, and how" to generate questions after reading a passage.
2. modeling use of facilitators--the teacher would model the generation of questions about the reading.
3. thinking out loud--the teacher models thought processes, showing choices and revisions.
4. anticipating difficult areas--during modeling and presentation, the teacher anticipates and discusses potential errors.
5. providing prompt or cue cards-- procedural facilitators written on cue cards for student use.
6. regulating the difficulty-- teach skills with simple problems, provide student practice, gradually increase task complexity.
7. provide half-done examples-- have students work out final solutions for half-completed problems.
8. reciprocal teaching-- have students and teachers rotate roles. Teacher provides support to students as they learn to lead discussions and ask questions.
9. providing checklists-- teach students self-checking procedures to help them regulate the quality of their responses.

Interaction between adults and children is particularly beneficial to children when they are at the **zone of proximal development.**

Zone of proximal development: the area where the child cannot solve a problem alone, but can be successful under adult guidance or in collaboration with a more advanced peer. This is where real learning is possible.

The Zone of Proximal Development and How it Relates to Other Learning Variables

Private speech This occurs when an adult helps a child to solve a problem or accomplish a task using verbal prompts and structuring. This scaffolding may be gradually reduced as the child takes over guidance.

Assessment Most classroom assessments tell what child can do alone, however, dynamic assessment begins by identifying the student's zone of proximal development and then asks the student to problem solve, all the time supplying prompts to see how he learns, adapts, and uses the guidance. The teacher can then use this information to plan instructional groups, peer tutoring, learning tasks, assignments, etc..

Teaching Students should be placed in situations where they have to reach to understand but where support is readily available from other students or the teacher. Sometimes the best teacher is another student who has discovered the solution to a problem because they are probably operating in the first student's zone of proximal development. Students need more than to discover on their own but they need facilitation and guidance and encouragement to use language to organize their thinking and to benefit from dialogue.

The Development of Language

An early view of language acquisition proposed that children learn a language through imitating and repeating those utterances that would bring about rewards. Closer examination reveals that children create their language, i.e., "Mommy sock" and "Milk allgone," and phrases never uttered by any adult. Moreover, adults rarely correct children's earliest utterances concerning themselves more with meaning and communication. Adults will simplify their language always staying a bit ahead of the child to advance the child's language development, a form of verbal scaffolding.

Chomsky and others believe that humans have built-in, universal grammars, and a set of rules that limit the range of language learning. It is likely that both biological and environmental factors play a role in language development.

Stages

1. First words - Once the first word is spoken, children slowly add up to ten words. After this, words increase rapidly. By 20 months, they'll have approximately 50 words. Language is more complex than it might appear, as one word can mean a lot. The meaning of single words can be very narrow or very wide in scope.

Holophrase: single words express whole phrases or complex ideas. **Example:** "Milk" may mean "I want more milk" or "I spilled my milk."

Overextension: overgeneralization of one word to mean an entire situation. **Example:** The child says "bird" and means "park" where you saw birds and swings and other children, but lacking the means to express all of that, says, "bird."

Underextension: undergeneralization by using a word to mean only one member of a category. **Example:** The child says, "dog" but means only his dog and no one else's.

2. First sentences - At about 18 months children begin to string together two word sentences.

Telegraphic speech: non-essential details are left out and the words that include the most meaning are included, as in a telegram. **Example:** "mommy sock" might mean that the child wants Mommy to put on her sock.

3. Learning grammar - As children learn the tenses of words they sometimes apply that tense to every word, correctly or not.

Overregularization: When children begin to learn rules they apply the rules to everything. **Example:** "I runned all the way home." This is a normal assimilation and children eventually learn to accommodate their grammar to be more consistent with how the rest of their culture speaks.

4. Learning vocabulary - Between the ages of two and four, children double their vocabulary every six months. Making up words is fun as well as playing with language in the form of silly chants, songs, and rhymes.

Language Development in the School Years

By age five or six most children have mastered the basics of their language. Of pronounced sounds, the *j, v, th, and zh* are the last to be mastered. Children will more often use the words they can pronounce. Word intonation sometimes confuses the meaning for children. **Example:** Even with proper intonation, the phrase "visiting relatives can be a nuisance" would probably confuse an early elementary school child.

By early elementary school children understand the meaning of passive sentences (they don't use it in normal conversation) and have also mastered basic word order.

Syntax: word order that corresponds to the rules of grammar.

Pre-puberty is a critical period for language development, especially for language growth . By the age of 6, average vocabulary is 8000 to 14,000 words and this increases by 5000 words between the ages of 9 to 11. In the early elementary years children have trouble understanding abstract concepts and may not understand sarcasm or some humor.

Pragmatics: the appropriate use of language to communicate. **Example:** Using a deeper tone to command a dog or simpler vocabulary when talking to a child, or waiting to take a turn when communicating with others.

Metalinguistic awareness: knowledge and understanding about language itself.

Language, Literacy, and Teaching

One goal of schooling is to promote oral language and reading and writing. Literacy has been shown to begin to develop as early as infancy. Literacy can be enhanced through a literacy rich environment. Teachers can enhance language environments by focusing not just on grammar but more on content and ideas. Reading aloud also promotes language development. Parents can play a crucial role in developing literacy by providing a literacy rich environment, reading to children and acquainting them with all forms of literature, while limiting television. As an educator, you will be in a good position to work with families where literacy is not a part of their lives.

Practice Tests

Essay Questions

1. With respect to acceleration of cognitive development, defend the Piagetian position that cognitive acceleration may possibly have deleterious (harmful) effects.

Cognitive Development and Language

2. A group of deaf children were found in a European orphanage. Remarkably, these children had created their own language for communication that no one had ever heard before. Explain why the Piagetian constructivist position can explain this phenomenon better than the Vygotskyian position.

Multiple Choice Questions

1. Central to the development of language and literacy in the early years
   a. are the student's home experiences
   b. is exposure to educational programs such as "Sesame Street"
   c. is the onset of spoken language by the child
   d. is the number of older siblings in the family

2. Which of the following is NOT one of the criteria for Piaget's stages
   a. The sequence of the stages does not vary
   b. The end point of a previous stage is the staring point for the next
   c. Stages are determined by the age of the child
   d. We know what stage represents the child's thinking by observing how they solve problems

3. Which of the following is consistent with Piaget's notions of constructing knowledge?
   a. students must be given a chance to actively experience the world
   b. active experience should include mental manipulation of ideas
   c. students need to interact with teachers and peers to test their thinking, be challenged, and receive feedback.
   d. all of the above

4. Theories proposed by Lev Vygotsky grant greater emphasis for cognitive development on
   a. changes in rates of growth in brain weight and skull size
   b. the child's culture
   c. genetically inherited abilities that manifest as IQ of the child
   d. how early the child acquires speech

5. Teachers can help students develop their capacities for formal thinking by
   a. using direct instruction to provide them with as much factual information as possible
   b. putting students in situations that challenge their thinking and reveal their shortcomings
   c. teaching them the rules for abstract reasoning and problem solving
   d. encouraging them to attend to their physical environment

6. A criticism of Piaget's theory of development is
   a. that Piaget underestimated the cognitive abilities of younger children
   b. that culture may play a greater part in determining cognitive differences among the children of the world
   c. that there are inconsistencies within a stage in terms of what a child can do
   d. all of the above

Cognitive Development and Language

7. Vygotsky suggested that private speech
    a. should be discouraged among school-age children
    b. increases with task difficulty
    c. occurs among those children who will later move their lips while reading silently
    d. none of the above

8. Adults who provide information and support necessary for the child to grow intellectually are using
    a. cognitive self-instruction
    b. imitative learning
    c. scaffolding
    d. collaborative learning

9. The area where a child cannot solve a problem alone, but can be successful under adult guidance or in collaboration with a more advanced peer is called
    a. the point of transition
    b. the ladder of learning
    c. zone of proximal development
    d. assisted learning

10. The basics of word order and sentence structure is called
    a. semantics
    b. grammar
    c. phonology
    d. syntax

Answer Key

Application One: Brain Terminology
1. e   2. a   3. c   4. f   5. d   6. b   7. b   8. a

Application Two: Matching Key Terms and Definitions
a. 2   b. 9   c. 4   d. 7   e. 5   f. 3   g. 6   h. 1   i. 8   The correct number is 15.

Application Three: The Preoperational Child
The term that can best be applied to this child's thinking is "egocentric". The child believes that since he/she can't see anyone, then no one can see him or her.

Essays
1. Research by David Elkind (1991) suggests that the pressure on parents and preschool teachers to create "superkids" who can read, write, and speak a second language, can be harmful to children. Elkind believes that preschool children who are pushed to achieve and are not given the opportunities for non-structured informal play are missing a very important aspect of their cognitive development, are showing symptomatic stress, and becoming dependent on adults for guidance. Early focus on "right" and "wrong" answers can lead to competition and self-esteem. It can also cause "academic burn-out".

Cognitive Development and Language

2. Piaget's theory posits that children, as biological organisms, must engage in adaptation within the environment in order to survive. Construction of a language system for communication is one such attempt at becoming intellectually proficient within one's environment. Vygotsky's theory places greater emphasis on the adults within the child's culture as providing the linguistic tools necessary for cognitive development. The children from the orphanage defy this notion that language must be "transmitted" from the environment, adults, and/ or able peers, and therefore addresses the notion that developing individuals will actively construct the means for communication even when incapable of hearing the culture's system of verbal communication.

Multiple Choice

1. a   2. c   3. d   4. b   5. b   6. d   7. b   8. c   9. c   10. d

Application Seven: Crossword Puzzle

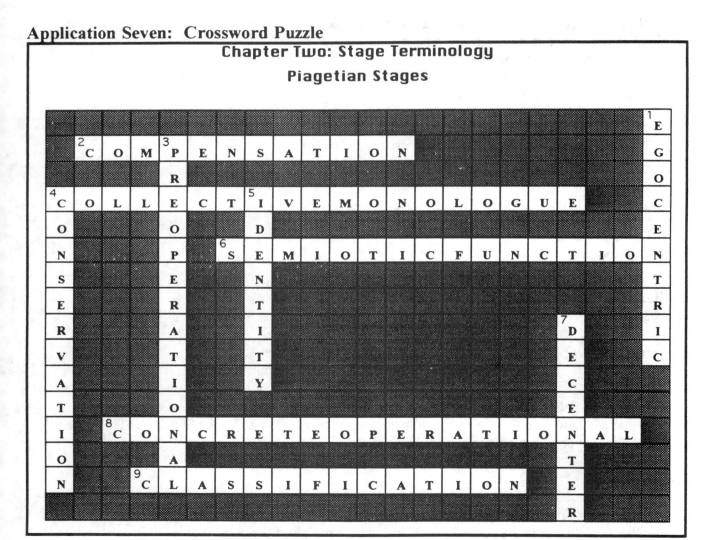

Chapter Three

Personal, Social, and Emotional Development

"Character is doing what's right when nobody's looking,"
J.C. Watts (R-OK, 2/4/97, Republican response to the State of the Union Address)

As educators, you will not only be required to advance the intellectual development of your students but also the emotional and social aspects of development. Erik Erikson studied child-rearing practices in many cultures and proposed a **psychosocial theory** of development.

Psychosocial Theory: Describes the relationship of the individual's emotional needs to the social environment.

Like Piaget, Erikson proposed a stage theory of development. According to Erikson, the individual encounters emotional and social **developmental crises.** How the crises are resolved at each stage, (conflicts between positive versus unhealthy alternatives) will influence the individual's approach and ultimate resolution of future crises.

Developmental Crises: A specific conflict whose resolution prepares the way for the next stage.

Preschool Years: Trust (stage 1), Autonomy (stage 2), and Initiative (stage 3)

Infants' first crucial aspects of development depend on whether their needs are met and they develop a sense of security and trust in their environment and in the adults who provide care for their well-being. This trust is important, because if the infant feels secure within his environment, then he feels confident to go out and explore the world apart from his secure home base. This positive resolution of the trust vs. mistrust conflict sets the stage for a positive resolution of stage 2, autonomy vs. shame/doubt. **Example:** Bobby is willing to stay at the neighbor's house while his parents go out for the evening because Bobby knows his parents will return. This gives Bobby the chance to have fun at a new household.

Autonomy: independence

If the infant feels secure within her environment, and knows that she has support at home, she will be willing to take initiative for exploring the world with a sense of autonomy and a willingness to assume greater responsibility for herself. Parents need to be supportive of children's efforts and encourage their attempts at independence regardless of the outcomes, lest the children feel doubt and shame about their abilities to succeed. **Example:** Amber's parents praise her for dressing herself, even when she comes in with her pants on backwards.

If the child has successfully resolved the autonomy crisis and has no doubts about his/her ability to succeed then the third stage will bring **initiative** to the child. Along with initiative, the child learns that some activities are not allowed and some impulses must be checked. **Example:** To avoid child-guilt, parents must assure children that the children are not "bad" when they engage in certain activities, but rather that the activities are not appropriate.

Initiative: Eagerness to engage in productive work.

Elementary and Middle School Years: Industry vs. Inferiority (stage 4)

Now is the time that demands are being made on children for performance in a work-related sense, either in the form of at-home chores or academic tasks at school. Children who up to this point have met with encouragement and support, will display an eagerness to function and be productive and take initiative to perform and perform well. If the child perseveres and is successful with his or her work efforts, he or she will find this rewarding and develop a sense of **industry**. If the child's attempts at productivity are unsuccessful or met with reproach or criticism, the child may develop a sense of inferiority and a decreased likelihood of engaging in productive work in the future.

Industry: Eagerness to engage in productive work. **Example:** Give children tasks within their capacity to perform and reward their efforts when they are successful. Do not give a six-year old your grandmother's china to wash after dinner, lest it backfire. Let your six-year old experience success with the unbreakable dishes.

Adolescence: The Search for Identity (stage 5)

This stage is marked by the adolescent's struggle to establish an **identity** for herself/himself separate from childhood identities. If conflicts regarding the adolescent's beliefs, abilities, drives, and future goals are not successfully resolved, then the adolescent may experience role confusion.

Identity: The complex answer to the question, "Who am I?"

Marcia proposed four alternatives to Erikson's Identity vs. Role Confusion. These alternatives are listed below:

1. **Identity Achievement:** Strong sense of commitment to life choices after free consideration of alternatives. **Example:** Adolescents who have explored many options, and been given support and freedom to make decisions, will establish a sense of identity and make choices with which they will be happy.

2. **Identity Foreclosure:** Acceptance of parental life choices without consideration of options. **Example:** Susan is pursuing a medical career because her mother was in medicine, and her mother before her, and she feels that she must carry on the tradition.

3. **Identity Diffusion:** Uncentered; confusion about who one is and what one wants. **Example:** John doesn't want to think about his future, and prefers to scrape by, day-to-day, doing odd jobs when he can find them.

4. **Moratorium:** Identity crisis; suspension of choices because of struggle; a healthy delay in decision making. **Example:** Juan is not sure if he is ready to enter college because he is not sure of his career interests. He decides instead to take a year to travel around the world to find "himself."

Personal, Social, and Emotional Development

Figure 3.1

Erikson's Theory of Psychosocial Development

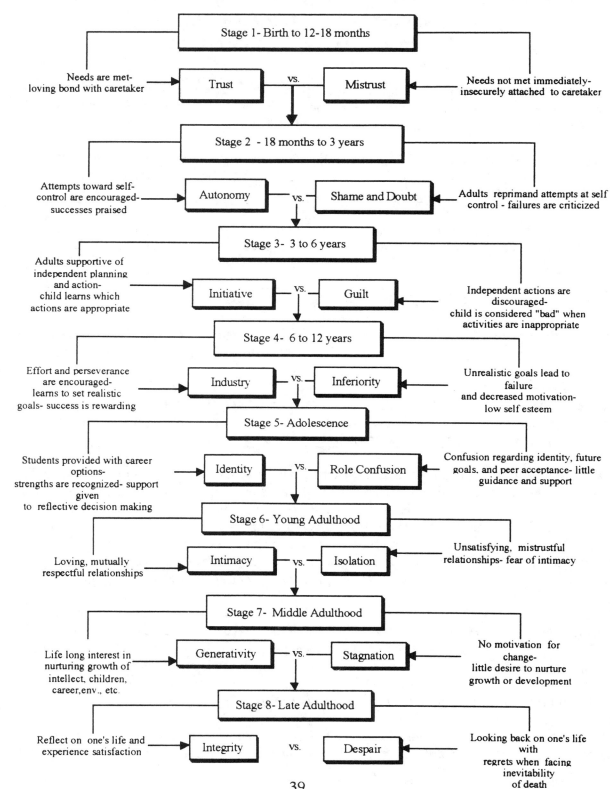

Beyond the School Years: (Intimacy vs. Isolation-stage 6, Generativity vs. Stagnation-stage 7, Ego Integrity vs. Despair-stage 8)

Intimacy vs. Isolation: If this conflict is resolved successfully, there is willingness to relate to another person on an intimate level beyond mutual sexual needs. If unsuccessfully resolved, the individual may avoid closeness and intimacy for fear of being hurt and instead may tend toward isolation.

Generativity vs. Stagnation: Sense of concern for future generations. If resolved successfully, individuals seek to nurture the growth of self and others. But if unsuccessfully resolved, the individual stagnates by remaining the same and not seeking to further develop.

Integrity vs. Despair: If successfully resolved the individual develops **integrity:** sense of self-acceptance, fulfillment, and acceptance of one's inevitable death. If unsuccessfully resolved the individual will look back on his or her life with despair and a sense of futility.

Application One: Psychosocial Development

Read each of the following scenarios to determine if you can identify the corresponding stage from Erikson or Marcia. After you have selected the stage, state whether the individual has achieved a positive or negation resolution to the conflict.

1. Jeff is a 26 year old, junior-high mathematics instructor. He enjoys teaching but feels he is ready for further professional development and makes the decision to attend graduate school in pursuit of advanced degrees. _Intimacy vs. Isolation_ (?) gen. vs. stag → pos

2. Rachel, a four-year old, just became a big sister to new baby, Olivia. Rachel's mom Laurie, tells Rachel, "I'm going to the basement to do some laundry. If Olivia wakes from her nap, come get me so I can change her diaper." Olivia wakes up and cries and Rachel picks her up, puts her on the floor, and changes her diaper. Rachel then flushes the diaper down the toilet. Seeing the toilet overflow, Rachel calls her mother who rescues Olivia, stops the flood, and then sits down to calmly explain to Rachel that, "It was very nice of you to want to help, but some things should be left to adults, because you could have dropped Olivia and flooded the house." _Industry vs. Inferiority (negative)_ init. v. guilt → pos

3. As a senior citizen, Joan is forced to sell her home. Her husband has died and left no insurance policy or savings for the future. Her social security is not enough to pay the taxes and a mortgage. Her grown children refuse to help her and most of her friends have passed on. She reflects on her life and thinks about all of the years she wasted, working as a waitress trying to make ends meet when she really wanted to become a photographer and travel the world. She is depressed realizing that those opportunities are gone forever. _Integrity vs. Despair (negative)_

4. Because she is such a helpful individual, Cali is selected from her sixth grade class to help out in the cafeteria at lunchtime. To reward her efforts, she is given free lunch all month long. _Industry vs. Inferiority (positive)_

5. As 20 month old Jennifer tries to take her first steps, she topples. Her mother gasps, quickly scoops her up and puts her back in her walker, fearful that she'll injure herself. *Autonomy vs Shame/Doubt (negative)*

6. Brian is a high-school freshmen and a loner. He relates better to computers than to his peers. Josh, his same-age cousin, recently came to live with Brian's family because of problems at home. Josh is a troubled youth who frequently drinks alcohol and smokes marijuana. He rapidly makes friends with classmates known to the other students as the "stoners." They invite Brian to "party" with them and he goes along, happy to have found some friends at last, but concerned about his participation in illegal activities. *Identity vs. Role Confusion (negative?)*

7. Becky loves Jason and Jason tells Becky he wants to marry her. Despite her religious convictions, she consents to have sexual relations with him. He promises to love and respect her always. The day after they make love for the first time, Becky goes to Jason's house only to find him in bed with another woman. She is devastated and swears never to look at another man again. *Intimacy vs. Isolation (neg)*

8. Four month old Carrie cries for most of the night because her single mother drinks herself to sleep every night and never wakes when Carrie cries. *Trust vs. Mistrust (negative)*

9. Juan Garcia comes from a family who has always encouraged him to do well in school, get involved in extra-curricular activities, and set goals for the future. Juan thinks that he would like to go to college, but he is not sure whether he would like to study agriculture and become a farmer like his father, or go into engineering. He decides that when he graduates high school, he will work on his father's farm for one year to help him to make a decision. *Identity vs. Role Confusion (positive)*

10. Le Chang does not want to pursue a medical career, but his parents insist that when he graduates from high school, he will apply to Yale and live with his relatives while he works on his degrees. Le respects his parents and goes along with their wishes. *Identity vs. Role Confusion (negative)*

Self-Concept and Self-Esteem

Society impacts individual growth and development on personal and social levels. The child's first conceptions of self are concrete, rule-bound, and largely determined by physical appearances. Self-perceptions become more abstract with time but **self-concepts** and **self-esteem** develop in accordance with the situations in our lives and how others respond to us.

Self-concept: a cognitive structure of ideas, feelings, and attitudes that people have about themselves. It's who we believe ourselves to be.

Self-Esteem: is an affective reaction; an evaluation of who you are. High self-esteem--we like ourselves; low self-esteem--we don't.

Personal, Social, and Emotional Development

Self-concepts are determined by a number of social-personal factors as well as academic factors. Success in school and social acceptance help to define self-concept and possibly self-esteem, especially for young adolescents. Situational circumstances determine self-concept relative to the comparison group. The development of self-concept occurs through constant comparisons of self- to- self and self- to- others. Examples of comparisons follow:

Comparisons

Personal-Internal

i.e., "I compare my math to my science performance."

i.e., "I compare my appearance today to my appearance yesterday."

Social-External

i.e., "I compare my math performance to math performance of my peers."

i.e., "I compare my popularity to that of my friends."

Application Two: Self-Esteem

Read the following descriptions of research supported self-esteem characteristics and select the students who most likely possess the characteristics. Some selections may be used twice. Check your responses in the answer key at the end of the chapter.

a. middle school or junior high students   b. high self-esteem students   c. 6th grade students
d. 1st grade students   e. 3rd grade girls   f. females
g. males   h. elementary school students

1. _a_ students' self-concepts become more negative and less stable.

2. _f_ more likely to be successful in school

3. _c_ students' reported self-esteem influenced by teacher feedback, caring, and grades

4. _a_ more favorable attitudes toward school, more positive behavior in the classroom, and greater popularity with other students

5. _b_ 80% surveyed believed themselves to be the best students in the class

6. _h_ boys and girls have comparable perceptions of their own abilities

7. _be_ feel confident, assertive, and authoritative about themselves

8. _a_ emerged from adolescence with poor self-image, constrained views of their future and their place in society, and much less confidence about themselves and their abilities

42

9. _____ by ninth grade and throughout high school, they gradually lower their perceptions of their own abilities compared to the opposite gender

10. _____ for most ethnic groups except for African-Americans, they are more confident about their abilities in school, particularly in math and science, than the opposite gender

11. _____ feelings of self-worth are more closely tied to physical appearance and social acceptance

School Life and Self-Esteem

School plays a major role in determining students' self-esteem. How school affects self-esteem:

Good and Weinstein (1986), school is a place where:
- children come to define self and ability
- friendships with peers are nurtured
- the role of a community member is played out
- self-esteem, interpersonal competence, social problem solving, and leadership develop

Hoge, Smit, and Hanson (1990) found that sixth grade students' self-esteem was related to:
- students' satisfaction with the school
- interesting classes and caring teachers
- teacher feedback and grades

Harter (1990) found:
- students who feel capable in a certain area and believe that the activity is important have higher self-esteem
- students must have legitimate success on tasks that matter to them

Personal and Collective Self-Esteem

Another major influence to our self-esteem comes from those groups with whom we associate.

Collective Self-Esteem: sense of the worth of the groups to which we belong. When the groups to which we belong are de-valued, loss of collective self-esteem can occur.

Many children from different ethnic groups hear messages that de-value their ethnic group. Since community patterns (majority culture) may differ from ethnic patterns (subculture), it may sometimes be difficult for ethnic minority students to establish an identity. Efforts must be made to encourage **ethnic**

pride so that students don't perceive differences as deficits. Students who have adopted the values from both cultures have a greater sense of identity and self-esteem. A great resource for increasing student self-esteem lies with their families.

Along with the development of identity, self-concept and self-esteem, comes an awareness of the separateness of self from others and an ability to **take the perspective of others.**

Perspective-taking ability: Understanding that others have different feelings and experiences. This increases as children mature.

Moral Development

Another aspect of development involves moral reasoning. Piaget called this stage of development **moral realism.** Here children believe rigidly in rules and do not think abstractly about the reasons for rule breaking. Everything is black and white with no shades of gray. Rule breakers should be punished regardless of circumstances.

Moral realism: stage of development wherein children see rules as absolute.

As children develop they begin to understand other's perspectives. As Selman suggested, they begin to understand that people have different information and situations and what will work in one situation may not be acceptable in another. A more abstract understanding of rules develops as does **morality of cooperation.**

Morality of Cooperation: Stage of development wherein children realize that people make rules and people can change them. When the rules are broken, severity of offense and intention are considered.

Kohlberg's Stages of Moral Development

Kohlberg proposed that the development of children's beliefs regarding right and wrong follows a logical sequence. Kohlberg studied the **moral reasoning** of both children and adults by presenting them with **moral dilemmas.**

Moral Reasoning: The thinking processes involved in judgments about questions of right and wrong.
Moral Dilemmas: Situations in which no choice is clearly and indisputably right.

Kohlberg divided moral development into three levels:

Level 1. Preconventional Moral Reasoning
Individuals make decisions based on others' rules and personal needs. There is no real consideration of right or wrong, but rather the individual makes judgments based on whether they may be punished for breaking a rule or rewarded for keeping a rule. Judgments are also made on the basis of individual needs.

Personal, Social, and Emotional Development

Example: Tom finds a wallet with the address of the owner inside but decides to keep the money because he figures no one will ever know who took the money and he could really use it to pay his bills

Level 2. Conventional Moral Reasoning
Individuals make decisions based on need for others' approval, family expectations, traditional values, the laws of society, and loyalty to country. Judgments are based on whether loved ones and legal structures deem the actions to be right or wrong and whether the individual also subscribes to these beliefs. **Example:** Tom finds a wallet with the address of the owner inside and returns the wallet, because to keep the wallet would be breaking the law.

Level 3. Postconventional Moral Reasoning
Judgments are made based on the belief in socially agreed upon standards of individual right similar to the constitution, and upon individual conscience, involving abstract concepts of justice, human dignity, and equality. Actions are driven more by personal morality than by societies' laws but when personal beliefs take precedence over the laws of society, there is a willingness to accept the consequences of one's actions. **Example:** Tom finds a wallet with no address inside but places an add in the paper in an effort to find the rightful owner because Tom believes that it is the right thing to do.

Application Three: Moral Dilemmas

Consider the following scenarios and discuss the actions from Kohlberg's three levels of morality.

1. Dr. Kevorkian, well-known for his active participation in assisting people with their own suicides
2. The soldiers, who under Calley's command, executed men, women, and children at the massacre at My Lai, March 16th, 1968
3. Individuals who bomb abortion clinics
4. Nameless firefighters who sacrifice their lives to save others
5. W.W.II Nazis under Hitler's rule
6. Protesters of the Vietnam War at Kent State University
7. Bonnie Parker and Clyde Barrow
8. The National Guard who killed the protesters at Kent State College
9. Boston tea party participants
10. Vietnam draft dodgers who were conscientious objectors and took service positions and desk jobs
11. Vietnam draft dodgers who went to Canada out of fear for life and limb

---

Application Four: Kohlberg's Stages of Moral Development

Match the following statements to the orientations within the different levels within Kohlberg's Stage Theory. Check your responses in the answer key.

a. good-boy-nice girl　　　b. personal reward　　　c. law and order
d. punishment/obedience　　e. universal ethics principle　f. social contract

1. _____ family expectations　　*a*
2. _____ individual values and conscience　　*e*
3. _____ personal needs determine right and wrong　*b*
4. _____ rules are obeyed to avoid punishment　*d*
5. _____ laws are absolute
6. _____ similar to the US constitution　　*f*
7. _____ authority must be upheld　*c*
8. _____ traditional values　*a, c*
9. _____ loyalty to country　*c, f, ?*

　　　Much of Kohlberg's theory has come under criticism because people exhibit different levels of reasoning in a non-sequential fashion and relative to the situation at hand. Furthermore, Kohlberg's theory doesn't differentiate between social conventions and true moral issues and it has been suggested that Level 3 is biased in favor of Western, male values. Carol Gilligan proposed an alternate theory based upon levels of caring that progress from (1) self-absorbed caring, to (2) caring for certain individuals and relationships, and finally, (3) to caring for all people and humanity. This theory is more consonant with female development. Actual research reveals that both men and women value caring and justice, however, women experience greater guilt when violating caring norms and men experience greater guilt when showing violent behaviors.

　　　As people develop, they become more **empathic.** Teachers can help to increase student empathy by encouraging student discussion regarding emotional issues and encouraging student mediation.

Empathy: the ability to feel an emotion as it is experienced by another person-to put yourself in another's shoes. Empathy helps us to understand one another and promote social responsibility.

　　　Friendships are an integral part of social development and like other aspects of development, follow a progressive evolution:-

1. Initially, children's friendships are as fleeting as their moment-to-moment encounters, and based on the immediate quality of their interactions.
2. At the next level, friendships are founded on concrete, stable characteristics and a greater desire to help one another.
3. Lastly, friends are established through mutual interests and values, loyalty, trust, and emotional support. Friendships are more permanent, and for girls, can be more intense, directed to one best friend, and less open to accepting new members to the group.

Personal, Social, and Emotional Development

Friendships, and acceptance by peers, can have a lasting effect upon the personal and social development of the individual. Teachers must be cognizant of difficulties within interpersonal relationships and seek to intervene when a student is being excluded or ostracized, especially in the middle-elementary school level.

Moral Behavior

Two influences on the development of moral behavior are, (1) direct instruction, supervision, rewards and punishment, and correction leading to **internalization**, and (2) modeling by caring generous adults who show concern for the rights and feelings of others.

Internalization: when children adopt the moral rules and principles of the authority figures who have guided them. Children are more likely to adopt the external standards as their own if they are given reasons when they are corrected for their actions.

Because students cheat, does not mean that they will be dishonest in other situations. Student reports suggest that over 97% of their peers have cheated. Teachers can help to prevent cheating by:
- avoiding placing students in high pressure situations
- helping them to prepare for tests, projects, and assignments
- emphasizing learning, not grades
- providing extra help for those who need it
- highlighting policies on cheating and reinforcing them consistently
- monitoring carefully to prevent cheating

Application Five: Characteristics of Students Who Cheat

Answer true or false to the following statements to assess your knowledge of student cheating. Check your responses in the answer key.

1. F Students will cheat because it increases their social acceptance.
2. T Students may cheat if the pressure to perform is great.
3. T If the chances of getting caught are slim, students are more likely to cheat.
4. T College students in the arts and humanities are more likely to cheat than students in engineering, business, and science.
5. T High achievers are more likely to cheat than low achievers.
6. F Students focusing on learning goals as opposed to performance goals (looking good in front of others) are less likely to cheat.
7. F Older and college-age males are more likely to cheat than their female counterparts.
8. T Students will cheat because of fear of failure.
9. T Students cite being too lazy to study as a reason for cheating.
10. F Parental pressure for good grades is not related to cheating.
11. T Students are more likely to cheat when they are behind or cramming for tests.

Personal, Social, and Emotional Development

As a classroom manager you will at some point be required to defuse **aggressive** behaviors by your students. Aggression is not to be confused with **assertiveness.**

Aggression: Bold, direct action that is intended to hurt someone else or take property; unprovoked attack.
Assertiveness: affirming or maintaining a legitimate right.

Modeling is a determining factor in aggressive behaviors. Listed below are some of the places where aggression can be observed:

1. **In the home:** Children who observed harsh punishment and violence in the home more likely to use violence to solve problems.

2. **Television:** (a.) 82% of programs have some violence, (b) children's' programs have 32 violent acts per hour; cartoons are the worst, (c) except for sleep, children spend more time watching television than anything else.

3. **Films and Video Games:** violence is frequently depicted by the "hero."

Socialization: The Home and School

Socialization: the ways in which members of a society encourage positive development for the immature members of the group. Two important influences on the socialization of children are the family and the school.

Characteristics of Today's Students:
- More will have one or no sibling
- May be part of a **blended family:** co-habitation with stepsisters or stepbrothers
- Some will live with "non-parent" adults, one parent, or in foster homes
- 25% of children under 18 live with one parent, usually the mother
- Almost 50% of the one-parent families have incomes below poverty level
- There is a growing number of latchkey children
- Experience social pressure to grow up too fast
- Pressured to cope with adult information from the media before they can cope with childhood problems

David Elkind suggests the "hurried child" is one who is expected to grow up too fast, to engage in formal learning before developmentally ready, may be subject to physical stress symptoms such as headaches, stomach aches, and behavioral problems, and further may experience early academic burn-out and decreased motivation. **Developmentally appropriate education** could lessen these effects if these preschools have materials and activities at a wide range of developmental levels, if children are permitted to follow their own direction, and teachers provide situations to support learning. If there is too much teacher direction, children may develop a sense of guilt versus initiative, diminished self-confidence, and may overly depend on others for direction.

Personal, Social, and Emotional Development

Developmentally Appropriate Education: educational programs and activities designed to meet the cognitive, emotional, social, and physical needs of students.

Divorce

The divorce rate in the United States is the highest in the world. This can possibly be a period of great loss for children:

- loss of parent in terms of residence
- loss of current home for less expensive home
- loss of friends, neighborhood and school due to relocation
- loss of toys, trips, recreation due to fewer finances
- loss of time with parent if custodial parent must work greater hours

Additionally, children may have to cope with parents' new partners or step-parents and step-siblings. The first two years after the divorce are worst for boys and girls. They may blame themselves or engage in behavioral or health disorders. Furthermore, there may be long-term personal and social problems. Teachers need to be receptive to symptomatic changes, avoid insensitive language, be supportive and help students maintain self-esteem. As unbiased individuals who are removed from the home environment, teachers can be wonderful resources to children who are suffering from personal and social problems.

Challenges for Children

Physical Development: Gross motor skills: voluntary body movements that involve control of the large muscles, improve from the years of 2 to 5. Give ample opportunities to develop physical coordination and balance with plenty of rest. **Fine-motor skills:** voluntary body movements that involve the small muscles are also developing. Experiences such as painting, clay-work, and scissors will refine these skills. 85% of the children will demonstrate right hand preferences but left hand students should be accommodated with special materials.

Throughout elementary school, there is wide variation in physical size, strength, and ability for both boys and girls. Girls may be larger than boys and downplay their physical advantage due to internal conflict.

Adolescence is another time for spurts in physical development. The beginning of sexual development is marked by **puberty.**

Puberty: The period in early adolescence when individuals begin to reach physical and sexual maturity. Girls begin puberty about two years ahead of boys and reach their final height by 16; boys will continue to grow until 18. Girls begin to develop breasts between the ages of 9 and 16, menstrual cycles begin between the ages of 11.5 and 14.5. For boys, the growth spurt begins between the ages of 12 and 13. Physical changes greatly influence identity. Early maturation has certain advantages for boys, but this is not the case for girls.

Children and Youth at Risk

Child Abuse: Unfortunately, many cases of child abuse go unreported. Parents are not the only people who abuse children, but also siblings, other relatives, and teachers. Many abusers could change their behaviors if they were to receive help. As a teacher, you must notify your principal, school psychologist, or social worker if you suspect abuse. Understand your state laws for dealing with abuse and your moral responsibility for involvement.

Teenage Sexuality and Pregnancy: About 80% of American men and 75% of American women have had sexual intercourse by the age of 19. There are many physical and emotional consequences of sexual activity:
- 1 million teenage girls become pregnant each year--30,000 younger than 15 years of age
- 1/2 of the pregnant adolescent girls become so in their first 6 months of sexual activity
- many teenage girls don't know when in their cycle they can become pregnant
- many girls will not prepare for sex because they don't want to appear sex-crazed
- adolescents need accurate information about sex and birth control

Eating Disorders: Today's standards for beauty and appearance sometimes lead to eating disorders due to excessive concern. Two such eating disorders are:

Bulimia: Eating disorder characterized by overeating, then getting rid of the food by self-induced vomiting or laxatives.

Anorexia Nervosa: Eating disorder characterized by very limited food intake. Anorexics lose 20 to 25% of their body weight and about 5% literally starve themselves to death.

Both of the above disorders occur more often with females than with males, although there has been an increase among male athletes. A teacher, sensitive to the situation, can be just the person to help with these problems.

Drug Abuse: High percentages of high school seniors (92) report some experience with alcohol. About 20% of seniors are daily smokers, and 30% have tried at least one illegal drug. Considering the conflicting messages sent to students via media and society, it is no small wonder drug use is increasing among youth. Successful educational programs teach students how to avoid drug usage with no loss of self-esteem and how to make responsible choices.

AIDS: The percentage of AIDS growth among adolescents is increasing at an alarming rate. In most cases, adolescents contract AIDS through intimate sexual contact or intravenous drug use. AIDS education should begin in the early years and continue through high school.

Suicide: The suicide rate is increasing among adolescents and even younger youth. There are certain warning signs that there is trouble:
- changes in eating and sleeping habits
- changes in grades

- changes in disposition, activity level, or friends
- giving away prized possessions
- depression or hyperactivity
- statements indicating that nothing matters or musings about death
- work or school absence

If you detect any warning signs, talk directly to the student and take the student seriously. Refer the student to a school counselor or school psychologist. Suicide is often a cry for help, not to be ignored.

Practice Tests

Essay Questions

1. Provide both pro and con arguments for values education in the schools.

2. As a means for addressing issues of morality, Kohlberg utilized moral dilemmas, giving students opportunities to clarify their values through interactive discourse and debate. Generate a moral dilemma, (appropriate at the high school level) for dealing with issues of cheating. Remember, this should be a dilemma for high school students and one that is not easily resolved. This dilemma is meant to promote discussion and debate by your students toward better understanding of their own morality. Check the answer key for a sample dilemma.

Multiple Choice:

1. Which of the following is not one of the goals of morals education in the schools?
   a. to help students to learn the skills of values analysis
   b. to teach students how to reason about moral issues through clarification
   c. to teach students what's right and what's wrong
   d. to help students learn higher levels of moral reasoning

2. With respect to the role that friendships play in the development of the child, adults who were rejected by peers as children
   a. are more capable of maintaining intimate relationships
   b. tend to have more problems like dropping out of school or committing crimes
   c. appear better able to cope with failure
   d. have difficulties forming close bonds with their own children

3. Regarding divorce, when parents have joint custody
   a. they may attend parent-teacher conferences on an alternating basis
   b. they are entitled to information *only while their child is residing with them*
   c. a court must determine their legal rights regarding educational decisions about the child
   d. both are entitled to receive information and attend parent-teacher conferences

51

Personal, Social, and Emotional Development

4. When students have chaotic and unpredictable home lives, they need
   a. teachers who set clear limits, are consistent, and enforce rules firmly but not punitively
   b. warm, firm structure in school
   c. teachers who respect students and show genuine concern
   d. all of the above

5. If as a teacher you suspect that one of your students is a victim of child abuse,
   a. you should contact the child's parents
   b. call the police
   c. report your suspicions to your principal, school psychologist, or social worker
   d. all of the above

6. Research indicates that giving adolescents accurate information about sex
   a. results in fewer unwanted pregnancies
   b. actually encourages them to experiment
   c. makes girls appear sex-crazed if they're prepared for intercourse
   d. has been the cause of a great number of civil lawsuits instigated by parents

7. According to Selman, when children understand that different perspectives may result because people have access to different information this is called
   a. undifferentiated perspective taking
   b. social-informational perspective-taking
   c. self-reflective perspective taking
   d. third-party perspective taking

8. A cognitive structure that is a belief about who you are, is called
   a. self-concept
   b. self-esteem
   c. self-efficacy
   d. collective self-esteem

9. It is sometimes difficult for ethnic-minority students to establish a clear identity because
   a. they are members of both a majority culture and a subculture
   b. they often hear and accept messages that de-value their group
   c. values, learning styles, and communication patterns of the student's subculture may be inconsistent with the expectations of the school and the larger community
   d. all of the above

10. Research on moral reasoning suggests that one difference in male-female reasoning is
    a. men feel more guilty when they are being inconsiderate
    b. men feel more guilty when they are untrustworthy
    c. men feel more guilty when they show violent behaviors
    d. men feel more guilty when they lack empathy toward others

Answer Key

Application One: Psychosocial Development

1. generativity vs. stagnation-positive
2. initiative vs. guilt-positive
3. ego integrity vs. despair-negative
4. industry vs. inferiority-positive
5. autonomy vs. shame/doubt-negative
6. identity vs. role confusion-negative
7. intimacy vs. isolation-negative
8. basic trust vs. basic mistrust-negative
9. identity vs. role confusion/moratorium-positive
10. identity vs. role confusion/identity foreclosure-negative

Application Two: Self-Esteem

1. a   2. b   3. c   4. b   5. d   6. h   7. e, b   8. f   9. f   10. g   11. a

Application Three: Moral Dilemmas

1. Kevorkian disregards the laws concerning suicide and follows his conscience and individual values while demonstrating a willingness to accept the consequences characteristic of Level 3
2. The soldiers held authority in higher regard than perhaps their own consciences and massacred men, women, and children, and obeyed military law, consistent with Level 2
3. Individuals who bomb abortion clinics may be seen as having moral convictions consonant with Level 3 in that they feel it is morally wrong to take life; but when one considers that they are serving their own purposes by breaking the law, possibly taking life themselves, and doing it anonymously to avoid consequences, then their actions more closely resemble Level 1.
4. These individuals are protecting others and doing what society would deem "good actions" consonant with Level 2, however, their willingness to die to save others is more characteristic of Level 3.
5. Nazis under Hitler's rule, may have committed atrocities because they were fearful for their own lives if they refused orders, consistent with Level 1 reasoning, or they may have believed in obeying laws of society and authority, consonant with Level 2, or they may have sacrificed their individual consciences to follow orders with which they disagreed in order to protect family and loved ones, willing to accept the consequences of their unconscionable actions, characteristic of Level 3. It is most likely that the majority reasoned from Level 2.
6. Vietnam protesters at Kent State were exercising their constitutional rights to assemble and their rights to free speech to protest a situation that they found to be immoral but were also willing to accept the consequences of their actions, consonant with Level 3.
7. Bonnie and Clyde sought only to benefit themselves and were not willing to accept the consequences of their actions as they broke numerous laws. Their actions can only be considered from Level 1.

8. The National Guard obeyed orders consistent with Level 2, but also responded in a self-defense mode when bricks were tossed at them by the protesters consonant with Level 1. Most of them probably responded from Level 2.

9. The Boston Tea Party participants sought to rectify a situation that they felt was unjust and what would later be considered to be "unconstitutional" while willing to accept the consequences in line with Level 3.

10. Draft dodgers who felt it was morally wrong to take another's life, in spite of it being condoned by the country, who were willing to accept the consequences of a desk-job, reasoned from Level 3.

11. Draft dodgers who were first and foremost concerned about their own well-being and the personal consequences of their actions (safety for themselves), demonstrated reasoning consistent with Level 1.

Application Four: Kohlberg's Stages of Moral Development

1. a   2. e   3. b   4. d   5. c   6. f   7. c   8. a, c   9. c, f

Application Five: Characteristics of Students Who Cheat

1. false   2. true   3. true   4. false   5. false   6. true
7. true   8. true   9. true   10. false   11. true

Essay Questions

1. In support of values education, one of the goals of educating youth is to produce good citizens who will work for the good of society. In a time of rising crime, drug use, violence, racial hatred, and the disintegration of the family, no one group can be expected to assume sole responsibility for the moral education of today's youth. Those opposed to values education, question whose morality will be taught, whose values, culture, or religion, and what happens when these values contradict family values? It is also argued that schools should not directly teach values but instead should help students clarify their own values.

2. **A moral dilemma for high school students regarding cheating**: Frank's science instructor grades on a curve with the highest 10% of the scores getting an "A" and the lowest 10% getting an "F." Frank's best friend Jack somehow obtained a copy of the science final exam and told Frank that other students also have a copy of the exam. Jack said that Frank would be stupid if he didn't look at the exam, especially since he was trying to get into an Ivy league college and his science grade would probably go down if he didn't get an "A." Considering that Frank's instructor grades on the curve, the students who had obtained copies of the exam would definitely get "A's" driving the curve higher for everyone else, decreasing their chances at getting a good grade. Should Frank report his classmates and friends? Should Frank look at the exam? What would you do in Frank's situation?

Multiple Choice:

1. c   2. b   3. d   4. d   5. c   6. a   7. b   8. a   9. d   10. c

Chapter Four

Learning Abilities and Learning Problems

"A child miseducated is a child lost."
John F. Kennedy

Language and Labeling

As educators, we will view all of students as exceptional and unique, but as a label, **exceptional students** comes to mean something very different in terms of their educational needs because their abilities significantly depart from average.

Exceptional Students: Students who have abilities or problems so significant that the students require special education or other services to reach their potential.

The use of labels is controversial. There are both advantages and disadvantages to assigning a label to a student because labels simultaneously help and stigmatize individuals.

Disadvantages:
1. labels do not tell the teacher which methods to use with individual students
2. labels can become self-fulfilling prophecies
3. labels may be viewed as permanent problems that cannot be changed
4. labels may be stigmas
5. labels may be mistaken for explanations
6. labels may emphasize the most negative aspect of the individual

Advantages:
1. for younger students, this may lead to a protective response from society
2. labels may open doors to special programs
3. labels help professionals communicate findings and provide information
4. labels help to secure financial assistance

Individual Differences in Intelligence

Definitions of **intelligence** are as diverse as the mental abilities that comprise intelligence.

Intelligence: Ability or abilities to acquire and use knowledge for solving problems and adapting to the world. Early notions of intelligence subscribed to one or more of three themes:
- the capacity to learn
- the total knowledge a person has acquired

- the ability to adapt to new situations and the environment in general

Today's experts agree that abstract reasoning, problem-solving, and decision making comprise intelligence but still argue as to whether it is one or many abilities. Following, are several theorists' positions on intelligence:

- Spearman (1927)- one factor, *g* or *general intelligence* needed to perform any mental task and *s* or *specific abilities* needed to perform specific tasks.
- Carroll (1993)-a few broad abilities and at least 70 specific abilities.
- Thurstone (1938)- verbal comprehension, memory, reasoning, ability to visualize spatial relationships, numerical ability, word fluency, and perceptual speed
- Guilford (1988)-**faces of intellect: 180 combinations** (6 operations x 5 contents x 6 products)
    - a. mental operations-processes of thinking:
        1. cognition (recognizing old information and discovering new)
        2. convergent thinking (finding one answer)
        3. divergent thinking (finding many possible solutions)
        4. evaluation (judgments about accuracy, value, etc.)
        5. immediate memory
        6. memory over time
    - b. contents-what we think about:
        1. visual content
        2. auditory content
        3. word meanings
        4. symbols
        5. behaviors

> Guilford's model broadens our notions of intelligence, however, when people are tested on these abilities, the abilities prove to be related. There is no explanation for the correlations between these supposed independent abilities

   - c. products-end results of our thinking:
        1. units
        2. classes
        3. relations
        4. systems
        5. transformations
        6. implications
- Gardner (1983, 1993)-**Multiple Intelligences:** Seven separate intelligences or abilities
    1. logical-mathematical: ability to handle logical or numerical patterns and long chains of reasoning
    2. linguistic: sensitivity to sounds, rhythms, word meanings, and different language functions
    3. musical: production and appreciation of rhythm, pitch, timbre, and forms of musical expressiveness
    4. spatial: accurate perceptions of visual/spatial world and mental transformations of initial spatial perceptions
    5. bodily-kinesthetic: skill at controlling bodily movements and handling objects
    6. interpersonal: ability to discern and respond appropriately to moods, temperaments, desires, and motivations of other people
    7. intrapersonal: knowledge of one's own feelings, strengths, weaknesses, desires, and intelligence, and ability to utilize this knowledge to guide behavior

> Research by Gardner and associates suggests that these intelligences may not be as independent as originally suspected but that in the interest of all individuals, these intelligences should be explored and cultivated.

- Sternberg (1985,1990)- **Triarchic Theory of Intelligence:** three processes of intelligence that are common to all people:
    a. analytic intelligence: defined in terms of **components:** basic problem-solving processes
        1. metacomponents: higher-order planning, strategy selection, and monitoring
        2. performance components: executing the strategies selected
        3. knowledge-acquisition components: **Example:** separating relevant from irrelevant information as you try to understand a new concept
    b. creativity: coping with new experiences
        1. **insight:** the ability to deal effectively with novel situations
        2. **automaticity:** learning to perform a behavior or thinking process so thoroughly that the performance is automatic and does not require effort
    c. practical intelligence: common sense, survival skills
        1. choosing environments in which one can succeed
        2. adapting to the environment
        3. reshaping the environment if necessary

Measurement of Intelligence

In 1904, Alfred Binet was commissioned by the French ministry to develop a test that would differentiate between those students who possessed the skills requisite to succeeding in a public school setting from those who would not. Binet and associate, Simon, developed 58 tests for children 3 to 13 for determining the **mental age** of a child.

Mental Age: In intelligence testing, a score based on average abilities for that age group. **Example:** John is four years old, but John can successfully answer the items passed by most six year olds, so John has a mental age of six.

An **intelligence quotient (IQ)** was added to Binet's test after it was brought to the US and revised at Stanford University to compare mental age to chronological age.

$$\text{Intelligence Quotient} = \frac{\text{mental age}}{\text{chronological age}} \times 100$$

> In time this formula proved insufficient because mental age does not increase in equal increments. Greater increases occur around the ages of 6 or 7 and then again around the ages of 11 or 12. This prompted the use of the **Deviation IQ.**

Deviation IQ: Score based on statistical comparison of individual's performance with the average performance of others in that age group.

IQ tests should be administered individually by a licensed psychologist as group administered tests are not as reliable. Teachers must be very cautious when interpreting IQ scores based on group tests.

Application One: IQ Myths and Facts

Read the following statements and determine whether they are myth or fact. Write true or false next to each statement. Check your responses in the answer key.

1. _____ The average IQ score is 115.
2. _____ Approximately 68% of the population scores between 85 and 115.
3. _____ IQ test scores are just as reliable for ethnic, minority groups as for white, native born Americans whose first language is Standard English.
4. _____ Intelligence test scores predict scholastic achievement very well.
5. _____ IQ scores and scholastic achievement are strongly related to success in later life.
6. _____ Individuals' IQ scores remain stable over the life of an individual.
7. _____ If a student scores poorly on an IQ test, he or she lacks innate ability to learn.
8. _____ Student's past experiences and learning have no bearing on IQ test scores.
9. _____ IQ tests provide accurate information about individual's overall intellectual ability
10. _____ IQ tests measure those limited abilities needed to do well in a scholastic setting.

Some theorists feel that intelligence is primarily inherited (nature) where others feel that it is environmental (nurture). Most psychologists believe that intelligence is due to both genetic and environmental factors, although it is impossible to determine the amount that each contributes to IQ. The problem with adopting a purely genetic approach to IQ is the belief that IQ is stable and not subject to improvement. As educators, we must believe that intelligence can be improved and that compensations can be made for lack of cognitive enrichment within the child's home or scholastic environment.

Ability Differences and Teaching

To adequately teach to the wide range of intellectual abilities within the classroom, many teachers use **between class ability grouping.**

Between Class Ability Grouping: System of grouping in which students are assigned to classes based on their measured ability or their achievements. This is also known as tracking. **Example:** college prep courses or honors classes, or remedial classes. Research reveals that this may be a good practice for high achieving students, but the problems associated with tracking low ability students are listed below:
◆ low ability classes receive lower-quality instruction in general
◆ teachers emphasize lower-level objectives and routine procedures with less academic focus

Learning Abilities and Learning Problems

- there are often more management problems leading to increased stress and decreased enthusiasm
- teachers' negative attitudes may mean low expectations are communicated to the students
- student self-esteem suffers upon assignment to the lower tracks
- attendance may drop with self esteem
- disproportionate number of minority students and economically disadvantaged are assigned to these classes which in effect becomes resegregation
- friendships become limited to students in the same ability range
- assignments to classes are often made on the basis of IQ which is not a good predictor of subject area performance

A more viable alternative are two forms of cross-grade grouping called the **non-graded elementary school** and the related **Joplin Plan.**

Non-graded elementary school/ Joplin Plan: Arrangement wherein students are grouped by ability in particular subjects, regardless of their ages or grades. This is more effective as long as the grouping allows the teacher to offer more direct instruction.

Another form of grouping is called frequently used in the elementary schools for reading is called: **Within Class Ability Grouping:** System of grouping in which students in a class are divided into two or three groups based on ability in an attempt to accommodate student differences.

Mental Retardation

Some differences in your students' intellectual functioning will be more extreme. About 1 to 1.5 percent of the population meets the AAMD's definition of **mental retardation.**

Mental Retardation: Significantly below-average intellectual and adaptive social behavior, apparent before the age of 18. Below average intellectual functioning is an IQ score less than 70 -75. This alone is not sufficient for diagnosing mental retardation, because in the past, a disproportionate number of minority individuals were diagnosed as mentally retarded due to low IQ scores but they showed no deficits in adaptive functioning and could survive quite well in society. Their IQ scores more likely reflected linguistic difficulty and cultural differences.

As a regular teacher you will probably work with mildly retarded children. In the early grades, these children will appear slow, but by third or fourth grade they will fall behind their classmates. By junior and senior high school there should be greater emphasis on vocational and self-care skills that will enable the individual to become self-sufficient. One such program is **transition programming.**

Transition Programming: Gradual preparation of exceptional students to move from high school into further education or training, employment, or community involvement.
See figure 4.1 for ways to adapt instruction for learner differences.

Gifted Students

Greater recognition is now being given to the fact that 50% of **gifted students** are not achieving to their potential and schools are not adequately meeting their needs.

Gifted Students: Very bright, creative, talented students with the following characteristics:
- significantly above average intellectual functioning (Renzulli and Reis, 1991)
- a high level of creativity (Renzulli and Reis, 1991)
- high level of task commitment and motivation to achieve in certain areas (Renzulli and Reis, 1991)
- larger, stronger, and healthier than the norm (Terman, et.al., 1925, 1947, 1959)
- walk sooner and are more athletic (Terman, et.al., 1925, 1947, 1959)
- more emotionally stable than their peers (Terman, et.al., 1925, 1947, 1959)
- better adjusted adults than the average (Terman, et.al., 1925, 1947, 1959)
- lower rates of delinquency, emotional difficulties, divorces, and drug problems (Terman, et.al., 1925, 1947, 1959)

Even though these findings seem to indicate that gifted children are well-adjusted and superior in many ways, they still encounter problems. Many gifted children experience boredom and frustration in school as well as ridicule from their peers and a sense of isolation. They may demonstrate great impatience when others do not share their interests and may place great expectations on themselves for peak performances. The greatest adjustment problems are found with those students who have IQs above 180. Furthermore, sex-differences in social adjustment and self-esteem favor gifted males over females with gifted girls perceiving their abilities lower than even non-gifted boys and girls.

Application Two: Matching Gifted and Talented

Read the following statements and select the term or phrase from the left column that corresponds to the statements on the right. Place your numbers from the blanks next to the same letters in the matrix below. If your answers are correct, all numbers across, down, and diagonally, will add up to the same number.

1. individual IQ test _____   a. gathering information, test scores, grades, examples of work, projects, portfolios, letters or ratings from teachers, and self-ratings

2. case study _____   b. moving quickly through the grades or particular subjects

3. group tests _____   c. giving students more thought provoking work while keeping them with their same age peers

4. enrichment _____   d. all have IQ scores in the top 1% in the nation, 140 and above

5. 10 to 50% _____   e. amount of time teachers successfully identify gifted students

6. above 180 IQ _____   f. tend to underestimate the IQs of very bright children

7. Terman's subjects _____   g. these individuals have the greatest adjustment problems

8. minority students _____   h. best single predictor of academic giftedness

9. acceleration _____   i. may be best identified by creativity tests or measures other than standardized IQ tests

A	B	C
D	E	F
G	H	I

What is the correct number _____ ?

Learning Abilities and Learning Problems

Figure 4.1

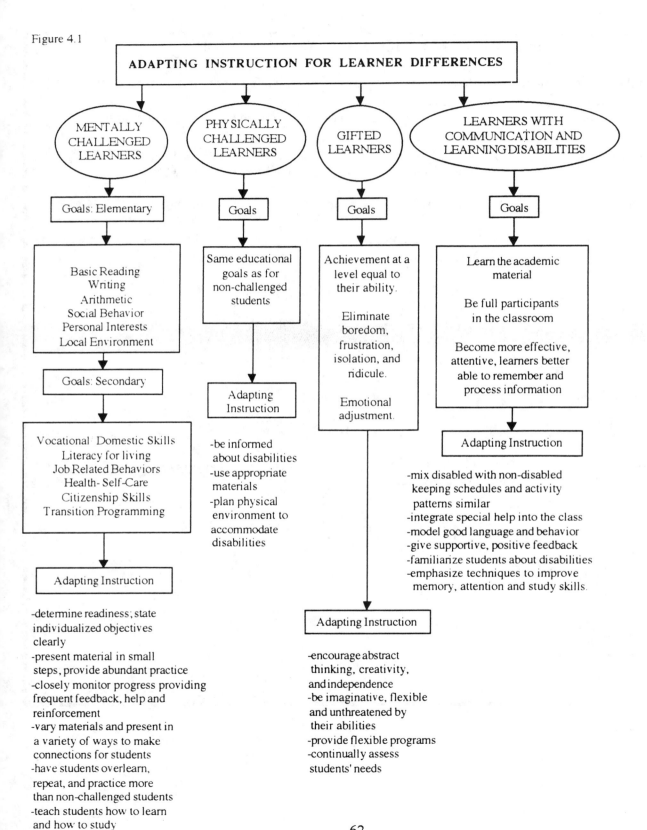

ADAPTING INSTRUCTION FOR LEARNER DIFFERENCES

MENTALLY CHALLENGED LEARNERS

Goals: Elementary

Basic Reading
Writing
Arithmetic
Social Behavior
Personal Interests
Local Environment

Goals: Secondary

Vocational Domestic Skills
Literacy for living
Job Related Behaviors
Health- Self-Care
Citizenship Skills
Transition Programming

Adapting Instruction

-determine readiness; state
individualized objectives
clearly
-present material in small
steps, provide abundant practice
-closely monitor progress providing
frequent feedback, help and
reinforcement
-vary materials and present in
a variety of ways to make
connections for students
-have students overlearn,
repeat, and practice more
than non-challenged students
-teach students how to learn
and how to study

PHYSICALLY CHALLENGED LEARNERS

Goals

Same educational
goals as for
non-challenged
students

Adapting
Instruction

-be informed
about disabilities
-use appropriate
materials
-plan physical
environment to
accommodate
disabilities

GIFTED LEARNERS

Goals

Achievement at a
level equal to
their ability.

Eliminate
boredom,
frustration,
isolation, and
ridicule.

Emotional
adjustment.

Adapting Instruction

-encourage abstract
thinking, creativity,
and independence
-be imaginative, flexible
and unthreatened by
their abilities
-provide flexible programs
-continually assess
students' needs

LEARNERS WITH COMMUNICATION AND LEARNING DISABILITIES

Goals

Learn the academic
material

Be full participants
in the classroom

Become more effective,
attentive, learners better
able to remember and
process information

Adapting Instruction

-mix disabled with non-disabled
keeping schedules and activity
patterns similar
-integrate special help into the class
-model good language and behavior
-give supportive, positive feedback
-familiarize students about disabilities
-emphasize techniques to improve
memory, attention and study skills.

Creativity

Many conceptions exist regarding what constitutes **creativity**. A general definition is:

Creativity: Imaginative, original thinking or problem solving. Creativity usually occurs within a particular area. Creativity requires (1) extensive knowledge, (2) flexibility, and (3) the continual reorganizing of ideas. Certainly, creativity embraces **restructuring** which is the ability to break set or break away from the usual, familiar mode of thinking.

Restructuring: Conceiving of a problem in a new or different way. **Example:** Karen is camping and it is raining. Her tent has a hole in the top and she has nothing with which to repair it. She sits in her tent, wearing a raincoat to keep dry, when she has a sudden insight, "Hey, if I put my raincoat over the hole in the tent, the tent will stay dry and I won't need to wear my raincoat inside the tent".

The assessment of creativity is a difficult task and for paper-and-pencil assessments has become equated with the measure of **divergent** as opposed to **convergent** thinking.

Divergent thinking: the ability to propose many different ideas or solutions.

Convergent thinking: a more common ability of identifying only one answer, more consistent with traditional expectations of student performance.

A widely used paper-and-pencil test of both verbal and graphic creativity was developed by Torrance and is called the Torrance Test of Creative Thinking (TTCT). Tests are timed and subjects are required, for example, to complete drawings from 30 parallel lines or 30 circles (for the graphic component) or to **brainstorm** verbal ideas, i.e., how many uses can you think of for a tin can or how many things can you come up with that are both solid and flexible.

Brainstorming: when individuals give rapid-fire responses, wild, free-flowing ideas without evaluation or judgment from others.

To score responses from the TTCT, the evaluator will consider the following criteria in scoring:

- **Originality:** when the given response occurs fewer than 5 or 10 times per 100 test subjects.
- **Fluency:** simply the number of responses within the allotted time
- **Flexibility:** number of different categories of responses

---

Application Three: Creative Thinking

This exercise is just for fun so that you can see how the TTCT might work. You will not be able to determine the originality of these responses, but you will be able to make educated guesses as to the flexibility and also come up with an accurate fluency score. Try to guess which responses might be considered original Check your responses against the answer key. The following were given in response to: "Name as many things as you can think of that are both solid and flexible".

licorice	rubber	plastic	old celery	bodies	marriages	cartilage
muscles	ideas	hair	spaghetti	gum	cloth	aluminum
fingernails	skin	Gumby	Silly Putty	Play Doh	tofu	taffy

1. Fluency score _____
2. Flexibility score _____
3. Originality score _____

Cognitive and Learning Styles

Variations in individuals' academic performance may in part, result from certain unique modes of functioning called **cognitive styles.**

Cognitive Styles: are self-consistent, characteristic modes of perceiving, remembering, thinking, problem solving, decision making, and organizing information, that relate to underlying personality trends.
Two cognitive styles are **(1) field dependence/field independence** and **(2) impulsive/reflective tempo.**

(1) Field Dependence: Cognitive style in which patterns are perceived as wholes. The figures in the foreground appear fused with the background and FD individuals have difficulty separating the parts from the whole. They are heavily reliant on the surrounding field for spatial cues and for orienting their own bodies within space. Because their focus is on the surrounding field, they attend to social information, having good memories for names and faces, work well in social groups, and prefer less analytical subjects as history and literature vs. mathematics and science. These individuals benefit from well structured, sequential assignments.

Field Independence: Cognitive style in which separate parts of a pattern are perceived and analyzed. This is the ability to perceive parts as distinct from the whole and disembed the figure from the ground. Because FI individuals are analytical, they do well in mathematics and science, but are not so people-oriented, preferring independent work and show less reliance upon the surrounding field for social or for spatial cues. These individuals can impose structure on a chaotic situation.

Because teachers will not always be able to discern students' styles, a variety of instructional strategies should be employed to respond to students' individual needs, weaknesses, and strengths.

Learning Abilities and Learning Problems

(2) Impulsive Tempo: Characterized by cognitive style of responding quickly but often inaccurately.
Example: Maria rapidly read the assigned passage but when asked what she had just read, she responded, "I don't know." She sped through the motions of reading without processing it's meaning.

Young children have a tendency toward impulsive behavior but become more **reflective** as they age, which is particularly important for some tasks such as reading. Children can be taught more effective learning strategies and to be more reflective through **self-instruction.**

Self-instruction: Talking yourself through the steps of a task.

Reflective Tempo: Characterized by cognitive style of responding slowly, carefully, and accurately. Even though reflection is a good quality, students who are too reflective deliberate too long, and have difficulty making choices and selecting the main idea. **Example:** Amanda sat in the restaurant, holding up her party for half an hour trying to decide on an item from the menu. "I don't know what to have. What are you having? Does this look good to you? Has anyone eaten this before? Maybe, I should just get a salad. What should I do?......." These individuals need help in focusing on the "meat of the matter" and working steadily to reach a goal.

Learning Styles and Preferences: Preferred ways of studying and learning, such as using pictures instead of text, working with other people versus alone, learning in structured or in unstructured situations, and so on. **Example:** One of my college students preferred to lie on the floor during class when taking her exams and told me that was how she studied and felt most comfortable. Since she was the only student with this request, it was easy to accommodate her and she performed quite well.

There are a variety of learning style inventories that examine many learning variables, such as, preferences for learning with structure, with peers, with music, with food, at different times of the day, with authority figures, independently, etc.. Some learning style inventories have been criticized for lacking reliability and validity, and many have suggested that teachers should present information in many modalities to prevent learners from becoming overly reliant on one modality. Other research, however, informs us that when students are instructed in their preferred style, their achievement is higher.

Another variable that appears to influence student achievement depends upon whether students adopt **a deep-processing approach vs. a surfacing processing approach**. Certainly, situational factors can influence this, but these are tendencies that individuals display.

Deep Processing Approach: when students see the learning materials or activities as a means for understanding some underlying concepts or meanings. These students tend to learn for the sake of learning.

Surface Processing Approach: when students focus on memorizing the learning materials, not understanding them. These students tend to be motivated by external rewards and performance evaluations.

With respect to all of the cognitive styles, no one teacher can possibly hope to accommodate all styles in the classroom but by varying instructional modalities, materials, physical environments, and groupings, everyone has the opportunity to learn within their preferred styles as well as experiencing other modalities.

Application Four: Identifying Cognitive and Learning Styles

Read the following descriptions of students as if they were your students and you were trying to determine their preferred learning modalities. Select the best response or responses (you may select more than one for each statement) from the list below. Check your responses in the answer key.

Reflective	Impulsive	Deep Processor
Surface Processor	Field Independent	Field Dependent

1. _____ Carrie Jackson was extremely upset when she failed her science exam. When asked what seemed to be her difficulty, Carrie responded, "I don't know. I studied real hard to memorize all of the definitions."

2. _____ Mitch Klett enjoys science and spends his free time trying to perform experiments that will enhance his understanding of scientific principles. He carefully plans out every detail of his experiments and becomes quite upset if anyone interrupts him during his planning stages. He is a solitary worker and dedicated to scientific advancement.

3. _____ Fred Smith frequently relies upon his friends for help in his geometry class. He laughs at his troubles stating, "It's just like pool. I just can't seem to see the angles." Fred asks everyone in class if they would consider forming a geometry support group for the mathematically challenged like himself.

4. _____ Bonnie Brown is a good reader, able to sound out some of the more difficult vocabulary words. When reading orally, she speaks so fast that no one else can keep pace to understand her and she needs to be constantly reminded to slow down. She approaches her classroom tasks in the same manner expressing her desire to be finished.

5. _____ Juan Rivera hangs back whenever his friends attempt something new or challenging. He only attempts those activities within his "comfort zone," what he already knows he can accomplish so that he doesn't lose face. He appears very worried about what other people think.

6. _____ Miko Ottawa gets lost every time she leaves the classroom. She says all of the hallways confuse her but she says she never forgets a face. "I guess I need a map to find my way around the school , although my map reading skills are almost as bad as my ability to follow directions. I guess I'll just keep asking directions from everyone I know."

7. _____ Janet Johnson wants to become an architect. She is very analytical, possesses good mathematical skills, and excels at drawing perspectives in her drafting class. The other students frequently rely on her for help, especially since she has such great organizational skills and is able to structure confusing situations so that others can comprehend.

Students With Learning Challenges

As teachers you will be required not only to respond to students' learning style differences but to the needs of those students with learning challenges. No teacher can hope to be an expert on all of the exceptionalities, unless your field is special education, but you can learn as much as possible about the specific disabilities you will encounter in your students. First, some terminology:

Disability: the inability to do something specific such as walk or hear.

Handicap: a relative term, referring to the difficulties that people with disabilities encounter in some situations. **Example:** a person in a wheelchair is handicapped when trying to ascend a flight of stairs but not when participating in a debate.

Woolfolk states in Chapter 4, "It is important that we do not create handicaps for people by way we react to their disabilities."

The school can help to insure that the physical environment of the school not create handicaps for students with disabilities by providing ramps, elevators, and accessible rooms.

Orthopedic Devices: Devices such as braces and wheelchairs that aid people with physical disabilities.

Epilepsy: Disorder marked by seizures and caused by abnormal electrical discharges in the brain.
* **partial seizure:** a seizure beginning in a localized area and involving only a small part of the brain.
* **generalized seizure:** a seizure involving a large portion of the brain. These seizures were once called grand mal, may last up to five minutes, followed by deep sleep or coma.

Seizures with convulsions require action by the teacher:
1. do not try to restrain their movements
2. lower the child gently to the floor, away from furniture or walls
3. move hard objects away
4. turn the child's head to the side and loosen any tight clothing
5. Never put anything in the child's mouth
6. If one seizure follows another, or if it lasts more than 10 minutes, seek medical help
7. Always find out from parents how the seizure is dealt with

* **Absence seizures:** were once called petit mal seizures and are so mild, they can easily go undetected. The student may briefly lose contact, stare, fail to respond to questions, drop objects, and miss what was happening for 30 seconds.

Cerebral Palsy: condition involving a range of motor or coordination difficulties due to brain damage. Cerebral palsy is often characterized by **spasticity**. Often, children with cerebral palsy have secondary handicaps such as hearing impairments, speech problems, or mild, mental retardation

Spasticity: Overly tight or tense muscles.

Hearing Impairment: teachers must be alert to signs of hearing difficulty such as turning one ear toward the speaker, misunderstanding conversation, not following directions, asking people to repeat what they've said, mispronouncing new words or names, being reluctant to participate, or being plagued by chronic earaches, sinus infections, or allergies. Hearing impaired children may require **speech reading, sign language, or finger spelling.**

Speech reading: Using visual cues to understand language.
Sign Language: Communication system of hand movements that symbolize words and concepts.
Finger Spelling: Communication system that "spells out" each letter with a hand position.

Vision Impairment: teachers must be alert to signs of seeing difficulty such as squinting, rubbing eyes, complaints of eyes itching, burning, redness, or encrustedness. Students may misread material on the board, describe their vision as blurred, be sensitive to light, or hold their heads at an odd angle. Mild vision problems could be corrected with lenses if they have **low vision** but 1 in 2500 students are **educationally blind.**

Low Vision: Vision limited to close objects.
Educationally Blind: Needing Braille and other special materials in order to learn.

Communication Disorders:

Communication disorders can result from any different sources because many factors contribute to the individual's ability to speak, i.e., hearing, inadequate language at home, or emotional problems. One form of disorder is **speech impairment**.

Speech Impairment: Inability to produce sounds effectively for speaking. Three forms of speech impairment are **articulation disorders, stuttering,** and **voicing problems.**

Articulation Disorders: Any of a variety of pronunciation difficulties, such as the substitution, distortion, or omission of sounds. **Example:** "I thought I thaw a putty tat," Tweetie Bird.

Stuttering: Repetitions, prolongations, and hesitations that lock flow of speech. **Example:** "I wa wa wa want some wa wa water."

Voicing Problems: Inappropriate pitch, quality, loudness, or intonation. **Example:** When I worked with children at a psychiatric institute, there was a girl who spoke in a monotone and was perceived as quite frightening by the other children there, when she stated, "I don't want to play with the children" in a deep-voiced monotone.

Emotional or Behavioral Disorders

Behavior is considered to be a problem when it deviates so far from normal that it interferes with the intellectual growth and development of the student and others. The behavioral problems are consistent across time and situations. Quay and Peterson have categorized five dimensions of emotional/behavioral disorders:

conduct disorders: demonstrated behaviors are aggressive, destructive, disobedient, uncooperative, distractible, disruptive, and persistent. Many of these children are disliked by children and adults and fail academically.

anxiety-withdrawal disorder: children who possess this disorder are anxious, withdrawn, shy, depressed, and hypersensitive, cry easily, have little confidence, few social skillls, and few friends.

attention problems immaturity: behaviors include short attention span, frequent daydreaming, little initiative, messiness, and poor coordination.

socialized aggression: aberrant behaviors demonstrated by youth who are reinforced for these behaviors by their culture, such as gang members.

psychotic behavior: most likely, you will not have to deal with students with bizarre, behaviors stemming from fantasies and ideas not related to reality.

Hyperactivity and Attention Disorders

Hyperactivity is a widely-used, much abused term that wasn't even in use 30 to 40 years ago. More boys than girls are being labeled as hyperactive. An increasing number of American youth are now on Ritalin or some other form of drug therapy to control their behaviors in despite the lack of evidence that these drugs lead to improvement in academic learning or peer relationships.

Hyperactivity: Behavior disorder marked by atypical, excessive restlessness and inattentiveness. The main problem encountered by these children is directing and maintaining attention in learning situations and the American Psychiatric Association has labeled this as **attention deficit-hyperactive disorder (ADHD).**

Attention Deficit-Hyperactive Disorder: Current term for disruptive behavior disorders marked by overactivity, excessive difficulty sustaining attention, or impulsiveness. These children have behaviors characterized by:
- more physically active and inattentive than other children
- difficulty responding appropriately and working steadily toward goals
- may have difficulty in controlling their behaviors

A promising approach toward more effective learning for these students combines instruction in learning and memory strategies with motivational training. Students learn "how" and "when" to apply these strategies and to take control. These skills need to be taught even if the students are on medication.

Learning Disabilities

Learning disabilities is a general term used to describe a broad group of disorders that may manifest as an imperfect ability to listen, speak, do mathematics, write, read, or reason. Most students with learning disabilities are of average or above average intelligence but demonstrate difficulties in one or two subject areas. Whereas, students with disabilities are not all alike, many possess the following characteristics:

- difficulties in one or more academic areas
- attention problems, hyperactivity, and impulsivity
- difficulty organizing and interpreting visual and auditory information
- disorders of thinking, memory, speech and hearing
- difficulty making and keeping friends
- lack effective ways to approach academic tasks; they don't know how to:
  1. focus on relevant information or get organized
  2. apply learning strategies or study skills
  3. change strategies when one isn't working
  4. evaluate their learning
  5. work independently to completion

Early diagnosis is especially important so that the learning disabled do not develop **learned helplessness.**

Learned Helplessness: The expectation, based on previous experiences with a lack of control, that all one's efforts will lead to failure.

Comparisons Between Mentally Challenged and Learning Disabled Students

	Mentally Challenged	**Learning Disabled**
IQ	lower than average less than 70	average or higher 100 and above
Adaptive Functioning	lower than average relative to same age peers	average or above
Academics	low overall in all subjects	average achievement and above except for one or two subject areas: depends on area of disability.
Causes	mild: unknown, may be due to prenatal influences moderate or severe: trauma, infections, brain disease	neurological dysfunction in the brain, resulting in an imperfect ability to read, write, think, speak, spell, or do mathematics
Symptoms	low motivation poor peer relations poor communication poor health (heart) poor motor skills memory disorders	hyperactivity perceptual/ motor problems emotional lability coordination deficits attention disorders impulsivity memory disorders twitching, glazed eyes

Integration, Mainstreaming, and Inclusion

In 1975, the **The Education for All Handicapped Children Act (Public Law 94-142)** mandated changes that would influence the appearance of handicapped children within the public school classroom. This law guarantees a free public education to every child between the ages of 3 and 21 regardless of how seriously handicapped toward **full inclusion**. Recently, there is a greater move toward **the regular education initiative.**

Full Inclusion: The integration of all students, including those with severe disabilities, into regular classes.

Regular Education Initiative: An educational movement that advocates giving regular education teachers, not special education teachers, responsibility for teaching mildly (and sometimes moderately) handicapped children.

In the 1990's Public Law 94-192 was amended by the **Individuals with Disabilities Education Act (IDEA)** which replaced the word "handicapped" with "disabled" and expanded the services for disabled students. Also in 1990, further changes were implemented by the **Americans with Disabilities Act (ADA).**

Americans with Disabilities Act (ADA): Legislation prohibiting discrimination against persons with disabilities in employment, transportation, public access, local government and communications.

Three key points to these laws and amendments are:

1. **Least Restrictive Environment:** Placement of each child in as normal an educational setting possible
2. **Individualized Education Program (IEP):** Annually revised program for an exceptional student, detailing present achievement level, goals, and strategies, drawn up by teachers, parents, specialists, and (if possible) student.
    a. includes student's present level of functioning
    b. goals for the year and measurable instructional objectives
    c. a list of specific services for the student
    d. a description of how fully the student will participate in the regular school program
    e. a schedule for implementation of the above
    f. plans for transitional services to move the student into adult life
3. Protection of the rights of disabled students and their parents

Whereas it is strongly recommended that wherever possible, provide services for disabled students within their own classroom, **resource rooms** may also be employed.

Resource Rooms: A classroom with special materials and a specially trained teacher. These rooms may also be used as crises centers, when the regular classroom teacher is unable to provide the kind of time and guidance necessary.

Learning Abilities and Learning Problems

More and more, special education and regular education teachers are combining forces to meet the needs of disabled students in a new approach called **cooperative teaching.** Both teachers exchange roles to make the best use of expertise, materials, and time, benefitting the regular as well as the disabled students.

Computers and Exceptional Students

Computers are seen as an educational boon for both disabled and non-disabled students. Some of the ways that computers have been found to benefit disabled students are listed below:

1. They can provide step-by-step tutoring, and repeat information as often as necessary
2. They are engaging and interactive, increasing motivation
3. They use images, sounds, and gamelike features
4. Programs are being developed to help hearing people use sign language
5. Hearing impaired benefit from visual programs
6. Programs will "speak" words for students with reading difficulties
7. For the writing disabled, word processors produce perfect penmanship
8. For gifted students, computers can be an enriching resource for sharing information and projects

Application Five: Identifying Key Terms and Definitions

Fill in the puzzle with the correct terms. Terms with two words will not have a space in between. Check your response in the answer key.

Clues

Down:
1. retardation caused by presence of an extra chromosome
2. overly tight or tense muscles, characteristic of some forms of cerebral palsy
3. repetitions, prolongations, and hesitations that block flow of speech
4. a disadvantage in a particular situation, sometimes caused by a disability
6. disorder marked by seizures and caused by abnormal electrical discharges in the brain
7. cognitive style of responding slowly, carefully, and accurately
8. cognitive style of responding quickly but inaccurately
9. condition involving a range of motor or coordination difficulties due to brain damage

Across:

5. significantly below-average intellectual and adaptive social behavior, evident before age 18
10. uncontrolled spontaneous firings of neurons in the brain
11. the inability to do something specific as walk or hear

Chapter 4: Key Terms
Learner Differences

Practice Tests

Essay Questions

1. Discuss the arguments for and against full inclusion of exceptional students.

2. Summarize some strategies for enhancing creativity among your students.

Multiple Choice Questions

1. The best predictor of divergent thinking is (are)
   a. student IQ
   b. fluency scores
   c. flexibility scores
   d. originality scores

2. Preschool children who spend more time in fantasy and pretend play
   a. engage in a higher frequency of behavior disorders in the classroom
   b. have higher resulting IQs
   c. are more creative
   d. possess greater intrapersonal intelligence

3. Highly related to standardized IQ scores are measures of
   a. scholastic achievement
   b. reflective/impulsive tempo
   c. field independence/dependence
   d. creativity

4. Which of the following is the single best predictor of academic giftedness?
   a. group achievement tests
   b. reading achievement scores
   c. midterm GPAs
   d. individual IQ tests

5. Which of the following is NOT something you should do if you suspect that a student in your class is having absence seizures?
   a. consult the school psychologist or nurse
   b. question the student to insure that they are understanding
   c. repeat yourself periodically
   d. try to gently rouse the child

6. Research indicates that hearing impaired children who learn manual approaches as opposed to those who learn only oral approaches
   a. perform better in academic subjects
   b. are more socially mature
   c. use sign language, finger spelling, or both
   d. all of the above

7. Students classified as having low vision
   a. can be helped with corrective lenses
   b. can read with the aid of a magnifying glass or large-print books
   c. must use hearing and touch as the primary learning channels
   d. rely solely on variable speed tape recorders

8. The ages at which most children can pronounce all English sounds in normal conversation are
   a. between the ages of 3 to 4
   b. between the ages of 4 to 6
   c. between the ages of 5 to 7
   d. between the ages of 6 to 8

9. Which of the following is NOT a side effect of the stimulants used with hyperactive children?
   a. weight gain
   b. increased heart rate
   c. nausea
   d. interference with growth rate

10. Within an IEP, the "rights of the parents and students" means that
    a. students may be assigned surrogate parents to participate in planning when the parents are unavailable
    b. confidentiality of school records must be maintained
    c. testing practices must not discriminate against students from different cultural backgrounds
    d. all of the above

Answer Key

Application One: IQ Myths and Facts
1. false   2. true   3. false   4. true   5. false
6. false   7. false   8. false   9. false   10. true

Application Two: Matching Gifted and Talented
a. 2   b. 9   c. 4   d. 7   e. 5   f. 3   g. 6   h. 1   i. 8   number=15

Application Three: Creative Thinking
1. fluency score=21
2. flexibility score=5 (toys, body parts, food, materials, and abstract ideas)

3. originality score= an educated guess might include marriage, Gumby, and ideas, but this is just a guess

Application Four: Identifying Cognitive and Learning Styles
1. Surface Processor
2. Deep Processor, Reflective, Field Independent
3. Field Dependent
4. Impulsive, Surface Processor
5. Surface Processor
6. Field Dependent
7. Field Independent

Learning Abilities and Learning Problems

Application Five: Identifying Key Terms and Definitions

Chapter 4: Key Terms
Learner Differences

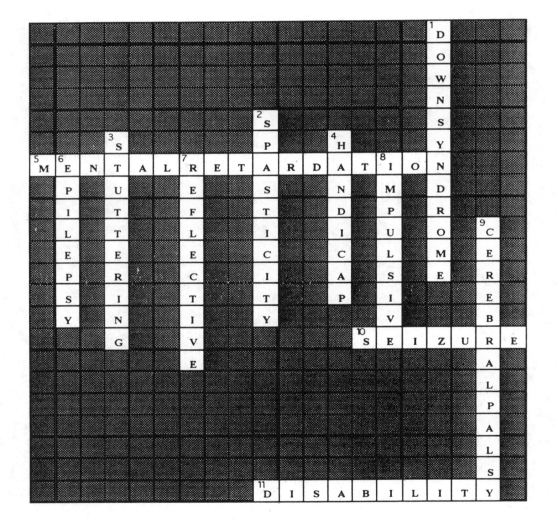

Learning Abilities and Learning Problems

Essays

1. In support of full inclusion, all children need to learn with and from other children. Exceptional children need to be in an environment that is as normal as possible; the "real world" with all of its real world experiences. Disabled students should not be denied the opportunity to participate in society for how else will they learn how to function in society and to become self-sufficient? Many say that special education has failed to help disabled students but the opponents of full inclusion suggest that these disabled students spend a portion of their time in regular classrooms. Therefore, the regular classrooms are also partially to blame. Opponents suggest that full inclusion places a tremendous burden on regular educators who have little preparation, support, and resources.

2. Encourage "no holds barred" wild ideas. Accept everyones' ideas with no judgments. Allow students to engage in rapid fire responses, calling out whatever comes to mind (within reason, of course). Permit some class projects to be designed, implemented, and evaluated by the students. Encourage problem solving toward multiple answers (divergent thinking) and celebrate diversity. Encourage debate and allow dissent. Provide an atmosphere where students feel safe to express their ideas and opinions.

Multiple Choice

1. b 2. c 3. a 4. d 5. d 6. d 7. b 8. d 9. a 10. d

Chapter Five

The Impact of Culture and Community

"Do not confine your children to your own learning for they were born in another time."
Hebrew Proverb

Our country is more culturally diverse than it has ever been since its inception. The immigrant influx during the past decade was larger than the total amount of immigrants to enter this country in the past century. One of the characteristics of today's immigrants is its youth with an average age of 13 to 41 years.

This means today's immigrants are primarily in their prime working and prime child bearing years. This will have a major impact on the number of minority students in the public school system. This will present new challenges to classroom educators because many minority students demonstrate lower academic achievement.

In the beginning of the 20th century, the immigrants who entered the country were expected to enter the cultural **melting pot** and to adopt the language, ways, and mores of those who had come before.

Melting Pot: A metaphor for the absorption and assimilation of immigrants into the mainstream of society so that ethnic differences vanish.

In the past few decades, educators suggested that because they had not become part of the melting pot, minority and poor students were culturally disadvantaged in school; hence poorer performance. This is explained by the **cultural deficit model.**

Cultural Deficit Model: A model that explains the school achievement problems of ethnic minority students by assuming that their home culture is inadequate and does not prepare them to succeed in school.

Today this notion is rejected and it is believed that no culture is deficient but instead, may be incompatible with the school culture. During the 60s and 70s, there was an increasing awareness of ethnic pride and a desire to become part of mainstream society while retaining cultural identity. **Multicultural education** is one way to address ethnic pride.

Multicultural Education: Education that teaches the value of cultural diversity through the expansion of educational curricula that includes the perspectives, histories, accomplishments, and concerns of non-European people and grants educational equality to all.

Culture and Group Membership

Groups create **culture**. Groups can be defined along regional, ethnic, religious, racial, gender, social class, or other lines. As each of us belong to many groups, we are also influenced by many cultures. Sometimes, the ideas and beliefs of one culture are incompatible with another.

Culture: The knowledge, values, attitudes, and traditions that guide the behavior of a group of people and allow them to solve the problems of living in their environment. Two cultural cautions are:

1. Much of the available research focuses on social class, gender, and ethnicity but real children are complex beings who belong to and are influenced by the many groups to which they belong.

2. Membership in a certain group does not determine behavior but makes certain behaviors more likely.

Social Class Differences

Socioeconomic Status (SES) has been categorized by four levels (upper, middle, working, and lower) although no single variable, not even income, is an effective measure of SES.

Socioeconomic Status (SES): Relative standing in the society based on income, power, background, and prestige. Social class is a strong characteristic uniting like individuals even beyond ethnic differences.

Characteristics of the poor:
- one in four Americans under the age of 18 lives in poverty
- poverty level is $13,359 for a family of four living in an urban area
- US has the highest rate of poverty for children of all developed nations
- the poverty rate is three times higher than most other industrialized countries
- twice as many children live outside as within large urban areas
- 65% of the poor children are white but the majority of the population is comprised of whites
- 36% of all Hispanic-American children live in poverty
- 44% of all African-American children live in poverty

Low-SES students may become part of a **resistance culture**.

Resistance Culture: Group values and beliefs about refusing to adopt the behaviors and attitudes of the majority culture. To succeed in school, many low-SES students believe that they must act "middle class" which may mean cooperating with teachers, studying, etc., and in effect, "selling out."

See Figure 5.1 for the educational influences of socioeconomic status.

The Impact of Culture and Community

Figure 5.1

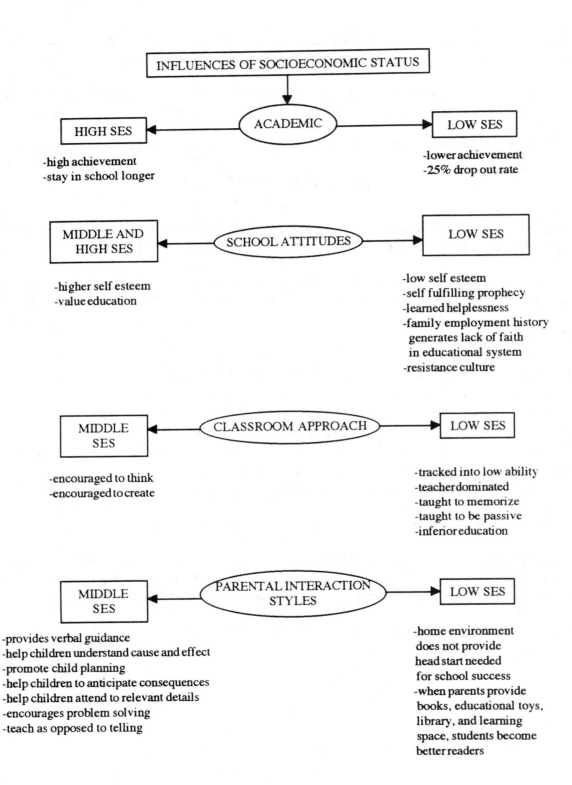

Ethnic and Racial Differences

Ethnicity: A cultural heritage shared by a group of people. This can be based upon common nationality, culture, language, religion or race.

Race: A group of people who share common biological traits that are seen as self-defining by the people of the group.

People often mistake the term **minority group** to mean particular ethnic or racial groups.

Minority Group: A group of people who have been socially disadvantaged--not always a minority in actual numbers. Sociologists use this term to label a group of people who receives unequal or discriminatory treatment.

There are visible and invisible signs of culture. The visible signs are things such as costume, music, food, etc.. The invisible differences may be things such as rules for conducting interpersonal relationships. For **example**, people from some cultures get very close to one another when conversing, but if you are from a culture that places greater distance between its members, then you might take affront at someone "invading your body space." Cultural conflicts are usually about the subtle, or invisible signs of culture, because when cultural differences meet, misunderstandings occur and members from different cultures may be perceived as rude, ignorant, or disrespectful.

It is a well established finding that some ethnic groups consistently achieve below average. We can look to cultural differences, discrimination, and the result of growing up in a low-SES environment as causal factors. Even after the *Brown v. the Board of Education of Topeka* ruling and the declaration that segregation is illegal there still appears to be other subtle forms of segregation. Too often, minority group students are placed in low ability tracks. However, when minority group students are placed in high quality schools with a predominance of middle class students, achievement and future outcomes improve.

The United States is a racist society, but education may be one of the best ways to combat **prejudice.** If schools emphasize acceptance and teach the value of all ethnic groups, attitudes may change.

Prejudice: Prejudgement, or irrational generalization about an entire category of people. Prejudice may take many forms: racial, ethnic, religious, political, geographic, gender, and sexual orientation.

Application One: Understanding Differences

Which of the scenarios listed below is consistent with what we know about ethnic and minority groups? When your decision is "inconsistent," explain your decision. Check your responses in the answer key.

1.　　The school counselor was working with a student from a different cultural background. The counselor was discussing career options, but upon receiving no acknowledgment from the student, repeated all of the information. Again, no response was forthcoming from the student, so the counselor assumed that the student was slow or just didn't care. _____

2.　　Hoa Carter's mother is from the Republic of China. Joan Smith's mother is from Iowa. Both are discussing their children's school failures and the probable causes. Hoa's mom blames the school system whereas Joan's mom states that Joan just doesn't put forth enough effort. _____

3.　　Danika is a five-year-old Black child. When she was told to choose between a white doll and a black doll, but that she should pick the one that is prettier and smarter, she chose the black doll because that is the one with which she was able to identify. _____

4.　　A group of non-Hispanic Americans living in L.A. were asked whether they believed that Hispanic Americans preferred to live off of welfare and the majority of the respondents stated that they disagreed and it was a ridiculous notion. _____

5.　　Teachers from the science and mathematics department surveyed their students about career goals in math and science. To their relief, they discovered that the majority of their students who planned to pursue careers in these areas were African American and Hispanic American _____

6.　　Nate Johnson's favorite television show was "All in the Family." One of his favorite authors is Rush Limbaugh. Nate's children frequently instigate racial conflict. _____

7.　　Jacque Renault is a high achieving, white male. His teacher gives him a tremendous amount of attention in class. _____

8.　　In Cali and Nick's reading group, the girls said they wanted to read a story about a boy for a change. _____

9.　　The school guidance counselor was extremely upset when Jennifer, who in her senior year would become valedictorian, stated that she did not want to take any more math and science courses. _____

10.　　Nicole Graham is an only child who comes from a white middle-class family. When asked what they value in Nicole, her parents respond "achievement, competitiveness, and emotional control."
_____

The Development of Prejudice

There are several theories as to why prejudices develop but several factors have been shown to relate to the appearance of prejudicial attitudes. It is generally thought to be a combination of both personal and social factors. Children may develop prejudices as a result of familial attitude, friends, media, advertising, and the entire environment around them. Extreme prejudice may also develop as a result of an **authoritarian personality.**

Authoritarian Personality: Rigidly conforming to belief that society is naturally competitive, with "better" people reaping its rewards.

Furthermore, we use schemas to structure and make sense of the world. Our experiences help us to construct our schemes of knowing, and as with everything we know, we also construct schemes about different groups of people, based upon characteristics we have encountered or what others have told us, called **stereotypes.**

Stereotypes: Schema that organizes knowledge or perceptions about a category.

When schemas result in negative stereotypes, then **discrimination** can ensue. Discrimination is prevalent within our society toward women and ethnic Americans. Discrimination can cause many problems for ethnic and minority groups because they must reconcile their identity with their ethnic group while trying to fit in with mainstream America.

Discrimination: Treating particular categories of people unequally.

Gender Differences

Differences do exist between men and women and these differences are both biological and environmental. Early on, interactions with our parents help to shape our notions of what it is to be male or female known as **gender schemas.**

Gender Schemas: Organized networks of knowledge about what it means to be male or female. **Example:** My friend's three year-old insisted that their postman was a woman because he had long hair and an earring. His appearance was inconsistent with her gender schemas.

Gender schemas help children to make sense of the world and guide their behavior. Little boys may avoid playing with dolls because it is inconsistent with their gender schemas about boy behaviors. Gender schemas help individuals to develop notions of **gender-role identity.**

Gender-Role Identity: Beliefs about characteristics and behaviors associated with one sex as opposed to the other.

Most people see themselves as possessing characteristics that are considered by society to be either "masculine" or "feminine." Nowadays, few individuals are rigidly masculine or rigidly feminine. Better adjusted individuals seem to possess both masculine and feminine characteristics depending on the situation. These individuals are considered to be **androgynous.**

The Impact of Culture and Community

Androgynous: Having some typically male and some typically female characteristics apparent in one individual.

Application Two: Gender-Role Stereotypes

To identify your own conceptions and stereotypes about gender, read the following statements and decide whether they apply to those of male or female gender as supported by research. Some statements may apply to both females and males.

1. _____ Prefer active, rough, noisy play

2. _____ By age 6, the ratio of playtime with same-sexed playmates is 11 to 1.

3. _____ Are played with more roughly and vigorously by their parents.

4. _____ Are touched more by parents as infants and kept at a greater distance as toddlers.

5. _____ Parents react more positively to emotional sensitivity.

6. _____ Parents react more positively to assertive behaviors.

7. _____ Encouraged to be affectionate and tender.

8. _____ Given more freedom to roam the neighborhood.

9. _____ Independence and initiative are encouraged.

10. _____ Protected longer from playing with scissors or crossing the street.

Reported to be a primary culprit in promoting the unequal treatment of males and females are schools themselves. Many educational factors can be seen to foster **gender biases.**

Gender Biases: Different views of males and females, often favoring one gender over the other.

A major source of gender bias can be found in textbooks where both females and males are portrayed in sexually stereotyped ways:

• Later grade materials omitted women altogether from illustrations and text. (before 1970)

• In a study of 2,760 stories from 134 books found the total number of stories dealing with males or male animals to be four times greater than the number dealing with females or female animals. (1975)

• Females tended to be shown in the home, behaving passively and expressing fear or incompetence. (1975)

- Males were usually more dominant, adventurous, and rescued females. (1975)
- Girls portrayed as more helpless than boys. (1990)

Still, another source of gender bias stems from classroom teachers' interactions with their students.
- Teachers interact more with boys than with girls
- Teachers ask more questions of males, give males more feedback (praise, criticism, and correction)
- Teachers give more specific and valuable comments to boys
- By college, men are twice as likely to initiate comments as women
- From preschool through college, girls receive 1,800 fewer hours of attention and instruction than boys
- Minority-group boys, like girls receive less teacher attention
- Boys are questioned 80% more than girls in science classes
- Boys dominate the use of equipment in science labs

Sex Differences in Mental Abilities

In the 1970's, research showed that males outperformed females on all tests of spatial ability and in mathematics. This has changed somewhat in the past 20 years. Sex differences favoring males still exist on spatial tests that require mental rotation of a figure in space, prediction of the trajectories of moving objects, and navigating. The differences in mathematics are diminishing with males still maintaining a slight edge over females but African-American females outperform their male counterparts in math and Asian-American females perform as well as Asian-American males in math and science.

Some researchers found that girls are better than boys on computational, logical, and abstract problems but boys do better on story and spatial relation problems. Sex differences in mathematics are greater among academically talented students. One explanation for the apparent differences may be due to the fact that girls take fewer mathematics courses than boys. When previous number of courses are equated, differences virtually disappear, except for high achieving boys and girls, that is. Academically qualified girls do not take advanced math and science courses, limit their college and career opportunities in these areas, hence, only 15% of the scientists, mathematicians, and engineers are women. Evidence indicates that teachers, are in part responsible for instilling in girls the belief that they aren't cut out for mathematics.

In schools where no gender differences in mathematics were found, teachers had strong backgrounds in mathematics, engineering, or science, not just general education. The brightest students, male and female were grouped together for math and there was a heavy emphasis on reasoning in the classes.

Language Differences in the Classroom

Culture affects communication. Children from different cultures and ethnic backgrounds experience many confusions in the classroom and one of the largest areas of confusion can stem from language and **dialect** differences.

Dialect: Rule-governed variation of a language spoken by a particular group.

Each dialect within a language system is logical, complex, and conforms to as many rules as **standard speech** but these rules will differ from dialect to dialect. **Example:** When we were growing up, everyone referred to the stream that flowed through our park as "the crick" versus the correct pronunciation of creek

Standard Speech: The most generally accepted and used form of a language.

The best teaching approach when one's students speak with a dialect is to accept their dialect as valid and a correct language system but to teach standard speech. To cope with linguistic diversity in the classroom, teachers:
* need to be sensitive to their own possible negative stereotypes about children who speak a different dialect
* should ensure comprehension by repeating instructions using different words and by asking students to paraphrase instructions or give examples
* check your chapter for further guidelines

Bilingualism

By the most recent reports, almost 25% of all students speak a first language other than English-- usually Spanish. Many problems are associated associated with **bilingualism**.

Bilingualism: Speaking two languages fluently. Two associated terms are:
English as a Second Language (ESL): Designation for programs and classes to teach English to students who are not native speakers of English.
Limited English Proficiency (LEP): Descriptive term for students who have limited mastery of English.

Some of the problems associated with bilingualism are:
1. you must be able to move back and forth between two cultures while maintaining a sense of identity
2. you must be able to master the knowledge necessary to communicate in two cultures
3. you may have to deal with potential discrimination

Some of the advantages of bilingualism are:
1. increased abilities at concept formation
2. increased creativity
3. knowledge of the workings of language
4. cognitive flexibility

These advantages hold true as long as there is no stigma attached to being bilingual and as long as students are not expected to abandon their first language.

Application Three : Myth or Fact-Bilingualism

Read the following statements and decide whether they are TRUE or FALSE. Check your responses in the answer key.

1. _____ Second language learning interferes with understanding in the first language.

2. _____ The more proficient the speaker is in the first language, the faster he or she will master the second language.

3. _____ When children simultaneously learn two languages, they will progress more slowly between the ages of one and two, because they have not yet figured out that they are learning two languages.

4. _____ When children are simultaneously learning two languages, their grammar for each language is as good as native **monolingual** speakers.

5. _____ The later we learn a second language, the more our pronunciation is near-native and accent free.

6. _____ Face-to-face communication skills (contextualized language skills) take about two years to master in a good quality language learning program.

7. _____ Mastering the academic uses of language like reading and doing grammar exercises (decontextualized language skills) takes about one more year to master than contextualized language skills.

Monolinguals: Individuals who speak only one language.

How should non-English speaking students be taught? We know that even when Spanish speaking students are taught other subjects in their native language and tested in Spanish also, they still score at the 32nd percentile on national tests. Two basic teaching approaches are:

- one that emphasizes making the transition to English as quickly as possible--proponents of this approach argue that valuable time will be lost if students are taught in their native language.

- and the other, that emphasizes the use of the native language for instruction of subjects until English skills are more fully developed (maintenance approach). Proponents of this approach suggest :

  a. to try to learn subjects in a foreign language is too difficult
  b. that teaching non-English speaking students in English only, may cause them to be **semilingual**.
  c. that teaching non-English speaking students in English only, sends the message that their language and culture are second class
  d. that by the time students have mastered English and let their home language deteriorate, they have to learn a second language in high school which would not have been necessary had the two languages been developed all along

A new approach to language learning is to create classes that mix students who are learning a second language with students who are native speakers with the goal for both groups to become fluent in both languages.

Semilingual: Not proficient in any language; speaking one or more languages inadequately.

Culturally Compatible Classrooms

Two decades of research supports the notion that when schools are changed to meet *the social organization, learning style*, and *sociolinguistic* needs of all students, then experiences and achievement also changes. It is the goals of most schools to create **culturally compatible classrooms.**

Culturally Compatible Classrooms: Classrooms in which procedures, rules, grouping strategies, attitudes, and teaching methods do not cause conflicts with the students' culturally influenced ways of learning and interacting.

Social organization means the ways people interact to accomplish a certain goal. Cooperative work groups are more effective, for example, with Hawaiian children than with Navajo children.

Learning Styles which were discussed in Chapter Four also differ for students from different ethnic backgrounds.

Sociolinguistics is the study of the formal and informal rules for how, when, about what, to who, and how long to speak in conversations within cultural groups. This includes **participation structures.**

Participation Structures: The formal and informal rules for how to take part in a given activity.

Most often, participation structures in school, match the communication rules found in middle class homes. Differences in these rules may cause frequent misunderstandings between teachers and students.

Application Four: Creating Culturally Compatible Classrooms

Research has provided us with generalized findings regarding ethnic differences in social organization, learning styles, and sociolinguistics. Read the learning style statements to match the corresponding ethnic group. Some statements may require more than one response. Check your responses in the answer key.
* Remember that there are dangers in stereotyping individuals based on group membership.

Hispanic Americans   African Americans
Native Americans   Asian Americans   Mexican Americans

1. _____ tend to be field dependent

2. _____ preferring holistic, concrete, social approaches to learning

3. _____ possess visual/global learning styles

4. _____ reason by inference rather than by logic, a tendency to approximate numbers, space, and time.

5. _____ show strong preferences for learning privately

6. _____ learn best in cooperative settings

7. _____ value teacher approval and work well in structured, quiet learning environments where there are clear goals

8. _____ tend to be more passive

9. _____ show greater dependence on nonverbal communication

10. _____ preference for energetic involvement in several simultaneous activities rather than routine, step-by-step learning

11. _____ dislike being made to compete with fellow students

Guiding Principles for Teaching Every Student Effectively

1. **Know your students**- Before you can engage in effective teaching, you must be able to understand your students' cultures, parents, home, and community environments. Try to bring parents into the classroom and don't wait until a student is in trouble before you meet with the family member. Watch how they interact in groups and spend non-teaching time with them.

2. **Respect your students**-Acceptance is an important first step toward helping your students develop self esteem. Once you know your students' strengths and accomplishments, you can help them to increase pride by highlighting their accomplishments and integrating their culture into the classroom.

3. **Teach your students**-Teach your students to read, write, speak, compute, think, and create. Do not limit your students' goals to basic skills. Focus on meaning and understanding and balance routine skill learning with novel and complex tasks. Provide context for skill learning that provides clear reasons for needing to learn the skills. Foster good attitudes about the academic content and eliminate redundancy in the curriculum. Finally, teach your students how to be students and how to act within the school environment. Review the chapter guidelines for more in depth strategies.

Practice Tests

Essay Questions

1. It states in your text "that even students who speak the same language as their teachers may still have trouble communicating, and thus learning school subjects, if their knowledge of pragmatics does not fit the school situation." Explain what is meant by this statement and what teachers can do about it.

2. Provide arguments as to whether multicultural education should emphasize similarities or differences.

Multiple Choice Questions

1. When SES and educational achievement are examined in research studies, results indicate that lack of income
   a. is the primary factor in determining lack of achievement
   b. is not related to decreased academic achievement
   c. is not as important for school achievement as family atmosphere variables
   d. is strongly correlated with lack of support for children's learning

2. What percentage of low SES students drop out of school?
   a. 10%
   b. 25%
   c. 35%
   d. 50%

3. Many students and teachers assume that low SES students are not very bright because
   a. they may wear old clothes
   b. they may speak ungrammatically
   c. they may be less familiar with books and school activities
   d. all of the above

The Impact of Culture and Community

4. Even though racial segregation is declared to be illegal, about one third of all black students still attend schools where members of minority groups make up _____ % of the student body.
   a. 10
   b. 25
   c. 50
   d. 90

5. Having a masculine or androgynous gender role identity versus a feminine gender role identity is associated with
   a. higher self-esteem
   b. tendencies toward aggressive behaviors
   c. competitive characteristics
   d. higher levels of achievement in school

6. Studies done by Sadker, Sadker, & Klein suggest that
   a. boys prefer to read about girls
   b. girls prefer to read about boys
   c. boys and girls enjoy reading about non-traditional females as much as traditional male characters
   d. boys and girls prefer to read about males in non-traditional roles

7. Males' superior spatial performance in navigating, mental rotation, and trajectory prediction is thought to result from
   a. evolution favoring these skills in males
   b. male participation in athletics
   c. males' more active play styles
   d. all of the above

8. Identifying the particular learning styles of a given ethnic group
   a. can help to provide the basis for grouping together similar individuals
   b. can become just one more basis for stereotyping
   c. is helpful because every individual in a group shares the same learning style
   d. it helps teachers to prejudge how a student will learn best

9. According to Suzuki, when Asian Americans are stereotyped as hardworking and passive
   a. they are channeled in disproportionate numbers into scientific/technical fields
   b. they may lack the ability to assert themselves verbally
   c. they may become overly conforming
   d. all of the above

10. When Hawaiian children's rules for responding allow that they "chime in" with contributions to a story despite it being considered an interruption in school, this is viewed as a difference in
    a. learning styles
    b. resistance culture
    c. participation structures
    d. second-language acquisition

Answer Key

Application One: Understanding Differences
1. consistent
2. inconsistent-mothers from the Republic of China attribute school failure to lack of effort more often than the Caucasian-American mothers.
3. inconsistent-studies done in the 1950's and in 1990, show that when black children were asked to pick the more attractive or smarter doll, they usually chose the white doll over the black doll.
4. inconsistent-78% of non-Hispanics believed Hispanics preferred to live off of welfare.
5. inconsistent-only 4% of the scientists, engineers, and mathematicians are African American or Hispanic American.
6. consistent
7. consistent
8. inconsistent-most stories are about boys and girls prefer to read about girls.
9. inconsistent-many guidance counselors would only protest if it were a boy in this same situation.
10. inconsistent- white middle-class parents value ladylike behavior for their daughters.

Application Two: Gender Role Stereotypes
1. males	2. females and males	3. males	4. males	5. females
6. males	7. females	8. males	9. males	10. females

Application Three: Myth or Fact-Bilingualism
1. False	2. True	3. True	4. False	5. False	6. True	7. False

Application Four: Creating Culturally Compatible Classrooms
1. Mexican Americans, Asian Americans
2. Mexican Americans
3. African Americans, Native Americans, Asian Americans
4. African Americans
5. Native Americans
6. Hispanic Americans, African Americans, Asian Americans
7. Asian Americans
8. Asian Americans
9. African Americans
10. African Americans
11. Hispanic Americans

Essay Questions
1. Even when students speak the same language as the teacher, as with the Hawaiian and Native American children, cultural differences may prevail in how these children interact with others in a scholastic setting. There are many unwritten rules for participation. If a child's interaction style conflicts with and is perceived by a teacher as something negative, that child will be less inclined to participate in the future. Teachers need to make rules for communication clear and explicit. Use cues to signal students when changes occur. Explain and demonstrate appropriate behavior. Be consistent in responding to students.

The Impact of Culture and Community

2. Many suggest that one of the chief aims of education is to foster commonality and to help students learn a public identity. To emphasize differences is to maintain divisions among groups of people when we are in a crisis state of racial bigotry. We should emphasize the commonalities that we share and collectively work together toward the same goals. Others suggest that knowledge of other societies and customs gives students choices that may be more meaningful to them than those offered to them by society. We are not in jeopardy of dividing an already divided country but instead should be learning HOW to value diversity and teach all students to affirm their feelings of worth.

Multiple Choice Questions
1. c　2. b　3. d　4. d　5. a　6. c　7. d　8. b　9. d　10. c

Chapter Six

Behavioral Views of Learning

"We are by nature observers and thereby learners. That is our permanent state."
Ralph Waldo Emerson

Most of us, if asked, could probably offer a definition of **learning.** As educators, we want to learning to continue long after our students leave the hallowed halls.

Learning: Process through which experience causes permanent change in knowledge or behavior.

This change may be intentional or not, good or bad, but brought about by the environment. These changes are not due to maturation. Temporary changes such as hunger or pain, are not learned responses either. Psychologists appear to embrace two separate notions regarding learning:

Behaviorists: believe that learning is evidenced by a change in behavior. Learning is observable.
Cognitivists: believe that learning is evidenced by a change in knowledge. Learning is not directly observable.

Behavioral Learning Theories: Explanations of learning that focus on external events as the cause of changes in observable behaviors.

Early Explanations of Learning: Contiguity and Classical Conditioning

One of the simplest forms of learning occurs through association. This is called **contiguity.** After repeated pairings an association is formed between two events. When one event or sensation **(stimulus)** occurs, it triggers recall of the other event **(response).**

Contiguity: Association of two events because of repeated pairings. **Example:** If a friend comes up to you and says, "Knock, knock" you respond, "Who's there?" Repeated pairings over time causes you to respond to the stimulus "knock, knock" with the age-old response, "who's there?"

Stimulus: Event that activates a behavior. **Example:** "Knock, knock"
Response: Observable reaction to a stimulus. **Example:** "Who's there?"

Contiguity learning is a basic component of the next three forms of learning that will be discussed from a behavioral perspective. The first of these is **classical conditioning.**

Classical Conditioning: Association of automatic or involuntary responses **(respondents)** with new stimuli. **Example:** An involuntary response is one that we cannot control, such as sweating.

Behavioral Views of Learning

Respondents: Responses (generally automatic or involuntary) elicited by specific stimuli.

Classical conditioning occurs when we respond involuntarily to something that wouldn't normally bring about that response. When asked to go in front of a room full of people, a three year old would not automatically break into a sweat, but an older student, who has repeatedly paired public appearances with uncontrolled nervous reactions, may break into a sweat at the mere mention of an oral report. Aspects of classical conditioning are easily understood by examining Pavlov's experiments with salivating dogs.

Pavlov is thought of as the father of classical conditioning and although he won the Nobel for his work on the digestive system, he is most widely remembered for his work with salivating dogs. Pavlov noticed that not only were the dogs salivating at the appearance of meat powder but also when Pavlov himself entered the room. To explain this phenomenon, Pavlov began his experiment.

a. Pavlov enters room and sounds a tuning fork, to which the dog made no response.
Neutral Stimulus: stimulus that does not automatically elicit a response. **Example:** tuning fork

b. Pavlov sounds fork and then presents food. The dog salivates to the food, constituting the food as an **Unconditioned stimulus (US):** Stimulus that automatically produces an emotional or physiological response (respondent). **Example:** the food

The salivation to the food is an **Unconditioned Response (UR):** Naturally occurring emotional or physiological response (respondent). **Example:** salivation to the food

This is where contiguity learning comes to play. Repeated paired associations of the tuning fork and food eventually result in the following scenario. The tuning fork is sounded, the dog is reminded of the food through paired associations, and salivates to the tuning fork before the food is presented.

c. Pavlov sounds the tuning fork and the dog salivates. The tuning fork is no longer a neutral stimulus but through contiguity learning has become what we call a **Conditioned Stimulus (CS):** Previously neutral stimulus that evokes an emotional or physiological response after conditioning. **Example:** tuning fork

d. The dog salivates but this time, the salivation is in response to what was previously a neutral stimulus. Now, the salivation is known as a **Conditioned Response (CR):** Learned response to a previously neutral stimulus. **Example:** salivation to the tuning fork, and salivation to Pavlov.

Three other processes are involved in classical conditioning:

Generalization: Responding in the same way to similar stimuli. **Example:** When we hear the police siren behind us, we respond in the same way regardless if the siren has a slightly different pitch. We pull over to the side of the road and we probably get a queasy feeling in our stomaches.
Discrimination: Responding differently to similar, but not identical stimuli. **Example:** Hearing an air raid siren would not produce the response of pulling over to the side of the road, but instead, you would probably continue to drive until you had located a fall-out shelter.
Extinction: Gradual disappearance of a learned response. In classical conditioning, this is accomplished by presenting the conditioned stimulus without the unconditioned stimulus. **Example:** Let's say that you started walking to college past a house with a vicious dog who charges at you baring his teeth, growling, and

barking. Luckily, his chain does not reach the sidewalk. Every time he barks and growls, you tremble, sweat, and your heart rate increases. After awhile, as soon as you approach this house, you begin to sweat and have fear reactions. The growling dog is the UCS, house is the CS, and your reaction is the CR. To get you over your fear, we must present the CS (house) without the UCS (scary dog) and eventually, the CR (your fear of the house) will be extinguished.

Application One: Classical Conditioning

Read the following scenario and identify each of the following components of classical conditioning. Check your responses in the answer key.

    Jennifer Costapolis just flew for the first time in her life. The minute the jet left the ground, Jennifer felt a pressure in her head, a ringing in her ears, and it felt as though someone had his hands on her heart, squeezing it until she couldn't breathe. She told her doctor and he prescribed tranquilizers for her, assuring her that she didn't have a heart attack, just a panic reaction.
    The next airline trip Jennifer took her seat on the plane and before they even taxied down the runway, she had the same reaction. The next trip, Jennifer had the reaction at the ticket counter and refused to even get on board.
    Jennifer decided it was time to do something and went to an organization who promised to help her conquer her fear of flying. The first step was to accompany Jennifer to the ticket counter, while talking, laughing and socializing to keep her mind off of being airborne. Tickets were purchased, a nice dinner was had, and Jennifer was returned home. This procedure was repeated until Jennifer indicated that she was ready to try sitting on the plane. Her companion accompanied her to a simulation plane, sat down with her, had a drink, ate a meal, listened to music, and then left the plane without ever leaving the ground. Jennifer had a great time and this process was repeated without panic reactions until Jennifer indicated that she was ready for a 15 minute commuter flight.

1. unconditioned stimulus _____

2. unconditioned response _____

3. neutral stimulus _____

4. conditioned stimulus _____

5. conditioned response _____

6. extinction _____

    Emotions can influence classroom learning, especially when these emotions are negative. Think about how you would handle a child who developed panic reactions everytime she had to take an exam. How would you work to eliminate the fear, anxiety, and embarrassment of a student who is afraid to do oral presentations in front of the class. How would you use principles of extinction to eliminate these involuntary responses?

Operant Conditioning: Trying New Responses

The second type of behavioral learning that incorporates contiguity learning is called **operant conditioning.** Whereas classical conditioning involves involuntary responses called respondents, operant conditioning involves voluntary responses to stimuli called **operants.**

Operant Conditioning: Learning in which voluntary behavior is strengthened or weakened by consequences or antecedents.

Operants: Voluntary (and generally goal-directed) behaviors emitted by a person or an animal.

With operant conditioning, an **antecedent** or stimulus occurs to which people choose to respond or not. If a person responds, this operant response is followed by **consequences** that will serve to determine the likelihood or unlikelihood of that person responding again. We can change behaviors by changing the antecedents or changing the consequences or both. We can't always tell which antecedents or stimuli cause behaviors, so to change behaviors, more often then not, we need to change behaviors through consequences. Two forms of consequences are **reinforcement** and **punishment.**

Antecedents: Events that precede an action. **Example:** see below **A B C**
Consequences: Events that follow an action. **Example:** see below **A B C**

Reinforcement: Use of consequences to strengthen a behavior. **Example:** Receiving a paycheck **(reinforcer)** at the end of the week increases the likelihood that you will return to work.

Reinforcer: Any event that follows a behavior and increases the chances that the behavior will occur again.

Punishment: Process that weakens or suppresses behavior. **Example:** Getting a pink slip at the end of the week decreases the likelihood that you will return to work.

Below, we find the **A-B-C's** of operant conditioning.

A antecedents (stimulus)	**B** behaviors (response)	**C** consequences (pun./rein.)
door bell rings	you answer the door	friends are at the door--this will increase the likelihood that you'll answer the door the next time it rings (rein.)
	OR	
door bell rings	you answer the door	it's the police, or the taxman, or a salesman--if this keeps happening you may never answer the door again (pun.)

Behavioral Views of Learning

Many of the findings from the field of behavioral psychology come from work done by Thorndike and B.F. Skinner (more commonly known as the father of behavioral psychology). Their experiments with cats, rats and pigeons placed in **Skinner Boxes** showed how animals' behaviors could be shaped by the chance reinforcements they encountered when acting on their environments.

Skinner Box: Experimental chamber designed to isolate stimulus-response connections.

There are two forms of reinforcement, **positive reinforcement** and **negative reinforcement.**

Positive Reinforcement: Strengthening behavior by presenting a desired stimulus after the behavior. **Example:** Positive reinforcement occurs when a student earns an "A" for effective study habits **OR** when a student is given attention when he or she is acting inappropriately in the classroom. **Do Not** confuse reinforcement with reward. A teacher may reprimand a child in class but if that child was "acting out" in order to receive attention, then the teacher actually reinforced the "acting out" behaviors. Remember, reinforcement is anything that increases a behavior, *either good or bad.*

Negative Reinforcement: Strengthening behavior by removing an **aversive (irritating or unpleasant)** stimulus. **Example:** Students in Ms. Tullen's class have to do homework every night, even on the weekends. Ms. Tullen tells her students that if they study hard and improve on the next exam, then they won't have to do homework on the weekends.

There are also two forms of punishment, **presentation punishment** and **removal punishment.**

Presentation Punishment: Decreasing the chances that a behavior will occur again by presenting an aversive stimulus following the behavior; also called Type I or positive punishment. **Example:** The teacher hands out detentions to students who are late to class.

Removal Punishment: Decreasing the chances that a behavior will occur again by removing a pleasant stimulus following the behavior; also called Type II or negative punishment. **Example:** The teacher tells the class that the next student who is caught fighting will lose recess privileges for the next month.

Always remember, **both reinforcement and punishment are defined by effect!!!!** If it doesn't increase behavior it is not reinforcement. If it doesn't decrease behavior, then it isn't punishment.

Reinforcement Schedules

The best way for people to learn a behavior is when they are **continuously reinforced.** Once the new behavior has been mastered, it is better to reinforce **intermittently** so that skills can be maintained without the expectation of constant reinforcement. We would like for our student's successes to be reinforcement enough without some additional, external reward.

Continuous Reinforcement Schedule: Presenting a reinforcer for every appropriate response.

Intermittent Reinforcement Schedule: Presenting a reinforcer after some but not all responses. Two types of intermittent schedules are **interval** and **ratio.**

Interval Schedule: Based on the amount of time between reinforcers.

Ratio Schedule: Based on the number of responses between reinforcers.

> Either of these schedules may be either **fixed** (predictable) or **variable** (unpredictable).

Fixed Interval	Reinforcement after a set period of time	Pizza party every Friday
Variable Interval	Reinforcement after varying lengths of time	Fishing
Fixed Ratio	Reinforcement after a set number of responses	Three news reports = 10 points
Variable Ratio	Reinforcement after a varying number of responses	Recess whenever the teacher feels that the students have completed enough worksheets

When the reinforcement schedule is fixed and students know when it is coming, they will work rapidly and steadily until reinforced and then productivity will drop after reinforcement. When students don't know when the reinforcement is coming, they will work steadily in anticipation of reinforcement and maintain the level of productivity since reinforcement may be coming again at any time or after any amount of responses. Variable schedules are best for maintaining steady levels of productivity.

Application Two: Modifying Behaviors

Read the following scenarios and decide whether positive reinforcement, negative reinforcement, presentation punishment, or removal punishment is being applied and state how it is influencing the behaviors.

1.   Trish wants to extend her bedtime from 9:00 to 9:30. Every night she argues with her mother and delays her bedtime procedure so that by the time she finally gets into bed it is 9:30._____

2.   Moira's newborn cries loudly. Moira tries changing her diaper, cuddling her, feeding her, and rocking her. When Moira hits upon the right behavior, the crying stops. _____

3.   Jimmy Snodgrass never gets any attention at home unless it is negative attention. His parents tell him he is a bad seed and will never amount to anything. When he goes to class, he makes rude noises to make everyone laugh and when his teacher says he sounds like a hog, he oinks loudly. His classmates laugh and tell him he is the "baddest dude in town". _____

4.   Carrie obtained a copy of her science exam prior to the exam. She shared the exam with all of her friends and they all obtained "A's." Her science instructor has not changed his exam in 10 years so many copies are in circulation throughout the school. _____

5.   Mr. Barkley told his class that if they behaved during assembly, his wife would bring in oatmeal scotchies for everyone to eat. The students had eaten the scotchies before and equated them with cardboard. When they went to assembly, Mr. Barkley's students started a near riot. _____

6.   Whenever it is time for Pablo to give an oral report in class, he goes to the nurses office where she allows him to lie down for the remainder of the period. _____

7.   Shirley Friedman uses cooperative learning structures in her classroom. When students' scores improve on their tests, the average amount of improvement scores determine the prizes awarded to each group. _____

8.   Tim Thompson was student teaching in Mr. Brown's history class. Everytime Mr.Brown left the class a spitball fight erupted and chaos ensued. Mr. Thompson never sent the unruly students to the office fearing a bad evaluation about his ability to discipline the class. _____

9.   Principal Gonzales decided to offer an incentive program to all of the students in the high school. Any student who showed improvement in GPA from the first to the second quarter or obtained a GPA of 3.00 or above would be allowed to attend a school-wide camping trip. _____

10.   The student teacher in Cali's classroom taught the students the bones of the body by having them play Simon Says "touch your clavicle, Simon Says touch your femur, etc." and offered small pumpkins to the winners as it was close to Halloween. _____

Application Three: Modifying Aggression

Examine the classroom situation in the cartoon on the next page and decide which strategy the teacher is using; positive reinforcement, negative reinforcement, presentation punishment, or removal punishment. Two responses are correct. Check your responses in the answer key

"Okay boys, I've had to call in the vice principal about your fighting. Play nice and I'll make him go away."

Behavioral Views of Learning

Whereas extinction can be applied in classical conditioning by presenting the conditioned stimulus without the unconditioned stimulus, it can also be used in operant conditioning. If the reinforcer is withheld, the behavior will disappear. How long do you think you would continue to go to your job if they withheld your paycheck and gave you a pat on the back instead? Sometimes, antecedents will provide cues as to what behaviors will be reinforced. This is called **stimulus control**.

Stimulus Control: Capacity for the presence or absence of antecedents to cause behaviors. **Example:** The teacher sets a timer (**cue**) and if the students get lined up before the buzzer goes off, they can have 10 extra minutes of playtime on the playground. The students are under stimulus control.

Cueing: Providing a stimulus that "sets up" a desired behavior. **Example:** In the above example, the timer is the cue.

Prompt: A reminder that follows a cue to make sure the person reacts to the cue. **Example:** In the above example, if after the teacher sets the timer, he says, "Now what are you supposed to do when I set the timer?" then his question becomes a prompt.

One of your primary teaching responsibilities will be to maintain classroom discipline and this can be effectively accomplished through **Applied Behavior Analysis.**

Applied Behavior Analysis: The application of behavioral learning principles to understand and change behavior. Applied Behavior Analysis is often equated with **Behavior Modification**.

Behavior Modification: Systematic application of antecedents and consequences to change behavior. **Example:** When the teacher sets the timer to give the students one minute to line up, that is the antecedent. When they successfully line up within a minutes time, they experience the reinforcing consequence of 10 extra minutes of recess. If they do not line up before the buzzer goes off, they will experience the punishing consequence of losing 10 minutes of recess time.

See Figure 6.2 for a concept map of Applied Behavioral Analysis. After you review the concept map, go to Application Four and apply the ABAB approach to the case study in Figure 6.3.

Behavioral Views of Learning

Figure 6.2

APPLIED BEHAVIORAL ANALYSIS- ABAB

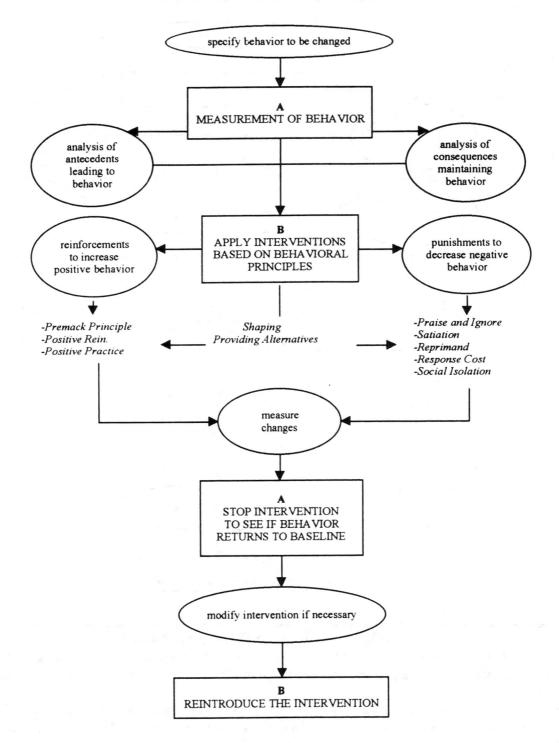

Figure 6.3

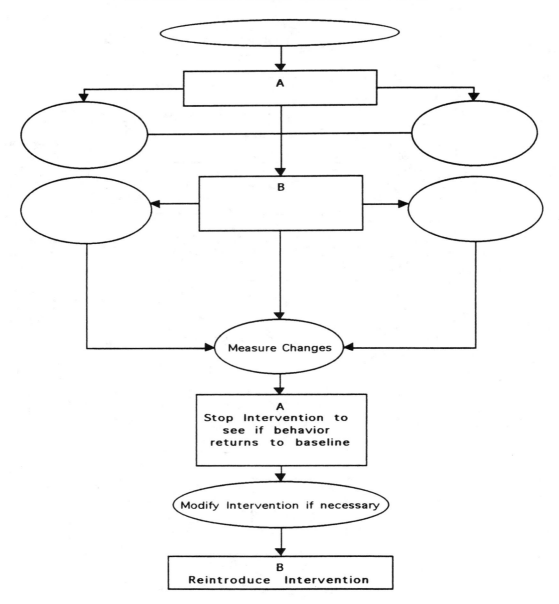

APPLIED BEHAVIORAL ANALYSIS- ABAB

(diagram labels:)

A

B

Measure Changes

A
Stop Intervention to
see if behavior
returns to baseline

Modify Intervention if necessary

B
Reintroduce Intervention

Application Four: ABAB-Case Study

Read the following case study and fill out the applied behavioral analysis chart in figure 6.3.
Establish the behavior to be changed and proceed to fill out the rest of the chart. Check your response in the
answer key.

 "Kevin does not like math class. Everyday, when the class is working on their math problems, Kevin does
everything in his power to disrupt his neighbors and amuse everyone in class. His classmates laugh, Kevin
loves the attention, and no one gets much work accomplished."

Intervention Methods

Methods for Encouraging Behaviors

Praise and Ignore Techniques: Research has shown that teachers can improve student behavior by ignoring rule breakers and praising students who are following the rules. Of course, this will not work in all situations and some behaviors just cannot be ignored.

Premack Principle: Principle stating that a more-preferred activity can serve as a reinforcer for a less-preferred activity. **Example:** "If you finish your math problems, you may read the book of your choice."

Shaping: Reinforcing each small step of progress toward a desired goal or behavior. **Example:** The first grade class is learning to write the alphabet. Instead of waiting until each student has perfectly mastered the letter "S," Ms. Harris circulates around the room, giving corrective feedback, and praising every slight improvement in form. A component of shaping is **task analysis.**

Task Analysis: System for breaking down a task hierarchically into basic skills and subskills. **Example:** Writing a research report requires that a student , (a) pick a topic, (b) go to the library (c) read the articles (d) summarize the articles, etc. At each step of the report writing, the teacher can reinforce its successful completion.

Positive Practice: Practicing correct responses immediately after errors. **Example:** The students entered the classroom pushing and shoving so Mr. Waters had them line up and practice going in and out in an orderly fashion.

Methods for Discouraging Behaviors

Negative Reinforcement: Strengthening a behavior by removing an aversive stimulus. Although this is usually used to increase a positive behavior, very often the increase of a positive behavior means the decrease of a negative behavior. **Example:** Let's say the students aren't studying. We want to decrease "their not-studying -behaviors" and increase their studying behaviors. Therefore, we might introduce an aversive stimulus such as a "weekly quiz" and when the students demonstrate improved study skills, the weekly quizzes will be removed.

Satiation: Requiring a person to repeat a problem behavior past the point of interest or motivation. **Example:** The students were throwing spit wads every time the teacher's back was turned. The teacher would turn around to discover a sea of wads on the floor. She decided to have the students make and throw wads for the next 30 minutes. They lost interest after 10 and never made another wad again.

Reprimands: Criticisms for misbehavior; rebukes. The most effective reprimands are those which are soft and private as opposed to loud and public and humiliating. **Example:** Mr. Slemmer walked over to Jason's desk and tapped him lightly on the shoulder, quietly telling him to get back on task.

Behavioral Views of Learning

Response Cost: Punishment by loss of reinforcers. **Example:** To stop their fighting, Mrs. Ortez gave Carrie and Stephanie each five circles. Everytime they fight, they lose a circle. When all of the circles are gone, they won't be allowed to go on the class trip.

Social Isolation: Removal of a disruptive student for 5 to 10 minutes. **Example:** Mr. Ross asked Matt to take his work into the "**time-out**" room so that he could complete it without distracting everyone around him.

Time Out: Technically, the removal of all reinforcement. In practice, isolation of a student from the rest of the class for a brief time. **Example:** Jackie was loving all of the laughter and attention from the class each time she fell out of her chair. Her teacher took her chair away and made her stand and sit on the floor for the rest of the day.

Whenever, you use punishment, make it part of a two-prong attack; stop the negative behavior and provide a positive alternative so that the individual doesn't replace one negative behavior with another.

Application Five: Matching Key Terms and Definitions
Operant Conditioning

Select the word from the left column that corresponds to the phrase on the right. Put the number of the matching word in the blank in front of the letters and next to the same letter in the matrix below. If your answers are correct, all numbers across, down, and diagonally, will add up to the same number.

1. Prompt   _____ a. Practicing correct responses immediately after errors

2. Positive Practice   _____ b. Reinforcing each small step of progress toward a desired goal or behavior

3. Response Cost   _____ c. Removal of a disruptive student for 5 to 10 minutes

4. Social Isolation   _____ d. Criticisms for behavior; rebukes

5. Satiation   _____ e. Requiring a person to repeat a behavior past the point of interest

6. Task Analysis   _____ f. Punishment by loss of reinforcers

7. Reprimands   _____ g. System for breaking down a task hierarchically into basic skills and subskills

8. Cueing   _____ h. A reminder that follows a cue to make sure the person reacts to the cue

9. Shaping   _____ i. Providing a stimulus that "sets up" a desired behavior

```
           A              B              C

           D              E              F

           G              H              I
```

What is the correct number_____ ?

Social Learning Theory

So far, we have discussed three types of learning from a behavioral perspective; contiguity learning, classical conditioning, and operant conditioning. The fourth type of learning is explained through **social cognitive theory.**

Social Cognitive Theory: Theory that emphasizes learning through the observation of others proposed by Albert Bandura.

Bandura differentiates between *the acquisition of knowledge (learning)* and the *observable behavior based on that knowledge (performance).* In other words, we may know more than we demonstrate and Bandura said that whether we demonstrate what we know depends in part on environmental situations and **reciprocal determinism.**

Reciprocal Determinism: An explanation of behavior that emphasizes the mutual effects of the individual and the environment on each other. **Example:** A 13 year old girl may know all of the answers in science class but may not volunteer any answers because she likes a boy in the class and doesn't want to appear "too smart."

Much of what we learn comes to us not through doing but through observing others, called **observational learning.** There are two main modes of observational learning. The first of these is **vicarious reinforcement.** The second mode of observational learning is **modeling.**

Observational Learning: Learning by observation and imitation of others. **Example:** We learn how to do the Macarena by observing others.

Vicarious Reinforcement: Increasing the chances that we will repeat a behavior by observing another person being reinforced for that behavior. Punishment can also have a vicarious effect and will decrease the likelihood of us repeating a behavior. **Example:** If you see a classmate get caught cheating, it will have a vicarious effect on you and you will probably be less likely to cheat as a result of witnessing your classmate being suspended.

Behavioral Views of Learning

Modeling: Changes in behavior, thinking, or emotions that occur through observing another person, the model. With modeling, the observer imitates the behavior of the model, even though the model receives no reinforcement or punishment. **Example:** Children may want to pretend to be Batman because he is so cool.

Observational learning is a very efficient way to learn. It eliminates much trial and error and does not require that the individual physically perform in order to learn. There are four components to observational learning:

- **attention:** Before teaching, make sure your students are attending. Direct their attention to specifics when requisite to their learning.
- **retention:** To imitate a behavior, you must remember it so provide you students with time for mental rehearsal or actual practice.
- **production:** Even though we may remember what we've learned through observation, doesn't mean we can perform smoothly without practice, feedback, and coaching.
- **motivation and reinforcement:** Before we'll perform a behavior, we must be motivated to do so. Once we perform the behavior, we're unlikely to continue to do so unless reinforced.

Many factors determine whether individuals will learn and perform the behaviors they observe.
1. Developmental Status-as people mature, they become better able to learn through observation.
2. Status of the Model-people are more likely to imitate prestigious, high-status models.
3. Vicarious Conditioning-by observing, people learn which behaviors are appropriate
4. Outcome Expectations-if outcomes are rewarding, the behaviors leading to them will be modeled.
5. Goal Setting-observers will imitate models who will help them to attain their own goals.
6. **Self-Efficacy**-observers who believe that they can succeed, are more likely to attempt to imitate others.

Self-efficacy: A person's sense of being able to deal effectively with a particular task. It is an individual's belief in his or her own ability to effect an outcome.

There are five possible outcomes of observational learning:

- **Teaching new behaviors:** So much of what we learn we learn by watching others; how to dress, our language and expressions, dancing, sports, chemistry, home economics, and wood shop to name a few. Teachers can be very effective models, even right down to modeling thinking processes such as problem solving if the steps are said aloud. Same age peers make the most effective models.
- **Encouraging already learned behaviors:** In a study by O'Connor a group of children who were social isolates observed a film where a boy was reinforced for his social interactions with others. Through vicarious reinforcement, these children increased their own social interactions. These children already knew how to interact but were encouraged through observation.
- **Strengthening or weakening inhibitions:** Effective discipline of one rule breaker may serve to inhibit others. Conversely, if a child is shy or inhibited, observing another child successfully giving an oral report and enjoying themselves may be just the needed encouragement.
- **Directing Attention:** Do you remember the whitewashing the fence routine from Tom Sawyer? He was able to direct everyone's attention to how much fun he was supposedly having. Utilize this strategy with peer models who enjoy working on computers, for example.
- **Arousing Emotion:** As the teacher, you can model enthusiasm and enjoyment about the learning process. You can insure that your students have a safe learning environment where they feel they can

try anything without fear of failure and ridicule. Make learning so much fun that it will have a **ripple effect**.

Ripple Effect: "Contagious" spreading of behaviors through imitation. **Example:** When we were in high school, we had a student teacher who would not discipline us. A few classmates would "hum" while he lectured. He never took action, so in time, even the most mild-mannered students were humming away with no fear of repudiation.

Self-Regulation and Cognitive Behavior Modification

As educators, one of our goals is to have students assume responsibilty for their own learning. One way to accomplish this is through the behavioral approach called **self-management.**

Self-Management: Use of behavioral learning principles to change your own behavior. Important components of self management include goal setting, recording and evaluating progress, and also **self-reinforcement.**

Self-Reinforcement: Providing yourself with positive consequences, contingent on accomplishing a particular behavior. **Example:** "If I finish reading Chapter 6 in my Woolfolk Educational Psychology Book, I'm going to treat myself to dinner, a movie, and a Caribbean vacation."

Cognitive Behavior Modification: Procedures based on both behavioral and cognitive learning principles for changing your own behavior by using self-talk and **self-instruction.**

Self-Instruction: Talking oneself through the steps of a task. **Example:** In Girl Scout camp, we were taught a special "friendship knot" for our neck bolas and to remember it, we would say, "over, under, around and through, a friendship knot for me and you."

Practice Tests

Essay Questions

1.   An issue that should be considered regarding the application of principles of behavior modification, is its effect on the individual subject to the strategy. Is it ethical to modify others' behaviors?

2.   A hot topic regarding the use of positive reinforcers is the effectiveness of the reward. According to Kohn, rewarding students for learning actually makes them less interested in the material. Discuss the pros and cons of providing extrinsic rewards for learning.

Multiple Choice Questions

1. To encourage persistence of response, which of the following schedules of reinforcement is most appropriate?
    a. variable interval
    b. continuous schedules
    c. fixed interval
    d. fixed ratio

2. When a more preferred activity serves as a reinforcer for a less preferred activity, this is called
    a. Premack principle
    b. positive practice
    c. shaping
    d. task analysis

3. Which of the following is **NOT** a strategy used to decrease behaviors?
    a. satiation
    b. reprimands
    c. positive practice
    d. response cost

4. Mr. Thompson told Stephanie that since she was quietly working on her project all through the class period, then she could be the first one to leave the hot classroom at recess. This is an example of
    a. presentation punishment
    b. positive reinforcement
    c. removal punishment
    d. negative reinforcement

5. Jimmy is afraid of heights. In P.E. class, the boys are learning how to climb the ropes. Recently, prior to P.E. Jimmy develops stomaache cramps and has to go to the nurse's office. This is an example of
    a. observational learning
    b. operant conditioning
    c. classical conditioning
    d. contiguity learning

6. In observational learning, observers are less likely to imitate the model
    a. if the model is a fictional character
    b. if the model is punished for an inappropriate behavior
    c. if the model is a same-age peer
    d. if the model is a high status individual

7. Which of the following is not one of the forms of reinforcement proposed by Bandura to encourage observational learning?
    a. direct reinforcement
    b. self reinforcement
    c. vicarious reinforcement
    d. negative reinforcement

8. When attempting to eliminate mildly disruptive behaviors in the classroom, the first recommended approach is to utilize
    a. soft and private reprimands
    b. praise and ignore techniques
    c. social isolation
    d. response cost

9. Which of the following is an example of the use of "response cost?"
    a. Joachim throws spit wads and is forced to continue past the point of interest
    b. Brandy is asked to leave the room
    c. The unruly students have lost their fifth chance and consequently, their recess
    d. Jackson was just given another red mark next to his name

10. When Pavlov's dog salivated when Pavlov entered the room, the dogs salivation is considered to be
    a. a neutral response
    b. an unconditioned response
    c. an unconditioned stimulus
    d. a conditioned response

Answer Key

Application One: Classical Conditioning
1. unconditioned stimulus-being off the ground
2. unconditioned response-pressure in the head, ringing in the ears, chest constriction
3. neutral stimulus-seat on the plane, ticket counter
4. conditioned stimulus-seat on the plane, ticket counter
5. conditioned response-anxiety reactions to the plane and ticket counter
6. extinction-presenting the plane seat and ticket counter without making Jennifer airborne

Application Two: Modifying Behaviors
1. Trish's arguing is being positively reinforced because she is getting what she wants, a later bedtime.
2 Moira's strategies are being negatively reinforced because when she hits on the right combination, the crying stops.
3. Jimmy's obnoxious behaviors are being positively reinforced by all the attention he is receiving.
4. Carrie's and her friend's cheating is being positively reinforced by the good grades they receive because their instructor has not updated his exams.
5. Mr. Barkley's students were experiencing presentation punishment over the threat of the "scotchies" and therefore decreased their good behavior to avoid punishment.

6. The nurse is negatively reinforcing Pablo's visits to her office because his visits allow him to escape an aversive situation; oral reports.
7. Shirley is positively reinforcing her student's improved performances on their exams.
8. Tim was positively reinforcing the students by allowing them to engage in the fun activity of throwing spitballs with no fear of repercussion.
9. Principal Gonzales positively reinforced the students who performed well with a class trip.
10. The student teacher positively reinforced the students learning by making it fun and by rewarding them with pumpkins.

Application Three: Modifying Aggression
Two responses are correct; (1) The teacher is trying to decrease their fighting through presentation punishment, the scary vice principal. (2) She is trying to increase their "playing nice behaviors" and says that once they demonstrate these positive behaviors, then she will make the aversive situation (the scary vice principal) go away. This is negative reinforcement.

Application Four: ABAB Case Study
See figure 6.3 on the last page.

Application Five: Matching Key Terms and Definitions, Operant Conditioning
a. 2   b. 9   c. 4   d. 7   e. 5   f. 3   g. 6   h. 1   i. 8   The number is 15.

Essays
1. We might object to principles of behavior modification from the premise that it is pure manipulation and what right does one individual in control have to manipulate another's behaviors. We could argue that every time we compliment another individual, we are in essence using positive reinforcement and increasing their behavior. Teachers need to be able to establish organization and control but what is too much control and when are behavioral principles abused? As indicated in your text, improvements in conduct won't necessarily ensure academic learning but in some situations, reinforcing academic skills may lead to improvements in conduct. Whenever behavioral principles are to be used, emphasis should be placed on academic learning because academic improvements generalize to other situations more successfully than do changes in classroom conduct.

2. Some psychologists fear that if students are rewarded for learning, then learning is not perceived as valuable in and of itself. It may be perceived that learning is something that is so aversive that students must be "paid off" in order to learn. Once the rewards end, it is argued that the motivation to perform may decline. Others suggest that everyone appreciates acknowledgement and praise for a job well done. Rewards can bolster the confidence of students who lack ability or interest in the task initially. Certainly, if students learn with the aid of rewards, they will not forget the material once the rewards have stopped. Furthermore, some students may not learn without the rewards. My daughter is a good student who works hard to get "A's" and has told me that she would work for the learning anyhow but that it is nice to get rewards and that it also provides additional incentive.

Multiple Choice
1. a   2. a   3. c   4. d   5. c   6. b   7. d   8. b   9. c   10. d

Application Four: ABAB

Figure 6.3

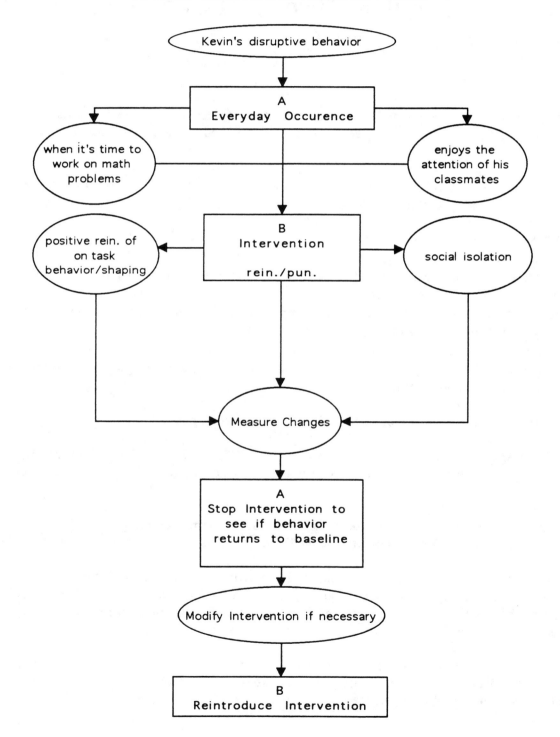

APPLIED BEHAVIORAL ANALYSIS- ABAB

Kevin's disruptive behavior

A
Everyday Occurence

when it's time to work on math problems

enjoys the attention of his classmates

positive rein. of on task behavior/shaping

B
Intervention
rein./pun.

social isolation

Measure Changes

A
Stop Intervention to see if behavior returns to baseline

Modify Intervention if necessary

B
Reintroduce Intervention

Chapter Seven

Cognitive Views of Learning

"Learning without thought is labor lost."
Confucius

The cognitive perspective had its origins in the philosophies of the ancient Greeks. Since that early time, educators and philosophers have been interested in how people think, learn concepts, and solve problems.

Cognitive View of Learning: A general approach that views learning as an active mental process of acquiring, remembering, and using knowledge.

Assumptions about the cognitive perspective:
- Knowledge is learned, and changes in knowledge make changes in behavior possible.
- Reinforcement is seen as a source of feedback about what is likely to happen if behaviors are repeated. Feedback is a source of information.
- People are seen as active learners who initiate experiences, seek out information to solve problems, and reorganize what they already know to achieve new insights.
- New cognitive approaches stress the construction of knowledge.
- Already acquired knowledge determines to a large extent what we will pay attention to, perceive, learn, remember, and forget in the future.

According to the cognitive perspective there are different kinds of knowledge.

General Knowledge: Information that is useful in many different kinds of tasks; information that applies to many situations. **Example:** How to add or subtract or make change, skills that are useful both in and out of school.

Domain Specific Knowledge: Information that is useful in a particular situation or that generally applies only to one specific topic. **Example:** Knowledge that a "roux" is a butter and flour mixture used in cooking.

Declarative Knowledge: Verbal information; facts; "knowing that" something is the case. **Example:** Information that can be taught through lectures or acquired through books, verbal exchange, Braille, sign language etc.. This is a broad category ranging from, the date of my brother's birthday, to mathematical rules, to knowledge of how to grow vegetables.

Procedural Knowledge: Knowledge that is demonstrated when we perform a task; "knowing how." **Example:** We may know what ingredients go into a cake (declarative knowledge) but how to combine them to make the cake is procedural knowledge.

116

Conditional Knowledge: "Knowing when and why" to use declarative and procedural knowledge.
Example: You may know what a kokanee is (declarative knowledge) and you may know how to catch one (procedural knowledge) but knowing under what conditions you should fish shallow or deep is conditional knowledge.

Application One: Behavioral and Cognitive Approaches

Read the following situations and decide whether each is more consistent with the behavioral or cognitive approach. Check the correctness of your responses in the answer key.

1. _____ Learning is the result of our attempts to make sense of the world.

2. _____ Reinforcement strengthens responses.

3. _____ Reinforcement is seen as a source of information.

4. _____ Learning can best be thought of as a stimulus-response paradigm.

5. _____ Our existing knowledge influences how and what we learn.

6. _____ People are passively influenced by environmental events.

7. _____ Much of the research in this area has been conducted in controlled laboratory settings.

8. _____ Experts in this area study a wide range of learning situations.

9. _____ People are active learners who initiate experiences.

10. _____ Their goal is to identify a few general laws of learning that apply to all higher organisms.

The Information Processing Model

Information processing views of memory rely on the computer as a model. Like a computer, the mind takes in data, stores the data, retrieves the data to work with it when necessary, and adapts and modifies the data. The whole system is guided by control processes that determine how and when the information will flow through the system.

Information Processing: Human mind's activity of taking in, storing, and using information.

See Figure 7.1 for a concept map of Memory Stores.

Cognitive Views of Learning

Figure 7.1

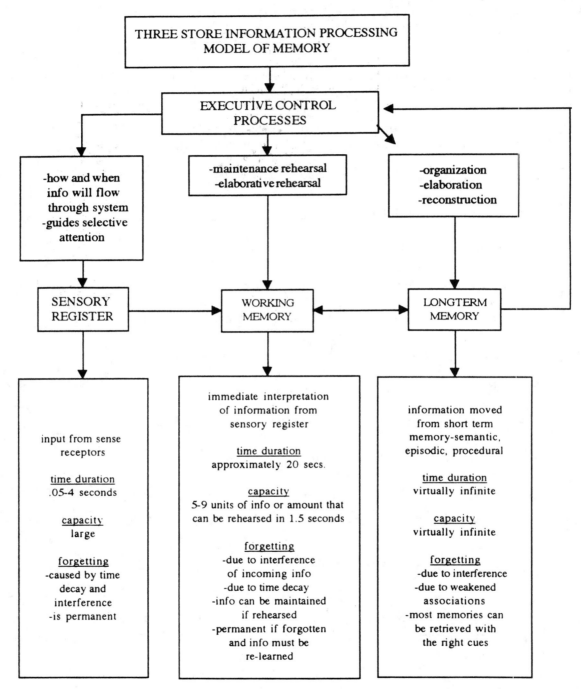

The Multi-Store Theory of Memory - Part 1 - The Sensory Register

All kinds of stimuli from the environment bombard our **receptors**.

Receptors: Parts of the human body that receive sensory information. **Example:** When you tap your arm, sense receptors detect the sensation. The sensation is held very briefly in the sensory memory also called the **sensory register** and then the sensation fades.

Sensory Register: System of receptors holding sensory information very briefly. The capacity of the sensory register is very large and it contains almost an exact image of the information as it occurred but we have no use for the retention of all stimuli exactly as seen, heard, smelled, felt, or tasted so this information lasts but a split second. .**Example:** Look around the room and close your eyes. You can retain an *exact* image of everything you saw but just for a second. Would you want to retain all of this information forever? It would be rather useless, don't you think? Some of this information, however, we do wish to retain by moving it into working memory.

The content of sensory memory resembles the sensations from the original stimulus. **Perception** and attention are critical at this stage.

Perception: Interpretation of sensory information. **Example:** How we interpret what we perceive is largely based on our past experiences and existing knowledge. For example, if you shout out the word "love" to a tennis pro, the pro will probably first perceive this as a zero score in tennis versus a deep emotional attachment.

Explanations of perception derive from **Gestalt** theorists who state that we tend to perceive things in their best form or most "meaningful whole." More current explanations of perception are **bottom up processing** and **top down processing.**

Gestalt: German for pattern or whole; Gestalt theorists hold that people organize their perceptions into coherent wholes.

Bottom-Up Processing (feature analysis): Perceiving based on noticing separate, defining features and assembling them into a recognizable pattern. **Example:** / \ / \ From my keyboard, this is back slash, forward slash, back slash, and forward slash. But for you to organize this into a meaningful whole, you probably perceive this as the letter "M" or perhaps a mountain range in Switzerland.

Top-Down Processing: Perceiving based on the content and the patterns you expect to occur in that situation. **Example:** If your were to fleetingly perceive a winged creature fly past the window of your house, even though it was a partial glimpse, you would probably perceive it as a "bird" and not a "bat" or a "fairy" because a bird would be more consistent with your interpretation of the global perception. You may be wrong, it could be a fairy, but to specifically determine that it was a fairy would require greater **attention** to the scene.

Attention: Focus on a stimulus. **Example: The first step in learning is ATTENTION!!!!!!** Did that get your attention? Without attention, no perception, no interpretation, no learning would take place. When teaching your students, employ the guidelines from your chapter for Gaining and Maintaining Attention, that are briefly summarized below:

- Use signals to direct student actions and inform them of what's coming.
- Make sure the purpose of the lesson or assignment is clear to students.
- Emphasize variety, curiosity, and surprise to maintain attention and **KEEP YOUR STUDENTS AWAKE AND EAGERLY ANTICIPATING YOUR NEXT MOVE!**
- Ask questions and provide frames for answering to help students focus on how they plan to study, what strategies they'll use and why the material is important. Help them attend to their own errors.

Part 2-Working Memory

The second component of the multistore theory of memory is **short term memory** synonymous with **working memory.**

Short Term Memory: **Working memory**, holding a limited amount of information briefly. Short term memory holds the information from the sensory register that your brain (after sifting through all of the sensory perceptions and selecting what is important based on past experience and knowledge) has interpreted and stored.

Working Memory: The information that you are focusing on at a given moment.

The capacity of working memory is limited to five to nine separate units of new information. This is why after meeting someone, and being told many units of information about that person, you very often have to ask "What's your name again?" The capacity for new information has been exceeded and unless you keep repeating that person's name over and over again, the most recent incoming information will push the other new information right out of working memory.

Another factor that influences the functioning of short term memory is its duration. Information can only be held for approximately 20 seconds without **maintenance rehearsal.**

Maintenance Rehearsal: Keeping information in working memory by repeating it to yourself. **Example:** Her name is Roberta, her name is Roberta, Roberta, Roberta, Roberta. As long as you say the name, it is in active use in working memory. The name "Roberta" is short enough that it fits the limitation of the **articulatory loop.**

Articulatory Loop: A rehearsal system of about 1.5 seconds.

Another form of rehearsal for keeping information in working memory and moving information from working to long term memory is **elaborative rehearsal.**

Elaborative Rehearsal: Keeping information in working memory by associating it with something else you already know. **Example:** When you meet Roberta, you don't need to engage in maintenance rehearsal because your mother's name is Roberta and by making the association, you can also move Roberta's name into long term memory. Another strategy for "expanding" the capacity of working memory is called "**chunking**".

Chunking: Grouping individual bits of data into meaningful larger units. **Example:** Our social security numbers are nine digits in length which is the maximum amount contained within working memory, but when given large strings of numbers, we usually chunk single digits into larger units. The social security numbers 1*2*8*2*5*3*6*9*8 become 128-25-36-98. That's four chunks instead of nine. Try to remember the number sequence both ways to determine which way is more effective.

Information in working memory can be lost or forgotten due to **decay**. Exceeding 20 seconds without rehearsal will cause the new information to be forgotten and exceeding the 5-to-9 units will ensure that some of the information will be forgotten. Forgetting is important because we need to empty working memory to make way for new information. Also, we would never want to retain every sentence we've ever read.

Decay: The weakening and fading of memories with the passage of time. **Example:** Your 20 seconds are up. What was the social security number written above? Unless you've been rehearsing the number all of the time, decay has probably removed the number from your working memory.

Part 3 - Long Term Memory

The final memory storage system from the multi-store theory is called **long term memory.**
Long Term Memory: Permanent store of knowledge. **Example:** You can remember your telephone number because it is stored permanently in long term memory.

Long term memory is said to be high in **memory strength.** The capacity of long term memory is virtually unlimited and once information is in long term memory, it is there permanently. When you're trying to recall information from long term memory when you're taking an exam, you may have your doubts as to the permanence of the information. It really is in there, however, the difficulty really lies with retrieval.

Memory Strength: The durability of a memory; if information is well learned, it is more durable.

Application Two: Memory Stores

Summarize below the different components of the three memory stores.

	Sensory Register	Working Memory	Long Term Memory
Capacity			
Duration			
Forgetting			

Several theories exist as to how information is stored in long term memory. Paivio suggested that information is stored as visual images, verbal images or both. But this theory is insufficient for explaining our memory of emotions, sounds (can you hear a melody in your head) and smells (can you smell chocolate brownies baking in the oven). Today, most psychologists distinguish between three categories of long term memory: **semantic, episodic, and procedural.**

Semantic Memory: Memory for meaning. These memories are stored as **propositions, images,** or **schemas.**

Propositional Network: Set of interconnected concepts and relationships in which long term information is held. A proposition is the smallest unit of information that can be judged to be true or false.

A propositional network is interconnected bits of information. **Example:** Washington DC is our nation's capital. You may have constructed a network that includes the capital, President Clinton, Washington Monument, cherry blossoms, etc. Recall of one proposition may influence recall of another and so on.

Images: Images are representations based on perceptions on the structure or appearance of the information. Images are not exact copies because perceptions are based on experiences or knowledge. **Example:** We can all construct an image of a flower, but our images and constructions differ greatly.

Schemas (also schemata): Basic structures for organizing information; concepts. **Example:** A schema for justice is complex and could not be adequately represented by either images or propositional networks.

Several types of schemas provide us with structures to help us perform and respond. Two such schemata are called **story grammars** and **scripts.**

Story Grammar: Typical structure or organization for a category of stories. **Example:** A typical story grammar for a love story might go like this, boy meets girl, boy and girl fall in love, misunderstanding occurs between boy and girl, boy and girl make up, everyone lives happily ever after.

Script: Schema or expected plan for the sequence of steps in a common event or everyday situation. **Example:** I have a script for showering, shampooing, conditioning, contact lenses, etc. and I apply the same script everyday.

Up to this point. we've been discussing aspects of memory that relate to the meaning of things and knowledge about many things. Some memories focus not so much on the meaning of the content but rather memory surrounding events at different times and different places, called **episodic memory** and memory for how to perform things, called **procedural memory.**

Episodic Memory: Long term memory for information tied to a particular time and place, especially memory for the events in a person's life. **Example:** I can remember the episode where I first watched *The Shining* at the house of my friends, and then none of us could get to sleep. The plot of the film, the time of year, and socializing with my friends is all part of my episodic memory.

Procedural Memory: Long term memory for how to do things. **Example:** No matter how old, you never really forget how to ride a bike.

Procedural memories are comprised condition-action rules sometimes called **productions.**

Productions: The contents of procedural memories; rules about what actions to take, given certain conditions. **Example:** When riding your bike around a corner, you must slow a bit and lean into the curve. The more practiced the procedure, the less you consciously think about these rules.

Storing and Retrieving Information in Long Term Memory

You might ask how we store information; creating semantic, episodic, and procedural memories. A key contingency for saving information is how we learn, process, and connect the new information with already existing knowledge, to begin with. Several strategies for encoding information are discussed below.

Elaboration: Adding and extending meaning by connecting new information to existing knowledge. **Example:** If I were to remember Phoenix, Arizona it might be difficult because neither name has any semantic meaning of its own. However, if I were to draw upon my existing knowledge of Greek mythology, then the word Phoenix would mean a mythological bird who rises up from the ashes. Elaborating further, ashes come from fire, fires are hot, deserts in Arizona are hot and I have just added many connections and new meanings to two words that had no meanings previously. Now when I think of Arizona, I think of deserts, heat, fire, ashes, and finally, Phoenix.

Material that is elaborated when first learned will be easier to recall later. When students elaborate for themselves, it is most effective, but whenever I have elaborated for myself, I share the elaborations with my students to help them remember. Another effective strategy, is to arrange information in such a fashion that it is logically grouped within your cognitive **organization**.

Organization: Ordered and logical network of relations. **Example:** To learn the bones of the body, you might teach your students all of the bones from the shoulders up, then those in the torso region and so on.

Context: The physical or emotional backdrop associated with an event. **Example:** The room in which you study becomes part of the associative structure of memory. As you are thinking about Pavlov, if you are looking at the clock on your wall, then the clock becomes part of the memory. If you see a similar clock on the wall while you are taking your exam, that clock will serve as a trigger for your recall of Pavlov.

An alternate theory called the **Levels of Processing Theory** suggests that how deeply you process information in the first place will influence later recall. **Example:** Level 1-I learn what a hammer is. Level 2- I learn what a hammer is and what it looks like. Level 3- I learn what a hammer is, what it looks like, and names for different types of hammers, i.e., ball peen, claw hammer, rock hammer, mallet. If I learn something to the depth of Level 3, I'll have an easier time accessing the information from long term memory.

Retrieving Material From Long Term Memory

Accessing information from long term memory is sometimes conscious, sometimes automatic. Information is retrieved into working memory through **the spread of activation.**

Spread of Activation: **Retrieval** of pieces of information based on their relatedness to one another. Remembering one bit of information activates (stimulates) recall of associated information. **Example:** When trying to recall the name of my high school shop teacher, I kept thinking of words like Mr. Wrench, Mr. Hammer and then finally, his real name, Mr. Tool.

Retrieval: Process of searching for and finding information in long term memory.

A sometimes less accurate method of retrieval of information from long term memory is called **reconstruction.**

Reconstruction: Recreating information by using memories, expectations, logic, and existing knowledge. This is a problem solving process that makes use of logic, cues, and other knowledge to construct a reasonable answer by filling in any missing parts. **Example:** People at crime scenes often reconstruct inaccurate reports because logic, cues, and their own schemata would often lead them to make the wrong conclusions.

Forgetting and Long Term Memory

When information is lost in working memory, it's lost for good and must be re-entered. Most psychologists believe that all information can be eventually retrieved from long term memory given the right cues. More recent research indicates that time decay and **interference** can erase some memories. New memories may interfere with old memories and old memories may interfere with new memories.

Interference: The process that occurs when remembering certain information is hampered by the presence of other information. **Example:** When the new year changes, how many of you continue to write the old year's date on your checks?

Long term memory is still the most important memory. Research supports the notion that teaching strategies that encourage student engagement and lead to higher levels of initial learning (such as those listed below), are associated with longer retention.

- frequent reviews and tests
- elaborated feedback
- high standards
- mastery learning
- active involvement on learning projects

Connectionism: An Alternative View of Memory

More recent explanations of memory suggest that knowledge is stored in patterns of connections in a vast network in the brain. **Connectionist Models** suggest that knowledge is stored in a network of connections rather than as rules, propositions, or schemas. Stronger connections suggest better recall.

Connectionist Models: Views of knowledge as being stored in patterns of connections among basic processing units in the brain.

Parallel Distributed Processing: Connectionist model that uses the brain's physical network of neuron's as a metaphor for memory networks.

Metacognition, Regulation, and Individual Differences

To explain individual differences in why some people learn and remember better than others may be a function of their **executive control processes.**

Executive Control Processes: Processes such as selective attention, rehearsal, elaboration, and organization that influence encoding, storage, and retrieval of information in memory. Sometimes these executive control processes are called **metacognitive skills** because they can be used intentionally to regulate cognition.

Metacognition: Knowledge about our own thinking processes.

Cognitive Monitoring: People's awareness and monitoring of their own thinking and learning strategies.

Metacognitive knowledge helps us to regulate thinking and learning by employing the following three skills:
- **Planning**: involves how much time to give to a task, which strategies to use, how to start, what resources to gather, what order to follow, what to skim and what to give intense attention, and so on.
- **Monitoring**: on line awareness of "How am I doing?", "Is this making sense?" and "Should I change strategies?"

- **Evaluation**: making judgments about the processes and outcomes of thinking and learning. "Is this paper sufficient?", "Should I get help?" and "Have I done an adequate job?" etc..

These strategies may be automatic in adults and as children grow older, they are more able to employ these strategies. Metacognitive abilities begin to develop around the ages of 5 to 7 and students should be taught these skills and reminded to use them because research has shown that superior metacognitive skills can compensate for lower levels of ability.

It is not clear whether the developmental increases in children's memory spans are due to changes in memory capacity or improvements in strategy use. Case has suggested that the amount of space in working memory is the same at each age but young children use up a lot of it trying to remember how to execute basic operations. As they age, the use of these strategies become more automatic so less space is used up in working memory. By the time children are 10 to 11 years old, they have adult-like working memories.

Besides developmental differences, there are individual differences in working memory. More efficient working memories have been associated with giftedness in the math and verbal areas.

With respect to long term memory, the major difference among individuals is knowledge. When students have more domain-specific declarative and procedural knowledge they are better at learning and remembering in that domain. The more you know, the easier it is to learn. In addition to a good sound knowledge base, interest plays a key component in how effectively people learn. How can teachers support the development of knowledge?

Development of Declarative Knowledge

The development of declarative, procedural, and conditional knowledge contributes to individual differences in intellectual functioning. To reiterate, to learn declarative knowledge is really to integrate new ideas with existing knowledge and construct an understanding. First, students need a good base of knowledge to build upon with further information. Strategies for accomplishing this are discussed below.

Rote Memorization: Remembering information by repetition without necessarily understanding the meaning of the information. **Example:** Sometimes, the material to be learned has no inherent meaning, e.g. the capitals of all the states in the United States, so memorization requires repeated practice versus semantic comprehension.

When you try to remember a long list of words, you may find your recall subject to the **serial position effect.**

Serial Position Effect: The tendency to remember the beginning and the end but not the middle of the list. **Example:** If you had to remember the names Bertha, Hubert, Hermione, Francis, Julietta, and Simone, you would probably remember Bertha and Simone best.

One way to combat the serial position effect is through the use of **part learning** and when combined with another strategy, **distributed practice**, more effective learning occurs. Unfortunately, many students engage in **massed practice.**

Cognitive Views of Learning

Part Learning: Breaking a list of rote items into shorter lists . **Example:** Bertha and Hubert would be on list one. Hermione and Francis would comprise the second and Julietta and Simone would be on the third list.

Distributed Practice: Practice in brief periods with rest intervals over time. **Example:** If your test is on Friday you would start to study Monday and then again Tuesday, Wednesday, and Thursday.

Massed Practice: Practice for a single extended period also known as cramming. **Example:** If your test is on Friday, you crack the book for the first time on Thursday night.

Distributed practice is the best strategy for a few reasons. The first reason is that distributed practice allows for deep level processing versus surface level processing where little other than memorization of definitions takes place. Distributed practice affords students the time to reflect and organize the new information and connect it to already existing knowledge. Massed practice does not afford students the time necessary to accomplish this. Secondly, with massed practice, once studying has ended, forgetting begins, and then it's test time. But with distributed practice, once studying ends, forgetting begins, but when you start studying again, this constitutes relearning and relearning is more efficient. Sometimes, when the material to be learned is difficult or doesn't have much inherent meaning, you can employ **mnemonics.**

Mnemonics: Techniques for remembering; also the art of memory. Many of these strategies use imagery. Examples of different types of mnemonics can be found below.

Loci Method: Techniques of associating items with specific places. **Example:** If you need to purchase a variety of items at the store, take an imaginary walk through your house and imagine the eggs in the fireplace, the celery coming out of the toilet, milk coming out of your faucet, and a cake in the bathtub, well you get the picture. And the picture or image will really help you with recall.

Peg-type Mnemonics: Systems of associating items with cue words. **Example:** This is similar to the loci method however, instead of memorizing furniture or rooms in your house, you would memorize pegs such as one is bun, two is shoe, three is tree. When you want to remember your grocery list you would envision a carton of eggs in a hamburger bun, grapes spilling out of a shoe, steaks hanging from the branches of a tree.

Acronym: Technique for remembering names, phrases, or steps by using the first letter of each word to form a new memorable word. **Example:** SCUBA--self contained underwater breathing apparatus. To help Cali remember the planets in order from the sun, I taught her the sentence My Very Eloquent Mother Just Sat Upon Nine Puppies. The first letters, MVEMJSUNP stand for Mercury, Venus, Earth, Mars, Jupiter, Saturn, Uranus, Neptune and Pluto.

Chain Mnemonics: Memory strategies that associate one element in a series with the next element. **Example:** To help Cali remember her address when she was four, I made up a song that went like this; 1824 Bryn Mawr Avenue, Haddon Heights NJ, I live there too. Each sentence rhymes and connects to the next sentence in a song.

Keyword Method: System of associating new words or concepts with similar sounding cue words. **Example:** To remember St. Paul, Minnesota, I envision Saint Paul drinking a "mini" or very tiny soda.

Cognitive Views of Learning

Mnemonics can be helpful but one problem is that many of them require self-generated imagery which may be difficult for younger children. Younger children would probably benefit more from chain mnemonics or mnemonics that you, as the teacher, provide. All in all, the best method for helping students to learn material is to make it meaningful so that they can process the material at a deep level versus reliance on rote memorization.

Application Three: Crossword Puzzle

Fill in the puzzle with the correct terms. Terms with two words will not have a space in between. Check your responses in the answer key.

Cognitive Terms and Definitions

Clues

Down:
1. the process of searching for and finding information in long-term memory
2. the weakening and fading of memories with the passage of time
4. knowledge about our own thinking processes
6. the type of knowledge that is useful in many different kinds of tasks; information that applies to many situations

Across:
3. the type of knowledge that is verbal information; facts; "knowing that" something is the case
5. German for pattern or whole
7. consciously applied skills to reach goals in a particular subject or problem area
8. focus on a stimulus
9. basic structures for organizing information or concepts
10. techniques for remembering

Becoming an Expert: Development of Procedural and Conditional Knowledge

Experts in a field possess great declarative, procedural, and conditional knowledge. Experts also have **automated basic skills**.

Automated Basic Skills: skills that are applied without conscious thought. **Example:** When you first learned how to ride a bike, you had to think about every step, but after awhile, you could jump on and ride away without much thought except to the traffic around you.

Most psychologists have identifies three stages in which behaviors become automated:
- **Cognitive Stage:** The initial learning of an automated skill when we rely on general problem-solving approaches to make sense of steps or procedures. **Example:** When learning to ride a bike, we make take each action step-by-step. We may pedal and try to keep our balance. We probably won't try to navigate a turn until we have good balance and even when we first try to turn the corner, we may stop pedaling.
- **Associative Stage:** Individual steps of a procedure are combined or "chunked" into larger units. **Example:** Back to the bike example, now when you turn the corner you can also simultaneously pedal or brake, but you're still concentrating on all of the processes.
- **Autonomous Stage:** Final stage in the learning of automated skills. The procedure is fine tuned and becomes "automatic." **Example:** Now you can pedal, turn, brake, ring the bell, and you don't really have to consciously concentrate on what you're doing.

An important aspect of making skills automatic is providing plenty of practice. Practice in real contexts helps students learn not only *how* to do a skill but *why* and *when*. All practiced actions do not become completely automatic and nor should they be. Some strategies should be consciously applied as is the case with **domain-specific strategies.**

Domain Specific Strategies: Consciously applied skills to reach goals in a particular subject or problem area. **Example:** Once your bicycling has become autonomous, your maneuvers when changing lanes may be automatic but your decision is conscious and based on the traffic conditions around you.

Application Four: Fill in the Blanks

Read the following statements and fill in the blanks with the best word or words to complete the sentence. Check your responses in the answer key.

1. I am trying to memorize a long list of terms for my anatomy test, but when I test myself, I find that I remember the first and last words from the list. This is an example of the _____.

2. Since my short term memory can hold only 5 to 9 units of information, I try to combine the single units into larger units which is called _____.

3. The term for my long-term memory for events connected to a particular time and place in my life is called _____.

4. The long term memory that holds information for "how to do things" is called _____ memory.

5. When I use NASA to remember National Aeronautic Space Administration, this is a good example of _____.

6. I just met my new, next- door neighbor and so that I can remember her name, I'm going to repeat it over and over again. This is called _____.

7. To combat the serial position effect, I'm going to take the long list that I have to memorize and break it into several shorter lists. This is called _____.

8. Sets of interconnected bits of information in which long-term knowledge is held are called _____.

9. As I follow my everyday sequence of events by walking to the College of Education, climbing the stairs, opening my office, getting my mail, answering my voice mail, and answering my email, I am reminded that "I'm just a character in the play of life," following one of its _____.

10. When you are able to play your computer games without thinking about what you're doing because you've done it thousands of times, this is called _____.

Constructivism and Situated Learning

All of the views of memory and learning discussed so far in this chapter view the human mind as a symbol processing system that converts sensory input into symbols and then processes these symbols into forms that can be held in memory. Challenging these notions is the **constructivist perspective** and **situated learning.**

Constructivist Perspective: View that emphasizes the active role of the learner in building understanding and making sense of information.

- Exogenous constructivism: focuses on the ways that individuals reconstruct outside reality by building accurate mental representations such as propositional networks, schemas, and condition-action production rules. This emphasis is on building accurate mental structures that reflect "the way things really are" in the external world.
- Endogenous constructivism: assumes new knowledge is abstracted from old knowledge and not from accurately mapping the outside world.
- Dialectical constructivism: suggests that knowledge grows through the interactions of internal (cognitive) and external (environmental and social) factors.
- Radical constructivism: suggests that we live in a relativistic world that can only be understood from individually unique perspectives. No individual's viewpoint is less correct than another's.

Situated Learning: Enculturation or adopting the norms, behaviors, skills, beliefs, language, and attitudes of a particular community. Learning in the real world is not like studying in school. Much of what is learned is specific to the situation in which it was learned. The implications are that students should learn skills and knowledge in meaningful contexts, with connections to real-life situations in which the knowledge and skills will be useful.

Practice Tests

Essay Questions

1.   Discuss the advantages and disadvantages of rote memorization. Reflect upon your experiences as a student and think about the situations in which rote memorization was an effective learning strategy.

2.   How does perception influence learning and why is it, that when all students in a classroom are presented with the same material and then are later asked to recall what they have learned, they don't all represent the material in the same way?

Multiple Choice

1. Mechanisms for seeing, hearing, tasting, smelling, and seeing are called
   a. the sensory register
   b. the sensory memory
   c. sensory information store
   d. none of the above

2. A problem solving process that makes use of logic, cues, and other knowledge to construct an answer is called
   a. retrieval
   b. spreading of activation
   c. reconstruction
   d. retention

3. Executive control processes describing peoples awareness of their cognitive machinery and how it works are called
   a. metacognitive skills
   b. organizational skills
   c. declarative skills
   d. mnemonics

4. The keyword method does not work well if
   a. it is difficult to identify a keyword for a particular item
   b. keywords may be more easily forgotten than vocabulary learned in other ways
   c. younger students have difficulty forming their own images
   d. all of the above

5. The best single method for helping students to learn is to
   a. organize the material for them
   b. make it meaningful
   c. provide them with mnemonics
   d. reinforce their learning with incentives and rewards

6. Which of the following is NOT one of the characteristics of *experts* functioning within an area?
   a. They function at the cognitive stage
   b. Their functioning has become proceduralized
   c. They possess extensive prerequisite knowledge
   d. They function at the autonomous stage

7. The field of constructivism that emphasizes building accurate mental structures that reflect the way things really are is called
   a. social constructivism
   b. exogenous constructivism
   c. endogenous constructivism
   d. dialectical constructivism

8. The long term semantic memory is the memory for
   a. syntax
   b. procedures
   c. meaning
   d. rules

9. The more deeply you process information, relative to its name, physical appearance, and function, you will have an easier time recalling information about it from long term memory. This notion is consistent with
   a. situated learning theories
   b. levels of processing theory
   c. associationistic theories
   d. constructivist theories

10. When you are studying to prepare for an exam, you hope to solidify all of the information in
    a. the sensory register
    b. working memory
    c. short term memory
    d. long-term memory

Answer Key

Application One: Behavioral and Cognitive Approaches
1. cognitive 2. behavioral 3. cognitive 4. behavioral 5. cognitive
6. behavioral 7. behavioral 8. cognitive 9. cognitive 10. behavioral

Application Two: Memory Stores

	Sensory Register	Working Memory	Long Term Memory
Capacity	Large	5 to 9 units of info	Infinite
Duration	.05-4 seconds	20 seconds	Infinite
Forgetting	time decay	interference & time decay	weak associations & interference

Application Three:

Cognitive Terms and Definitions

Application Four: Fill in the blanks

1. serial position effect
2. chunking
3. episodic memory
4. procedural
5. an acronym

6. maintenance rehearsal
7. part learning
8. propositional networks
9. scripts
10. automaticity

Essays

1. Those who argue against rote memorization suggest that it opens the door for memorization of terms and definitions with little comprehension of the meaning. Without understanding, there would be little application of learning beyond the academic setting. Therefore, learning that can't be applied would become useless and obsolete.

2. What people learn is never an exact replica of what they have read or been told. All people perceive based on what they already know and then they *interpret* what they have perceived based on what they already know. Perceptions are not pure but rather the meaning we give to the sensory data. Individual differences will also account for student differences in perception and learning.

Multiple Choice

1. d   2. c   3. a   4. d   5. b   6. a   7. b   8. c   9. b   10. d

Chapter Eight

Complex Cognitive Processes

"What is education but a process by which a person begins to learn how to learn?"
Peter Ustinov

Of great importance to all of us who are or will be educators, is that our students comprehend what we teach them beyond rote memorization for the purpose of achieving a grade on an exam. Ideally, they should be able to understand and remember information to routinely apply it outside of the school setting. This involves a good understanding of **concepts** and relationships among concepts.

Concept: A general category of ideas, objects, people, or experiences whose members share certain properties. **Example:** An example of a concept is a *bird*. Concepts help us to organize vast amounts of information. There are many, many different kinds of birds but by categorizing birds into 10 or more groups we can deal with the diversity within this concept.

Traditionally, people have believed that members of a concept share **defining attributes.** **Defining Attributes:** Distinctive features shared by members of a category. **Example:** A defining attribute for the concept *bird* might be that they all have feathers.

When teaching students about concepts you will generally help them to understand the concepts by giving them the example of a **prototype.**

Prototype: Best representative of a category. **Example:** For the concept *bird*, the best representative may be a "robin."

Whereas a robin may come to most people's minds when asked to provide an example of a *bird*, some members may not be as great an example as other members of the concept *bird*, which brings us to **graded membership.**

Graded Membership: The extent to which something belongs to a category. **Example:** A robin is a better example of the concept *bird* than perhaps a penguin.

Another way to explain concept learning is by identifying members of a category by referring to its **exemplars.**

Exemplars: A specific example or memory of a given category that is used to classify an item. **Example:** You may have an exemplar of a swimming pool, like the one in your backyard, against which you make comparisons of any other swimming pools you will encounter.

Prototypes are probably built from experiences with many exemplars. Eventually, all of the memories of every swimming pool you have ever encountered will blend together over time creating the swimming pool prototype. We also recognize concepts through our schematic knowledge attached to that concept. We may have schemes that say "swimming pools can be indoors/outdoors, above ground/below ground, inflatable, plastic, concrete," etc..

Teaching Concepts

Whereas children most readily learn about concepts on the basis of best examples and defining attributes, teaching of concepts utilizes both of these to teach concept attainment through hypothesis testing. To teach a concept you will need the following four components:

- name of the concept
- definition of the concept
- examples and non-examples (to set the boundaries, e.g. a bat is not a *bird*)
- relevant and irrelevant attributes

Exercise: For Concept Development, Go On A Safari

Cali and I play this game in the car but it can be played anywhere with as many people as you like. It's a great game for helping students to understand the notion of shared attributes. The game begins by someone saying, "I'm going on a safari and I'm going to bring a nail and a dime." (you can bring any two items as long as they share a defining attribute or have a common bond). Then it becomes the next person's turn to say what they're bringing and they must pick two items that share the defining attribute of the dime and the nail, (they won't know right away what the defining attribute is). Now, if you picked dime and nail because they're both metals, then the next person would have to bring something like a fork and a can, and you would say, "You can come on the safari," because their items possess the defining attribute. BUT, if you picked nail and dime because both are four-letter words, and the next person said fork and can, you would say, "Sorry, but you can't come on the safari," (because "can" only has three letters) You go on like this with everyone getting more turns (even the people who couldn't go on the safari right away) until someone is able to say what the defining attribute is. Hint: dime and nail could also share the attribute of being small enough to hide in your hand, or fit in a pocket, etc.. The person who starts must make that decision.

Furthermore, whenever you are teaching concepts, you will achieve greater success when you can graphically represent the concept which you are trying to teach. See Application One for an example of how this works.

Application One: Concept Formation

Examine the following examples and nonexamples of Elgnathgir. By comparing the examples to the non-examples, determine the defining attributes and which of the figures on the third row are examples of Elgnathgir. Check your responses in the answer key.

These are examples of Elgnathgir

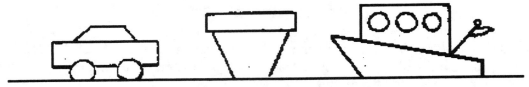

These are non-examples of Elgnathgir

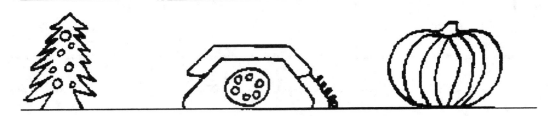

Which of the following are Elgnathgir?

Complex Cognitive Processes

Start your lesson with a prototype to help students establish the category. Along with a definition include less typical examples to prevent **undergeneralization** and nonexamples to prevent **overgeneralization.**

Undergeneralization: Exclusion of a true member of a category; limiting a category. **Example:** Some students may not think to include "ostrich" within the concept of *bird* since ostriches can't fly.

Overgeneralization: Inclusion of nonmembers in a category; overextending a concept. **Example:** Some students may think a "bat" is a *bird* since it has wings and can fly.

As students examine examples and non-examples they should be forming hypotheses about the concepts much as you did in the exercise in Application One. Ask your students to reflect on their problem solving processes and document their findings. This will help to develop their metacognitive strategies. A useful strategy for students above the primary grades is **concept mapping.**

Concept Mapping: Student's diagram of his or her understanding of a concept.

Problem Solving

Now, more than ever, in our age of rapidly changing information and technological advances, it becomes crucial that educational programs produce students who are capable of solving **problems**, versus memorizing static information. Students who are taught to be effective **problem solvers** will be better prepared for the world of the future.

Problem: Any situation in which you are trying to reach some goal and must find a means to do so.

Problem Solving: Creating new solutions for problems.

Within the field of psychology there is dispute as to whether problem solving strategies are specific to the problem area or whether there are general strategies that can be useful in many areas. Usually, we start with general strategies and as we become more expert within the field we develop specific strategies.

General problem solving has five stages that correspond to the acronym IDEAL .
- I   Identify problems and opportunities
- D   Define goals and represent the problem
- E   Explore possible strategies
- A   Anticipate outcomes and Act
- L   Look back and Learn

Problems should be presented as opportunities and their solution should be approached from a variety of angles. Help students to focus their attention on relevant material and ignore the irrelevant details. When dealing with word problems, **linguistic comprehension** is a necessary component.

Linguistic Comprehension: Understanding the meaning of sentences. **Example:** When the problem says "Jack has five more apples than Jill who has two. How many do they have together?" what this really means is to set up an addition problem, 5+2=X. This may be a difficult sentence to understand because it subscribes to **part-whole relations.**

Part-Whole Relations: These are problems in which students have trouble figuring out what is part of what as in the example above. Another type of problem that presents difficulty for students are **relational propositions.**

Relational Propositions: describes the relationship between two rates, amounts, and so on. **Example:** One train is traveling 90 MPH due west. Another train, that is 100 miles away from the first train is slowly traveling east toward the first train at a rate of 45 MPH or half the rate of the first train. How long will it take for the two trains to intersect?

A much easier word problem for students is one that assigns value to something called **assignment propositions.**

Assignment Propositions: Simply assign value to something. **Example:** The suit cost $120.00.

Students often encounter difficulties with word problems when they translate the problem-when they decide what type of problem they are encountering. If they inaccurately believe a problem to be a relational problem of distance and it is instead a relational problem of time, then their approach will be off and they will activate the wrong schemas for problem solving.

To help students improve translation and schema selection we have to teach them to move from general to specific problem solving strategies. It appears that students benefit from seeing many different kinds of example problems worked out correctly for them. The best examples are those that do not require students to integrate several sources of information. Give students practice in the following:
- recognizing and categorizing a variety of problem types
- representing problems in pictures, symbols, graphs or in words
- selecting relevant or irrelevant information in problems

If students encounter a problem that suggests an immediate solution, they probably haven't really solved a new problem. More likely, what has occurred is called **schema-driven problem solving.**

Schema-Driven Problem Solving: Recognizing a problem as a "disguised" version of an old problem for which one already has a solution.

If you do not have an immediate solution that comes to mind, then you must employ one of two procedures; **algorithms** or **heuristics.**

Algorithms: Step-by-step procedure for solving a problem; prescription for solutions. **Example:** 2 X 3 + 5=K would yield a very different answer from 2 X (3+5) =K. You have to know the rules for multiplication.

Heuristics: General strategy used in attempting to solve problems. Several heuristics are listed below.

Complex Cognitive Processes

- **Means-Ends Analysis:** Heuristic in which the goal is divided into subgoals and then a means for solving each subgoal is figured out. **Example:** A semester long project could be divided into step-by-step components, each completed by the end of every week, building toward the final goal.
- **Working Backward Strategy:** Heuristic in which one starts with the goal and moves backward to solve the problem. **Example:** Start with the final goal of the semester long project, and working backwards, figure out when each aspect of the project should be completed.
- **Analogical Thinking:** Heuristic in which one limits the search for solutions to situations that are similar to the one at hand. **Example:** The person who invented Velcro found his particular solution in nature, in the burrs that attach themselves to your socks as you walk through the woods.

Another strategy that will aid in the problem solving process, that being **verbalization.**

Verbalization: Putting your problem solving plan into words and giving reasons for selecting it.

Complex Cognitive Processes

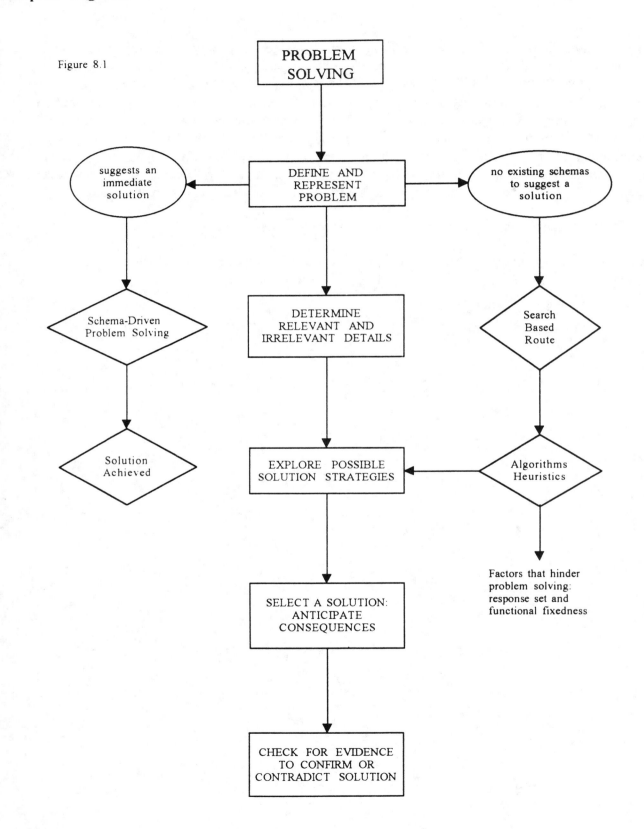

Figure 8.1

PROBLEM SOLVING

suggests an immediate solution

DEFINE AND REPRESENT PROBLEM

no existing schemas to suggest a solution

Schema-Driven Problem Solving

DETERMINE RELEVANT AND IRRELEVANT DETAILS

Search Based Route

Solution Achieved

EXPLORE POSSIBLE SOLUTION STRATEGIES

Algorithms Heuristics

Factors that hinder problem solving: response set and functional fixedness

SELECT A SOLUTION: ANTICIPATE CONSEQUENCES

CHECK FOR EVIDENCE TO CONFIRM OR CONTRADICT SOLUTION

Factors that Hinder Problem Solving

People often fail to solve problems because they seldom consider unconventional uses for materials that have a specific function. This is called **functional fixedness**. Another impediment to solving problem is **response set.**

Functional Fixedness: Inability to use objects or tools in a new way. **Example:** Unable to extract my computer disk from my lap top, I called a friend who said I needed a Mac disk extraction tool to put into the little hole above the disk slot. Stating that I didn't own one of those, he laughed and said it was nothing more than a straightened out paper clip. He was NOT suffering from functional fixedness.

Response Set: Rigidity; tendency to respond in the most familiar way. **Example:** See Application Two for an example to test your response set.

Application Two: Response Set

Examine the picture below. Should you accept the mission, your problem is to determine exactly what you see in the water below. Check your response in the answer key.

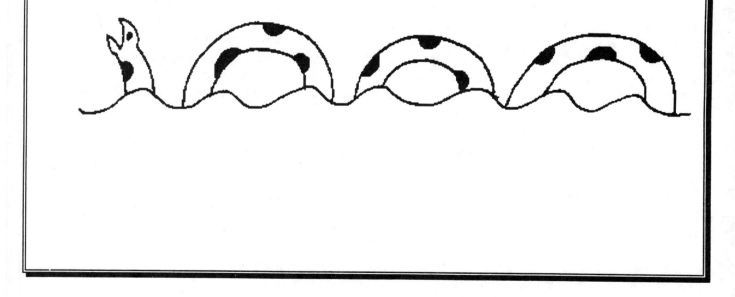

Both response set and functional fixedness prevent us from looking at problems divergently, or from many different angles. Opening your mind to divergent thought processes might lead to what Gestaltists call **insight.**

Insight: Sudden realization of a solution. **Example:** A boy lost his shuttlecock in the tree. He jumped up try reach it in the branch but was a bit too short. He shook the tree. It didn't budge. He stared down at the ground and noticed fallen branches lying at his feet. "Aha," he thought. He picked up a branch and used it to knock his shuttlecock out of the tree.

Effective Problem Solving: What do the Experts Do?

You might wonder what it is that experts possess that enables them to be such effective problem solvers. We know that experts possess certain abilities that beginners or novices lack.

- Experts generally possess a great deal of knowledge about the subject area and many schemas available.
- Experts can also recognize the patterns needed to solve a problem very quickly
- Experts also have a large store of productions or condition-action schemas so they know what action to take in various conditions
- Understanding the problem and choosing the solution happen almost simultaneously
- Experts' knowledge is elaborated, well-practiced, and organized to make for easy retrieval
- Experts plan out solutions and monitor progress

Expert teachers also possess skills that set them apart from novice teachers. Expert teachers have automatic teaching routines, they work from integrated sets of principles, they look for patterns revealing similarities, they focus on analyzing problems and mentally applying different principles to develop solutions. Expert teachers are expert problem solvers because they can meet the needs of their students by figuring out the best way to clear their confusion and help them to expand upon what they know. Expert teachers also must be able to analyze students' misconceptions and inaccuracies so that students don't develop misleading representations of problems. Sometimes students must be taught to "unlearn" common sense ideas.

Learning Strategies and Tactics

Key to becoming an expert and accomplishing learning goals are **learning strategies** and **learning tactics.** Your use of these strategies and tactics reflects your metacognitive knowledge. Teaching these skills to students has become a top priority in education. Some important principles for accomplishing these goals are outlined below the following definitions.

Learning Strategies: General plans for approaching learning tasks.

Learning Tactics: Specific techniques for learning, such as using mnemonics or outlining a passage.

- expose students to a number of very specific strategies and tactics
- teach conditional knowledge about when, where, and why to use various strategies

Complex Cognitive Processes

- motivate students to use the strategies they have learned
- ensure that students have the appropriate schemas for making sense of the material

The following strategies should be taught to students because all too often we assume that students automatically know how to effectively employ these tactics when they don't.

1. underlining and highlighting-key phrases and important topics
2. taking notes- to focus attention on important ideas
3. visual tools-graphic organizers and mapping to comprehend relationships
4. **PQ4R**- a method for studying text that involves six steps: Preview, Question, Read, Reflect, Recite, Review.

Application Three: Learning Tactics-What Should You Do?

Read the following statements and decide whether they accurately reflect what the experts know about their usage by writing "True" or "False" before each statement. Check your responses in the answer key.

1. _____ Students never seem to underline or highlight enough material.

2. _____ Limiting how much students underline to three sentences per paragraph improves their learning.

3. _____ Note taking during class helps to encode it into long term memory.

4. _____ Note taking aids learning even when students don't review them before a test.

5. _____ Note taking may distract you from actually listening to and making sense of the lecture.

6. _____ To record key ideas in your own words, you must translate, connect, elaborate, and organize.

7. _____ The use of graphic organizers and mapping is not as effective as underlining or highlighting.

8. _____ The "P" in PQ4R, stands for "Problem solving."

9. _____ The PQ4R method is most appropriate for children before fifth grade when they need to establish study skills..

10. _____ The use of PQ4R forces students to engage in distributed practice.

Even under the best conditions when we have taught students what to learn, how to learn, how to study, and how to apply metacognitive skills, how do we teach them to think? Many programs have been developed for the direct teaching of thinking skills, called **Stand-Alone Thinking Skills Programs.**

Complex Cognitive Processes

Stand-Alone Thinking Skills Programs: Programs that teach thinking skills directly without the need for extensive subject matter knowledge. Students who have had trouble with the standard curriculum may experience success and enhanced self esteem with these programs but a disadvantage is that they may not be able to generalize these skills to specific subject areas.

Teachers can teach good thinking skills by modeling good thinking aloud, providing direct instruction about how to analyze causes, and giving the students practice through interaction in using the skills. Many of these components can be found in methods that support **critical thinking.**

Critical Thinking: Evaluating conclusions by logically and systematically examining the problem, the evidence, and the solution. A crucial component in approaches designed to develop critical thinking is that enough practice be given that the thinking skills become practically automatic. This is the only way that **transfer** can occur.

Transfer: Influence of previously learned material on new material. **Example:** Now that I know how to drive a car with a standard transmission (four on the floor) I will be able to drive my boyfriend's truck which is also standard but has three on the column.

Two kinds of transfer are called **low-road** and **high-road transfer.**

Low-Road Transfer: Spontaneous and automatic transfer of highly practiced skills, with little need for reflective thinking. **Example:** I can move from one computer to another with relative ease because I have experience working with both Macs and IBMs.

High-Road Transfer: Application of abstract knowledge learned in one situation to a different situation. **Example:** In a study I conducted, I trained individuals to improve their performance on a spatial task. At a later date, I gave them a different spatial task and their performances revealed that spatial skills had transferred from one task to another.

Unfortunately, learning does not always transfer because learning occurs in specific situations and students may not always transfer their learning from one situation to another. Greater transfer will occur if students are provided with the opportunities for **overlearning.** Positive transfer is encouraged when skills are used under conditions similar to those that will exist when the skills are needed later.

Overlearning: Practicing a task past the point of mastery to combat forgetting and improve transfer. **Example:** You have overlearned how to ride a bike so well that you will never forget how and you can probably ride any bike that you encounter (as long as it has two wheels).

Application Four: Identifying the Problem

Read the following problems that require linguistic comprehension. See if you are able to identify the types of word problems represented there. Will you activate the correct schemas? Check your responses in the answer key.

relational proposition   assignment proposition   part-whole relations

1. There is a 30-60% off sale at the mens' store where John buys his suits. He sees a suit he likes and the regular price of the suit is $120.00 discounted by 30%. Another suit that John admires has a regular price of $180.00 and it is discounted by 60%. John wants to purchase the suit that will cost him the least amount. Which suit offers John the best savings? _____

2. A goose is flying back and forth between two trains that are 270 miles apart and approaching each other at a speed of 90 MPH. It's a fast goose (flying 45 MPH). How many times will the goose fly back and forth before the two trains meet? _____

3. Apples cost $.35 a pound. You buy 10 pounds of apples. How much money will you need?
_____

4. Jeffrey weighs 10 times as much as Cubby, who weighs 16 lbs. If Cubby loses half of her body weight, how many times more than Cubby will Jeff weigh? _____

5. A pool has a depth of 8 feet and an area of 32 feet. It's being filled at a rate of 2 cubic feet per minute. How long will it take to fill it up? _____

Application Five: Matching Key Terms and Definitions
Transfer

Select the word from the left column that best matches the definition on the right. Put the number of the matching word in the blank in front of the letters and in the matrix below containing the same letter. If your numbers are correct, all numbers across, down, and diagonally will add up to the same number.

1. Transfer   _____   a. Spontaneous and automatic transfer of highly practiced skills

2. Low-road transfer   _____   b. Previous learning correctly applied to new situation

3. High-road transfer   _____   c. Learning from one situation is applied in second, similar situation

4. Specific transfer   _____   d. Looking back on previous problems for transfer cues

5. Forward transfer   _____   e. Looking ahead to applying knowledge

6. General transfer _____   f. Application of abstract knowledge learned in one situation to a different situation

7. Backward reaching transfer _____   g. Solving problems based on previously learned principles and attitudes

8. Negative transfer _____   h. Influence of previously learned material on new material

9. Positive transfer _____   i. Previously learned material hinders learning of new material

A   B   C

D   E   F

G   H   I

What is the number? _____

Practice Tests

Essay Questions

1. Describe Phye's three stages of strategic transfer.

2. Why is it sometimes necessary to help students "unlearn" common sense ideas?

Multiple Choice

1.   When teaching concepts to your students, the most effective sequence is
   a. prototype, less obvious examples, nonexamples
   b. nonexamples, less obvious examples, prototypes
   c. less obvious examples, nonexamples, prototypes
   d. less obvious examples, prototypes, nonexamples

Complex Cognitive Processes

2.   A prototype for the concept of liquids might be
        a. mercury
        b. glass
        c. milk
        d. water

3.   Exemplars are best defined as
        a. the best representation of a concept or category
        b. a specific example or memory of a given category
        c. a category with a "fuzzy" boundary
        d. abstract concepts

4.   Exclusion of a true member of a category results in what we call
        a. negative transfer
        b. overgeneralization
        c. undergeneralization
        d. specific transfer

5.   The error rate for recalling relational propositions is about _____ times higher than the error rate for assignment propositions.
        a. two
        b. three
        c. four
        d. five

6.   Your interpretation of a word problem is called
        a. a translation
        b. a linguistic schema
        c. a relational proposition
        d. a search-based route

7.   Because they involve the attempt to apply familiar but inappropriate strategies to a new situation. functional fixedness and response set are examples of
        a. backward-reaching transfer
        b. negative transfer
        c. overlearning
        d. situated learning

8.   Which of the following best illustrates the notion of functional fixedness?
        a. a man who can't find his hammer uses a rock to hammer a nail back into a floor board
        b. a woman who can't find the cork for a half finished bottle of wine, pours the wine into a jar
        c. a woman who has her Xmas tree wrapped in a plastic tarp doesn't know how she will get it to the curb because she has no wheelbarrow and doesn't think to drag it out in the plastic
        d. A woman can't find her turkey pins so she straightens out some paperclips to use instead

9. A step-by-step procedure for solving a problem is called a(n)
   a. analogy
   b. heuristic
   c. means-ends analysis
   d. algorithm

10. Which of the following is NOT characteristic of "expert" problem solving?
   a. experts use pattern recognition to represent a problem quickly
   b. experts have a large store of condition-action schemata
   c. experts have misconceptions or intuitive notions about a subject
   d. experts have a fund of declarative, procedural, and conditional knowledge

Answer Key

Application One: Concept Formation
The defining attribute of Elgnathgir is that it must have right angles somewhere in the figure. On the last line, the only figure that subscribes to the defining attribute is the house.

Application Two: Response Set
If you automatically assumed that this was one sea serpent or one sea snake, then you are responding from a response set. Open your thinking to many options and always look beneath the surface, pardon the pun.

Application Three: Learning Tactics-What Should You Do?

1. False   2. False   3. True   4. True   5. True
6. True   7. False   8. False   9. False   10. True

Application Four: Identifying the Problem

1. part whole relations-it's hard for students to understand what is really being asked
2. relational proposition-it's a rate and distance problem
3. assignment proposition-simple assignment of a cost to a product
4. part whole relations-Jeff's weight won't change but his weight is defined in relation to Cubby
5. relational proposition-it's a rate and volume problem

Application Five: Matching Key Terms and Definitions, Transfer

a. 2   b. 9   c. 4   d. 7   e. 5   f. 3   g. 6   h. 1   i. 8   The number is 15.

Essays:

1. In the acquisition phase, students should not only receive instruction about a strategy and how to use it, they should practice the strategy and practice being aware of when and how they are using it. In the retention phase, more practice with feedback helps students perfect their strategy use. In the transfer phase, the teacher should provide new problems that can be solved with the same strategy, even though the problems appear different on the surface. To increase motivation, inform students that strategy usage will help them solve many problems and accomplish different tasks.

2. Many novices or beginners approach subject areas with misunderstandings because up to the point where formal instruction begins, most of their knowledge has been constructed through perception and intuition. Many of their ideas about the physical world are wrong. For example, many young children believe that the sun follows them wherever they go, because they see the sun wherever they go. Teachers must first find out what children believe and what they think they know and then begin to clear up misconceptions and help them to formulate schemas based on accurate information and concepts.

Multiple Choice

1. a   2. d   3. b   4. c   5. b   6. a   7. b   8. c   9. d   10. c

Chapter Nine

Learning and Instruction

"Minds are like parachutes. They only function when they are open."
Sir James Dewar

Before you begin your classroom instruction you must determine the goals of teaching. What changes in your students would you like to take place? Written down, these goals take the form of **instructional objectives.**

Instructional Objectives: Clear statement of what students are intended to learn through instruction. **Example:** The students will be able to explain the democratic form of governance.

There are different types of objectives for different learning goals. **Behavioral Objectives** use words like *list, define, add, or calculate*, but **cognitive objectives** use terms like *comprehend, recognize, create*, and *apply.*

Behavioral Objectives: Instructional objectives stated in terms of observable behaviors. **Example:** Students will be able to list capitals for every US state.

Cognitive Objectives: Instructional objectives stated in terms of higher level thinking operations. **Example:** Within mathematics, the students will be able to apply estimation procedures to arrive at close approximations of the actual results.

Instructional Objectives

Several experts in the field have outlined their notions of educational objectives and what should be included therein. These are outlined below.

Mager: Objectives should be so **specific** that they clearly state what students will be doing when demonstrating their achievement and how you will know they are doing it. These objectives are thought of as **behavioral** and there are three components:
1. describes what the student must do
2. lists the conditions under which the behavior will occur
3. gives the criteria for acceptable performance

Gronlund: Objectives should be stated first in **general** terms followed by a few specific sample behaviors. This is generally thought to be a **cognitive** approach. The rationale behind this widely used approach is that teachers could never list all of the behaviors that might be listed in problem-solving, for example, so it's better to state a few general objectives and clarify them with specific examples.

Bloom's Taxonomy: Bloom and colleagues developed a **taxonomy** (classification system) of educational objectives that cover three different areas of learning: **Cognitive, affective, and psychomotor.** The most widely used and developed objectives are in the cognitive domain.

Bloom's Cognitive Objectives from simple to complex:
* **knowledge:** recalling information and facts
* **comprehension:** understanding, translating the information into your own words
* **application:** using information to solve problems
* **analysis:** breaking down information into parts and revealing organization
* **synthesis:** creating a new idea, product, solution
* **evaluation:** judging something against a standard

When the material to be learned is loosely structured, providing students with the objectives may give them the necessary framework for understanding why the material is important and what are the ultimate goals of achievement. In this case, knowing objectives appears to improve achievement but when the activities are structured and organized, knowing objectives appears to have little effect on achievement.

Application One: Identifying Domains of Objectives
Choose the domain which best describes each statement below--Affective, Cognitive, or Psychomotor.

_____ 1. Climb the ropes and touch the gymnasium ceiling in 4 out of 5 attempts

_____ 2. Compare the gross national product of Mexico to that of the US

_____ 3. Determine the volume of a pool with a 15 foot diameter and 4 foot height

_____ 4. Select poetic literary works that you find emotionally moving and explain why

_____ 5. Using your knowledge of the periodic table, perform an experiment using NaCl and H_2O and write the principle that you discover

---

        6. Devise a routine set to music on the uneven parallel bars in gymnastics class

        7. Demonstrate an understanding of number estimation

        8. Show that students can work cooperatively on a community improvement project

---

Behavioral Models of Teaching

Two forms of instruction that make use of objectives are **mastery learning** and **direct instruction.** Each will be discussed separately.

Mastery Learning: An approach to teaching and grading that assumes, given enough time and the proper instruction, students can master any learning objective and should do so before moving on to the next topic.
- teachers break course into units of study
- each unit has several objectives to be mastered
- mastery usually means a score of 80-90% on a test or assessment
- students are informed of the objectives and criteria
- students may recycle through the material and retest to achieve the minimum or surpass the minimum
- those who achieve mastery are given enrichment exercises
- those who need more help work with teachers, peers, tutors, etc..

This approach is especially good for topics where a good understanding of **basic skills** is necessary. **Basic Skills:** Clearly structured knowledge that is needed for later learning and that can be taught step-by-step. **Example:** It would be fruitless to move into decimals before understanding fractions.

Advantages:	Disadvantages:
*when the focus is on key concepts and foundation skills for future learning	*teachers must have a variety of materials for students who need to recycle through objectives
*very successful when students are given extra time for learning	*some will be frustrated by the need to recycle
*advanced students are not held back	*faster students may be held back while slower students catch up
*self-motivated students will learn much more and achieve a better understanding	*individual differences persist

154

Another approach that focuses more on the whole group than on individuals is **direct instruction.**

Direct Instruction/Explicit Teaching: Instruction for mastery of basic skills. This approach, was tested by research and found to be effective for whole groups because the emphasis is on the instruction of basic skills and those types of skills that are assessed by standardized tests. Group averages improve, but the achievement of individuals may not and when the objectives are in the high level cognitive domain (writing creatively, solving complex problems, etc.) then this approach may not be suitable. Another term for direct instruction is **active teaching.**

Active Teaching: Teaching characterized by high levels of teacher explanation, demonstration, and interaction with students.

Rosenshine summarizes six teaching functions of direct instruction:
- **Review and check the previous day's work:** reteach if necessary
- **Present new material:** teach in small steps providing examples and non-examples
- **Provide guided practice:** question students, give practice problems
- **Give feedback and correctives:** examine student answers and reteach if necessary
- **Provide independent practice:** provide opportunities for students to apply new learning on their own and in groups working toward a goal of 95% success rate. Skills should be overlearned and automatic.
- **Review weekly and monthly:** include review items as homework to consolidate learning

Critics of direct instruction suggest that it is limited to lower level objectives, is based on traditional teaching methods, discourages independent work, and ignores innovative models. The student is seen as a passive vessel waiting to be filled up with knowledge rather than an active constructor of knowledge. Proponents, however, suggest that when implemented properly with plenty of guided and independent practice and feedback, students will learn actively.

Cognitive Models of Teaching

When the emphasis is on concept development and the relationships between concepts, information processing models and cognitive models are appropriate. Three proponents of the cognitive approach are Jerome Bruner, David Ausubel, and Robert Gagne'.

According to Bruner, students will learn the most when they focus on the **subject structure** and **coding system** of the area under study. Bruner suggests that students must be active in order to grasp the subject structure and they must identify key principles for themselves rather than blindly accept teachers' explanations. This can be accomplished through **discovery learning.**

Subject Structure: According to Bruner, the fundamental framework of ideas.

Coding System: A hierarchy of ideas or concepts.

Discovery Learning: Bruner's approach, in which students work on their own to discover basic principles. **Example:** Some of my students employed a lesson in discovery learning to help kindergarten children learn their secondary colors. See the description of the lesson below.

Discovery Learning in the Classroom

My students wanted a group of kindergarten children to discover for themselves which primary colors combined to make the secondary colors. The K children already knew their primary colors; red, yellow, and blue. Here is where the fun began........ My students went into the classroom dressed as clowns with multi-colored clown wigs and costumes. Using themselves as color models, they asked the K children to identify each color by pointing to their own costumes and wigs. Having established that the children knew the primary colors, my students brought forth a number of flasks containing colored water; red, blue, and yellow. They placed empty flasks on a table and while the K students observed, combined red and blue water into an empty flask and asked the children if they could tell them what was happening. The children shouted out their observations, "Red and blue make purple!" The children then took over the lesson, experimenting with combinations and recording their data via a color chart in which, for example, a yellow piece of paper and a red piece of paper were placed and made to equal an orange piece of paper. The children continued in this fashion until they had completed a color chart with all of the combinations they had observed. They were very proud of their discoveries and the lesson ended with all of the children decorating iced cupcakes with varying combinations of colored sugar. Their learning was fun and rewarding!

In a discovery lesson, the teacher provides examples and the students work with these examples to "discover" the underlying principles and rules. This type of reasoning is known as **inductive reasoning** and as it is sometimes called, **Eg-Rule Method**. This method requires **intuitive thinking** on the part of students.

Inductive Reasoning: Formulating general principles based on knowledge of examples and details.

Eg- Rule Method: Teaching or learning by moving from specific examples to general rules.

Intuitive Thinking: Making imaginative leaps to correct perceptions or workable solutions.

Unfortunately, traditional education often discourages intuitive thinking tending more toward coming up with one correct answer, safe and uncreative. Whereas in Bruner's discovery learning the teacher organizes the classroom so that students can make intuitive guesses and discoveries, sometimes this may occur within too haphazard a situation. When more guidance and structure is required for learning to take place, **guided discovery** would be more appropriate.

Guided Discovery: An adaptation of discovery learning, in which the teacher provides some direction. **Example:** The "color" lesson above is a good example of guided discovery.

Learning and Instruction

Whereas there are many advantages to discovery learning, it is not appropriate for every situation. For example, how long do you think it would take you to "discover" the theory of relativity? Some topics can be learned more efficiently and much quicker when they are taught directly which brings us to Ausubel's theory of **Expository Teaching/Reception Learning.** According to Ausubel, people acquire knowledge through reception rather than through discovery. By reception, Ausubel does not mean rote memorization but rather the connection of information, ideas, and the relationships among ideas through **meaningful verbal learning.** Exposition is taken to mean explanation and presentation of materials in a carefully organized, sequenced, and usable form. This type of learning relies upon **deductive reasoning** and is sometimes called the **Rule-eg method.**

Expository Teaching: Ausubel's method--teachers present material in complete, organized form, moving from the broadest to the most specific concepts.

Meaningful Verbal Learning: Focused and organized relationships among ideas and verbal information.

Deductive Reasoning: Drawing conclusions by applying rules or principles; logically moving from a general rule or principle to a specific solution.

Rule-Eg Method: Teaching or learning by moving from general principles to specific examples.

The best learning occurs when there is a connection between what the student already knows and the material to be learned. To help accomplish this, always begin a lesson with an **advance organizer**.
Advance Organizer: Statement of inclusive concepts to introduce and sum up material that follows.

As with any type of teaching, expository methods work better in some situations than in others. This approach works best when one wants to teach about the relationships between concepts and of course, students must have working knowledge of the concepts in the first place. It is also more effective for students in later elementary grades and beyond.

Contrary to Ausubel and Bruner, Gagne' demonstrates less concern for how learning is accomplished but rather expresses a greater interest in the quality, permanence, and usefulness of the learning. Steps in Gagne's Instructional Events Model are as follows:
- gain student's attention
- inform students of objectives and arouse motivation
- bring existing schemas into working memory-remind students about what they already know
- present new material, making connections and highlighting key features
- support new information with examples, exercises, explanations
- engage students in active responding-provide feedback
- provide opportunities for practice

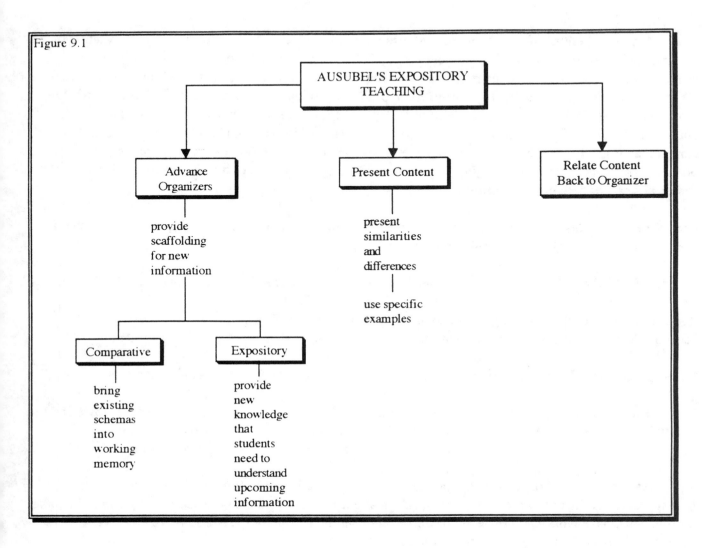

Figure 9.1

Constructivist and Situated Learning

Constructivist approaches are gaining in popularity across all academic subject areas. Definitions may vary but in general, responsibility is placed within the students for constructing their knowledge.

Constructivist Approaches: View that emphasizes the active role of the learner in building understanding and making sense of information.

Central to constructivist approaches are the following themes:
- **Complex Learning Environments:** Problems and learning situations that mimic the ill-structured nature of real life. Don't give students stripped down unrealistic problems but try to provide them with authentic tasks and activities similar to what they will encounter in the real world.

- **Social Negotiation:** Aspect of learning process that relies on collaboration with others and respect for different perspectives. Students must be able to talk and listen to each other.
- **Multiple Representations of Content:** Considering various problems using various analogies, examples, and metaphors.
- **Understanding that knowledge is constructed:** Understanding that different assumptions and different experiences lead to different knowledge with an awareness that different influences shape our thinking.
- **Student-Centered Instruction:** Student actively assumes responsibility for his/her learning.

I want to give you an example that embraces all of the themes listed above.

An Example of a True Constructivist Approach

Last summer at The University of Idaho, professors, college students, public school educators, and public school students all came together for a week-long workshop. We all became students, to learn technology in a realistic setting and apply it to a real life problem that we have in Moscow, Idaho. Moscow, Idaho is located in the middle of millions of acres of wheat. A stream runs through our town called Paradise Creek. It is polluted by fertilizer run-off from our wheat fields.

1. **The complex learning environment and real life problem** - how to reclaim the once beautiful and wild-life inhabited, Paradise Creek.

2. **The social negotiation aspect**-we formed diverse teams of people who would learn how to access information from the internet, do field testing of the water, devise spread sheets with data, capture photos with quick take computer cameras, work with local environmentalists and scientists, and at the end of the week, combine forces to present all of our findings in a hyperstudio media presentation. It was a group effort.

3. **Multiple representations of content**- we researched water quality through information gathered from scientists, environmentalists, scientific literature, and field testing.

4. **Understanding that knowledge is constructed**- no one *Told* us how to approach this task. We came together, we brainstormed, we relied upon what we knew already.

5. **Student Centered**- We were all students of the project, we were students with a problem to solve, and we were learning every step of the way, from every mistake we made and from every insight we gained.

An offshoot of the constructivist approach, although Dewey conceptualized this approach as early as 1910, is **inquiry learning**.

Inquiry Learning: Approach in which the teacher presents a puzzling situation and students solve the problem by gatering data and testing their conclusions. Inquiry teaching allows students to learn process and content at the same time (much as in the above example). Key components to this approach are:

- formulate hypotheses to explain the event or solve the problem
- collect data to test the hypotheses
- draw conclusions

- reflect on the original problem and on the thinking processes needed to solve it

Group Work and Cooperation in Learning

Many individuals mistakenly believe that **Cooperative Learning** is group learning. Group learning is accomplished by a division of labor among a number of students with a common goal. Students learn by doing and by teaching each other, however, sometimes one or two members of the group end up doing all of the work for the rest of the group. Cooperative learning involves much, much more.

Cooperative Learning: Arrangement in which students work in mixed-ability groups and are responsible for each other's learning yet each individual performs his or her own work and is accountable for his or her own grade.

In the early 1990's John Dewey criticized the competitive emphasis of American schools and encouraged educators to downplay the competitive emphasis in favor of structuring schools to be democratic learning communities. Today, cooperative learning is embraced by constructivists for different reasons.

Exogenous constructivists: These information processing theorists value group discussions for helping participants rehearse, elaborate, and expand upon their knowledge.

Endogenous constructivists: These Piagetians favor the type of group interactions that generate conflict and disequilibration that lead an individual to question his or her understanding, try out new ideas, or as Piaget (1985) said, "to go beyond his current state and strike out in new directions."

Social constructivists: Vygotskian, dialectical theorists value cooperative learning for the social interaction aspect because according to them, higher mental functions such as reasoning, comprehension, and critical thinking all originate in social interactions.

Cooperative learning structures are the brainchild of Johnson and Johnson (1985). They list five elements that define cooperative learning groups:
- face-to-face interaction--close together and not across the room
- positive interdependence--for support explanations and guidance
- individual accountability--will be individually assessed and graded
- collaborative skills--giving each other constructive feedback, reaching consensus
- group processing--monitor relationships to ensure effective group dynamics

Setting up cooperative groups: Usually, if the goal of the group is to review, practice, and rehearse information, 4 or 5 students is about the right size. If the goal is problem solving or computer work, then 2 or 4 members work best. Generally, the groups of students are balanced for ability, gender, and ethnicity. It is the responsibility of the group to insure that all team members comprehend the material. High ability students help low ability students and improve their own performances by teaching others. Research suggests that giving good explanations appears to be even more important for learning than receiving explanations. Some teachers assign roles to students to encourage cooperation and full participation. Roles differ contingent upon the goals of the group. Several types of cooperative groups are defined below:

Jigsaw: An early format for cooperative learning emphasizing high interdependence.

Reciprocal Questioning: Approach where groups of two or three students ask and answer each other's questions after a lesson or presentation.

Scripted Cooperation: A method for learning in pairs.

Instructional Conversation: Situation in which students learn through interactions with teachers and other students.

Cognitive Apprenticeship: A relationship in which a less experienced learner acquires knowledge and skills under the guidance of an expert.

Application Two: Identifying Cooperative Structures

Read the following statements and match each with the corresponding type of cooperative learning structure. Check your responses in the answer key.

Jigsaw   Reciprocal Questioning   Scripted Cooperation
Instructional Conversations   Cognitive Apprenticeships

1. _____ The students create questions, then take turns asking and answering.

2. _____ Each group member is given part of the material to be learned by the whole group and becomes an expert on her or his piece.

3. _____ In reading, both partners read a passage, then one gives an oral summary and the other gives feedback. Then they switch roles of summarizer and listener.

4. _____ After a lesson or presentation by the teacher, students work in pairs or triads to ask and answer questions about the material.

5. _____ Students have to teach each other so everyone's contribution is important.

6. _____ The master knows a great deal about the subject.

7. _____ Students return to the group bringing their expertise to the learning sessions.

8. _____ Students work together in pairs on almost any task.

9. _____ This is more effective than traditional discussion groups because it seems to encourage deeper thinking about the material.

10. _____ The knowledgeable guide provides models, demonstrations, corrections and a motivating personal bond.

11. _____ The teacher provides question stems and students are taught how to develop specific questions on the lesson material.

12. _____ The performances required of the learner are real and grow more complex as the learner become more competent.

13. _____ In the end, students take an individual test over all the material and earn points for their learning team score.

14. _____ Teams can work for rewards or simply recognition.

15. _____ This provides an alternative to the dominance of teacher talk

16. _____ The teacher's goal is to keep everyone engaged in a substantive discussion helping students construct their own understandings.

Cognitive and Constructivist Approaches to Reading, Mathematics, and Science

Learning to read and write: For years the debate has raged as to whether students should be taught to read and write through code-based (phonics) approaches or through meaning- based (**whole language**) approaches that focus on the meaning of the text. Advocates of whole language believe that reading is a natural process much like mastering your own language. They feel that words should not be presented out of text and broken into little abstract pieces. Teaching and learning are seen as reciprocal and collaborative and teachers and students make decisions together about the curriculum.

Whole Language Perspective: A philosophical approach to teaching and learning that stresses learning through authentic, real-life tasks. This approach emphasizes using language to learn, integrating learning across skills and subjects, and respecting the language abilities of student and teacher.

Advocates of whole language also insist that the curriculum should be integrated combining spelling, listening, reading, and writing across all subject areas, even math and science. There are many advantages to whole language however, advocates of code-based approaches have shown that skill in recognizing sounds and words supports reading. The more fluent and automatic you are in identifying words, the more effective you will be in getting meaning from context. An effective method for enhancing reading comprehension is called **reciprocal teaching.**

Reciprocal Teaching: A method, based on modeling, to teach reading comprehension strategies. The goal is to help students understand and think deeply about what they read. To accomplish this, students engage in four strategies:

- summarizing the content of the passage
- asking a question about the central point
- clarifying the difficult parts of the material
- predicting what will come next

Skilled readers will apply these skills almost automatically but poor readers seldom do or don't know how. It is important for the teacher to explain and model these strategies and encourage the students to practice. Research shows that after 20 hours of practice with this approach, many students who were in the bottom quarter of their class moved up to the average level or above on tests of reading comprehension.

Learning and Teaching Mathematics: Because of the way mathematics has been taught in the past, there is a great need for constructivist approaches. Many students feel that mathematics doesn't make sense and most of it is a lot of memorization. I can remember when Cali's third grade teacher told them that when they were subtracting the number nine from a two digit number in the teens, the answer would always be the sum of the two numbers that comprised the numerator, like this:

$$
\begin{array}{ccc}
18 & 15 & 13 \\
-09 & -09 & -09 \\
\hline
9 & 6 & 4
\end{array}
$$

She said this would work because (a) 1+8=9 and (b) 1+5 =6 and (c) 1+3=4. Mathematically, this made no sense to the third graders and they engaged in yet another instance of mathematical false learning. It's no wonder so many students are math phobic.

Constructivist approaches embrace the following: The thinking processes of the *students* should be the focus of attention. One topic should be considered in depth rather than trying to cover many topics. Assessment should be ongoing and mutually shared by teacher and students.

Learning Science: Howard Gardner has suggested that the key to understanding science is for students to directly examine their own theories and confront their shortcomings. My colleagues who teach science methods from a constructivist approach have a favorite phrase that they utilize to promote confrontation and growth. They believe strongly in the introduction of *discrepant events.* For change to take place students must go through six stages:

- initial discomfort with their own ideas and beliefs
- attempts to explain away inconsistencies between their theories and evidence presented to them
- attempts to adjust measurements or observations to fit personal theories
- doubt

163

Learning and Instruction

- vacillation
- conceptual change

For this to happen in the classroom teachers must be committed to teaching for student understanding rather than "covering the curriculum."

Application Three: Matching Key Terms and Definitions

To check your comprehension, see if you can come up with terms to match the definitions below. Remember, some of the terms may have two words but there will be no space in between words. Check your responses in the answer key.

Clues

Down:
1. Classification system
2. Drawing conclusions by applying rules or principles
4. According to Bruner, the fundamental framework of ideas
5. Making imaginative leaps to correct perceptions or workable solutions
6. Statement of inclusive concepts to introduce and sum up material that follows
7. Clearly structured knowledge that is needed for later learning and that can be taught step by step
9. Clear statements of what students are intended to learn through instruction
10. A type of teaching method, based on modeling, to teach reading comprehension strategies
11. A hierarchy of ideas or concepts
12. A type of reasoning where general principles are formulated based on knowledge of examples and details

Across:
3. Teaching method where teachers present material in complete, organized form, moving from broadest to more specific concepts
8. View that emphasizes the active role of the learner in building understanding and making sense of information

---

Key Terms and Definitions

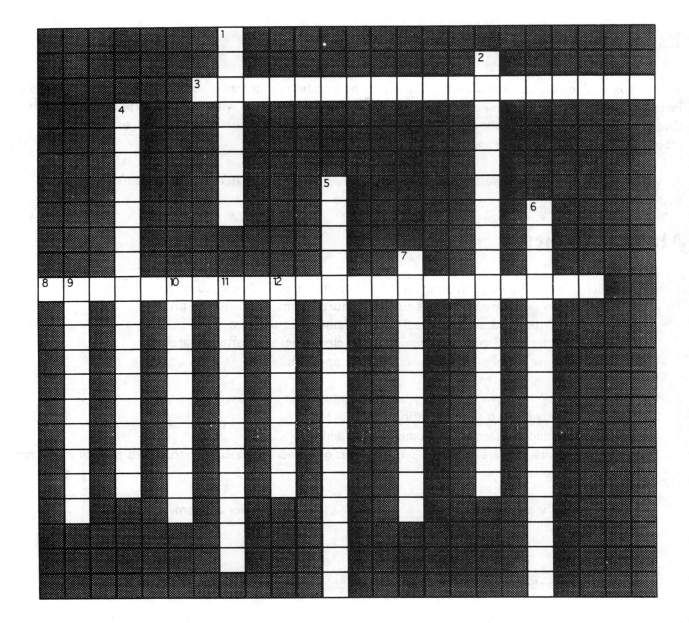

Practice Tests

Essay Questions

1.   Some educators favor discovery methods in the classroom whereas other educators feel that this is an inefficient method of instruction and much more could be accomplished with direct or expository methods. Cite some instances in which the discovery approach would be particularly effective and some in which other methods would be more appropriate.

2. What are some of the misuses of group learning and problems associated with cooperative learning structures?

Multiple Choice:

1.   In which of the following situations is it NOT useful to provide objectives for students?
     a. with loosely structured activities such as lectures, films, and research projects
     b. with very structured materials such as programmed instruction
     c. if the importance of some information is not clear from the learning materials
     d. if the purpose of the activities is not readily apparent

2.   The Keller plan is a form of mastery learning and is most often used
     a. with students in need of remediation
     b. with ungraded classrooms of elementary students
     c. with students who are unable to work at their own pace but need the structured pace of a program
     d. with college students

3.   Mastery usually means a score of _____ on a test or other assessment.
     a. 80 to 90 %
     b. 75%
     c. 100%
     d. none of the above

4.   Discovery learning is often called
     a. Rule-eg method
     b. deductive reasoning
     c. Eg-rule method
     d.   expository learning

Learning and Instruction

5. Characteristic of Ausubel's expository teaching approach is (are)
    a. meaningful rather than rote reception learning
    b. materials presented in a carefully organized, sequenced, and finished form
    c. deductive reasoning from the rule or principle to examples
    d. all of the above

6. Expository organizers
    a. bring into working memory already existing schemas
    b. provide new knowledge that students will need to understand upcoming information
    c. is actually just a statement of historical or background information
    d. remind you of what you already know

7. Relative to cooperative learning structures, for shy and introverted students,
    a. teachers should assign them the leader role to help them overcome awkwardness
    b. they should not be pressured to participate until they feel comfortable with the group
    c. an adult should sit in on the group to promote interaction
    d. individual learning may be a better approach

8. After 20 hours of practice with this approach, many students who were at the bottom quarter of their class moved up to the average level or above on tests of reading comprehension.
    a. reciprocal teaching where students learn to summarize the content of a passage, ask questions about central points, clarify material and predict what will come next
    b. cognitive apprenticeships where young people work with knowledgeable guides
    c. instructional conversations which are seen as an alternative to teacher dominated interactions
    d. scripted cooperation where students work in pairs to learn a topic

9. One of the reasons that so many students have difficulty understanding mathematics is that
    a. abstract reasoning is required before students are developmentally ready
    b. people believe mathematics to be mostly the memorization of formulas
    c. students are left to construct their own mathematical concepts
    d. algorithms often confuse the correct selection of problem solving approaches

10. Which of the following is NOT one of the criticisms levied against direct instruction?
    a. it is limited to lower level objectives
    b. that it is based on non-traditional teaching methods
    c. that it ignores innovative models
    d. that it discourages students' independent thinking

Answer Key

Application One: Identiying Domains of Objectives
1. psychomotor   2. cognitive   3. cognitive   4. affective
5. cognitive   6. psychomotor 7. cognitive   8. affective

Application Two: Identifying Cooperative Structures
1. reciprocal questioning   2. jigsaw   3. scripted cooperation   4. reciprocal questioning
5. jigsaw   6. cognitive apprenticeship   7. jigsaw
8. scripted cooperation   9. reciprocal questioning   10. cognitive apprenticeship
11. reciprocal questioning 12. cognitive apprenticeship   13. jigsaw
14. jigsaw   15. instructional conversations
16. instructional conversations

Application Three: Key Terms and Definitions

Key Terms and Definitions

```
. . . . . T . . . . . . . . . D . . . . . .
. . . . . A . . . . . . . . . D . . . . . .
. . . . E X P O S I T O R Y T E A C H I N G
S . . . . O . . . . . . . . . D . . . . . .
U . . . . N . . . . . . . . . U . . . . . .
B . . . . O . . . . . . . . . C . . . . . .
J . . . . M . . . . . I . . . T . . . . . .
E . . . . Y . . . . . N . . . I . . . A . .
C . . . . . . . . . . T . . . V . . . D . .
T . . . . . . . . . . U B . . E . . . V . .
C O N S T R U C T I V I S T A P P R O A C H
. B . T . E . O . N . T I . . . . E . N . .
. J . R . C . D . D . I I . . . . A . C . .
. E . U . I . I . U . V C . . . . S . E . .
. C . C . P . N . C . E S . . . . O . O . .
. T . T . R . G . T . T K . . . . N . R . .
. I . U . O . S . I . H I . . . . I . G . .
. V . R . C . Y . V . I L . . . . N . A . .
. E . E . A . S . E . N L . . . . G . N . .
. S . . . L . T . . . K S . . . . . . I . .
. . . . . . . E . . . I . . . . . . . Z . .
. . . . . . . M . . . N . . . . . . . E . .
. . . . . . . . . . . G . . . . . . . R . .
```

Essays

1.   If the objective is for students to be able to describe the taste of harmless PTC paper then discovery learning would be a great instructional method. If the objectives are to complete an observational study of teenage mall behavior, then discovery learning would be a good method. However, if the objectives are for the student to understand the rules and trends of the periodic table, they are far too complex and hidden for the average learner to inquire about through discovery learning and a didactic method would be called for. If the objectives are for the students to speak French or to examine the effects of sulfuric acid on skin, then once again, discovery methods would be inappropriate. Whereas discovery methods are purported to produce long term transfer of learning, direct methods tend to require less time, less preparation and fewer materials so when planning instructional methodology, take objectives, time and other variables into consideration.

2. Without careful planning and monitoring by the teacher, group interactions can hinder learning and reduce rather than improve social relations in classes. If one student plays the dominant role, or some students fail to contribute, then interactions can be unproductive and unreflective. Although the high ability students generally benefit from playing the role of instructor, sometimes they resent being cast in the role of the person who has all of the information. Sometimes, socializing takes precedence over learning the material and dialectical reflections may usurp completion of projects. Also, students may reinforce each other's misunderstandings. Lastly, some may become convinced that they can't learn without the support of the group.

Multiple Choice
1. b   2. d   3. a   4. c   5. d   6. b   7. d   8. a   9. b   10. b

Chapter Ten

Motivation: Issues and Explanations

"Did you know that the Chinese use the same word for crisis and for opportunity?"
Lisa Simpson
(The Simpsons, Oct. 29, 1996)

One of the greatest challenges of your teaching career will be to motivate your students toward self-actualization, achievement, success, and love of learning. What is **motivation?**

Motivation: an internal state that arouses, directs, and maintains behavior.

Motivation is a complex issue and many variables function to determine whether individuals will be motivated. Psychologists explain motivation in terms of personal **traits** and temporary **states.**

Trait: Long-term characteristic **Example:** My brother Greg has been motivated to work to acquire money ever since we were very small children.

State: Temporary situation in which you are momentarily motivated. **Example:** You may not be motivated to study every night but the night before your exam, you will probably be in a high state of motivation to study.

In addition to traits and states of motivation which address the time duration and persistence of motivation, psychologists also discuss the source of motivation; whether it is **intrinsic** or **extrinsic.**

Intrinsic Motivation: Motivation associated with activities that are their own reward. The source of motivation comes from within ourselves. **Example:** I enjoy painting. I may not be any good and I may never receive any recognition for my artwork or any financial remuneration, but I do like to dabble.

Intrinsic motivation is what drives us to do something when we really don't have to do anything. It certainly explains what drives us to do what we do in our free time. As educators, we would love to think that all of our students are intrinsically motivated to learn and that the source for the motivation comes from within, but realistically, we have to admit that many of our students would not put forth effort unless they were **extrinsically motivated.**

Extrinsic Motivation: Motivation created by external factors like rewards and punishments. The source of motivation comes from the environment. We are not really interested in the activity for its own sake but for what it will gain us. **Example:** Desiring an "A" motivates you to study. Desiring a paycheck, motivates you to show up to your job on time.

Motivation: Issues and Explanations

Looking at a behavior, it is very difficult to tell whether the behavior is intrinsically or extrinsically motivated. Once again, the difference between the two lies with whether or not the individual has an internal or external **locus of causality.**

Locus of Causality: The location--internal or external-- of the cause of the behavior.

Application One: Locus of Causality

Read the following statements and for each one determine whether it is intrinsic, extrinsic, state, trait or some combination thereof. Check your responses in the answer key.

1.   "I really hate English but I'm going to study sentence diagramming so that I get an "A" and maintain my already high GPA." _____

2.   "Ever since I was just a small child, I could not sit idle for more than a minute. I always have to be up doing something because life is too short and I don't want to waste it being a lazy slug."

_____

3.   "I would prefer to spend my entire life lying on the couch watching television and it has been this way for as long as I can remember. I hate to exert energy." _____

4.   "Children are such trying little creatures and I'd rather not spend any time around them, but I babysit so that I can enhance my wardrobe." _____

5.   "I truly hate to exercise, but I think I'll stick with my exercise routine until I lose 10 pounds because there is this really cute guy who I would just love to go out with if he would sit up and take notice of me."

_____

6.   "I'm participating in the **I Love to Read Program** for two reasons: For every 20 hours we spend reading, we get rewarded with a new book and also, because I truly love to read." _____

7.   " I'm going to stick with my cooking class because it is so much fun, and I feel so accomplished when I cook a great meal for my friends. I also get to eat some really great food." _____

8.   " My parents said that if I get all "A's" in my Spanish class all year, they will send me to Spain with the Spanish club. I guess I can put up with Spanish for that." _____

9.   "I'm going to try real hard to remember my homework because I lost points on my grade the last three times I forgot it. I'm in jeopardy of getting a 'D'." _____

10.   "I love to sing all of the time. It makes me feel so happy and carefree." _____

Motivation: Issues and Explanations

In school, both intrinsic and extrinsic motivation are important. Some subjects are intrinsically motivating to students but to expect that all subjects are equally interesting to all students is a bit unrealistic. To encourage our students to perform, sometimes we must rely on **rewards** and **incentives.**

Rewards: An attractive object or event supplied as a consequence of a behavior. **Example:** If you study real hard, you'll get an "A."

Incentive: An object or event that encourages or discourages a behavior. **Example:** If you arrive late to class without an excuse (at least a really good excuse) you'll be given a detention.

As with all other aspects of education, we can examine motivation from a number of psychological schools of thought.

Behavioral Approaches to Motivation: As you might anticipate, behavioralists look to the external environment for supplying the motivation to perform or not to perform. Incentives hold the promise of something good to be gained or punishments to be avoided, contingent upon behaviors. Rewards serve to maintain behaviors as getting an "A" will reinforce good study habits. To motivate students, we must acknowledge and reward their successes, and help them to see the personal gains of their learning.

Humanistic Approaches to Motivation: This approach to motivation emphasizes personal freedom, choice, self-determination, and striving for personal growth. Humanistic psychologists emphasize the role of needs in determining whether we are motivated to perform. According to the humanists, we are born with the natural tendency or need to strive to achieve to our fullest potentialities. To motivate students we must appeal to their affective domains--their sense of competence, self-esteem, autonomy, and self-actualization.

Cognitive Approaches to Motivation: Cognitivists believe that behavior is determined by our thinking; by goals, expectations, attributions, schemas and the desire to be competent, intellectually functioning individuals. People respond not to external events or physical conditions but rather to their interpretations of these events. In cognitive theories, people are born with intrinsic curiousity and motivation, seeking to problem solve as a form of adaptive behavior. To motivate students, we must stimulate their natural curiousity and support their beliefs about their abilities to succeed.

Social Learning Approaches to Motivation: A blend of both behavioral and cognitive approaches, social learning theorists take into consideration the external outcomes of behavior and the internal beliefs and expectations. Feather explains motivation by the **expectancy X value** formula. While it is difficult to come up with an actual measure of motivation, this formula looks at motivation as a product of an individual's expectations for success times the value of achieving the goal. To motivate students, we must focus on helping them to set realistic goals and expectations and to value the outcomes of their learning.

Expectancy X Value Theories: Explanations of motivation that emphasize individual's expectations for success combined with their valuing of the goal. **Example:** I may value the notion of becoming a super-model (heavens knows, I could use the money) but considering I'm a short, middle-aged woman, my expectations for success are at about zero. Even though the value may be high, when multiplied by zero, the product is zero, therefore my motivation is zero. I guess I'll stick to teaching........

Application Two: Psychological Theories of Motivation

Read the following activities and for each one determine if it describes motivation from a Behavioral, Humanistic, Cognitive, or Social Learning Theorist perspective. Check your responses in the answer key.

1.   Becky has organized a study group for her physics class. In addition to wanting to enhance her understanding of physics, Becky wants to increase her social acceptance within her peer group because she is a transfer student and doesn't know anyone. _____

2.   John has high expectations that someday he will become a lawyer. From past experience he knows he can present a good argument and he values his ability to engage in undefeatable verbal repartee. To further hone his skills, he decides to join the debating team. _____

3.   Jenny is striving for good grades this semester because her father promised her a new car if she could bring all of her "Fs" up to "Cs." _____

4.   Sarah wants to experience first hand how plant photosynthesis works and asked her teacher if she could do an experiment to improve her understanding of the process. _____

5.   Fred has joined as many extra-curricular clubs as possible because he feels a strong need for affiliation due to the fact that his home-life is fraught with turmoil and abuse. _____

6.   Samantha has a difficult time getting up in the morning so she purchased three alarm clocks and placed them all around her room because if she gets one more detention she's grounded. _____

7.   Cali greatly values her job working with marine animals and works hard to advance within the program because she expects to become a marine biologist. _____

8.   Francis wants to learn how to operate a computer because he knows he will be able to access lots of valuable information about ecosystems from the internet and greatly improve his understanding.

_____

Motivation to Learn in School

Aside from everything else that we would like to see our students do, most of all we would like to increase **student motivation to learn.**

Student Motivation to Learn: The tendency to work hard on academic activities because one believes they are worthwhile. **Example:** I was very motivated to learn how to operate a computer because I knew it would enable me to do things such as this study guide.

According to Brophy, motivation to learn can be construed as both a general trait and a situation-specific state. As teachers we have three major goals:

- to get our students productively involved with the work of the class; to create a state of motivation
- to develop in our students the trait of being motivated to learn so they will be able to educate themselves throughout a lifetime
- to have our students be cognitively engaged--planning concentration on the goal, metacognitive awareness of what you intend to learn and how you intend to learn it, actively searching for new information, clear perceptions of feedback, pride, and satisfaction in achievement, and no anxiety or fear of failure

Goals and Motivation

In order for an individual to achieve, there must be the realistic setting of **goals.**

Goals: What an individual strives to accomplish. There are four reasons why goal setting improves performance:

- goals direct our attention to the task at hand
- goals mobilize efforts-the harder the goal, the greater the effort
- goals increase persistence
- goals promote the development of new strategies when the old strategies fall short

In classrooms, there are two main categories of goals: **learning** and **performance goals.**

Learning Goal: A personal intention to improve abilities and understand, no matter how performance suffers. **Example:** I have a personal learning goal to be able to improve my skiing skills. If I have a learning goal then I am a **task-involved learner.**

Task-involved Learners: Students who focus on mastering the task or solving the problem. **Example:** I am more concerned with becoming a good skiier than looking like a graceful skiier.

Performance Goal: A personal intention to seem competent or perform well in the eyes of others. **Example:** If I had performance goals, I would be more concerned with how absurd I look face-plowing down the slopes versus improving my skills. As well as I ski, if I had performance goals, I probably would never leave the lodge. If I had performance goals, I would be an **ego-involved learner.**

Ego-involved Learner: Students who focus on how well they are performing and how they are judged by others. **Example:** If I were worried that everyone was watching me fall down the slopes and passing judgment on me as an uncoordinated klutz, then I would be an ego-involved learner.

A student who is ego-involved with classwork may have the following characteristics:
1. uses shortcuts to complete tasks
2. cheats/copies classmates' papers
3. seeks attention for good performance
4. only works hard on graded asssignments

5. is upset by and hides papers with low grades
6. compares grades with classmates
7. chooses tasks that are most likely to result in positive evaluations
8. is uncomfortable with assignments that have unclear evaluation criteria

Feedback and Goal Acceptance

Two factors that influence effective goal setting in the classroom are feedback and goal acceptance. With feedback, you need accurate information as to "where you are" and how far you have to go. Feedback gives students valuable information about the success or failure of their efforts, whether they have achieved their goals, and how far to increase their goals for the future. Feedback is most effective when it emphasizes progress.

The second factor, goal acceptance, addresses the likelihood of students to adopt teacher-generated goals or develop their own goals. If students adopt goals, it is likely that they will demonstrate higher motivation toward the task. Students are more likely to adopt goals that are clear, specific, reasonable, moderately challenging, and attainable within a relatively short amount of time.

Needs and Motivation

One of the most renowned humanistic theories was developed by Maslow and examines the role of needs in determining motivation. A need is defined as a state of deprivation that motivates a person to take action toward a goal, whether it be physiological, psychological, emotional, or intellectual needs. Maslow has suggested that humans have a **hierarchy of needs** that begins with the most basic needs for survival and culminates with the highest level needs for self-actualization.

Hierarchy of Needs: Maslow's model of seven levels of human needs, from basic physiological requirements to the need for **self-actualization**.

Self-Actualization: Fulfilling one's potential.

Maslow suggested that humans will sequentially fulfill their needs on each level before moving onto the next level. Maslow called the lower level needs **deficiency needs** and upper level needs, **being needs**. With deficiency needs, as each is fulfilled, the motivation to fulfill it, decreases. But with being needs, as the individual fulfills each level, the motivation supposedly increases. For instance, as a person's need for intellectual achievement is fulfilled, according to Maslow, the person will be even more motivated toward fulfilling the need for even further intellectual achievement.

Deficiency Needs: Maslow's four lower level needs, which must be satisfied first.
Being Needs: Maslow's three higher-level needs, sometimes called growth needs.

1. **Physiological Needs:** sleep, thirst, hunger
2. **Safety Needs:** freedom from danger, anxiety, and threat to psychological well-being
3. **Love Needs:** acceptance from parents, teachers, peers, and significant others
4. **Esteem Needs:** self-efficacy, competency, belief in one's abilities often validated by others

Motivation: Issues and Explanations

5. **Intellectual Achievement Needs:** need to understand and grow intellectually
6. **Aesthetic Needs:** appreciation for beauty, culture, literature, music, the arts
7. **Needs for Self-Actualization:** attempt to realize personal potential, striving to become the best that you can be.

Application Three: Maslow's Hierarchy of Needs

Read each of the following statements to determine which need level from Maslow's hierarchy is being addressed. Check your responses in the answer key.

Physiological	Safety	Love	Esteem
Intellectual	Aesthetic	Self-Actualization	

1.   For today's writing project, I want you to be able to express in poetic form how deeply you care for someone. It can be one of your friends in this class, your parents, grandparents or siblings. It can be your boyfriend or girlfriend or a teacher or neighbor. I want you to think about how they make you feel and try to draw analogies between how they make you feel and beautiful things in nature. I want you to get in touch with your emotions and reflect on how important this person is to your life. _____

2.   Since the springtime weather is delightful, we're going outside for today's art class. Find a place that appeals to you for it's beauty or tranquility and take out your pastels and draw what you feel. When everyone has finished, we're going to have a sidewalk art show and I want you to select the three works that have the greatest emotional impact for you. Explain why. _____

3.   Climbing walls are a lot of fun, but they're also dangerous. We will be learning safety procedures for rappelling and the proper use of equipment. You will be responsible for each other's safety, this is a team effort. Do not be fearful, WE WILL NOT LET YOU FALL. _____

4.   In this home economics class we will be studying the physiological effects of proper nutrition on the functioning of our brains. The body and brain need fuel to operate, just like your cars. I want you to chart the meals you eat for a one month period and note changes in your own functioning, e.g., describe your energy level, your functioning in school, your concentration, your complexion, etc.. _____

5.   Today we're going to focus on long-term goal setting. Now that you're in high school, you should be thinking about what you would like to do with your lives. What are your strengths? What will make you happy? How can you use all of your wonderful gifts and talents to your best advantage? How do you plan to be the best that you can be? Have you given any thought to how you will proceed? _____

6.   Today we will entertain nominations for class officers. Remember to base your nominations on qualities of competence and dedication. This should be more than a popularity contest. This is your student government and you want representatives who will capably do their best to insure that your needs are met and your issues are dealt with intelligently. _____

7.   We will be holding a poster contest for anyone who would like to do research on a scientific topic of your choice. The results of your research will be presented and judged at the science fair. This will provide you with the opportunity to explore scientific topics that we would not normally have the time to examine within the usual framework f our science classes. _____

Implications of Maslow's theory for the classroom are that before our students will be motivated to fulfill the need for intellectual achievement, their lower level needs must first be met. Students who come to school hurt, sick, distraught over parental divorce, abuse, homelessness, etc., will not be motivated to perform academically.

Achievement Motivation

Consonant with the trait of motivation is a term that describes how some individuals constantly strive for excellence in a field soley for achievement's sake. This is called **achievement motivation.**

Achievement Motivation: Desire to excel; impetus to strive for excellence and success. This is generally viewed as a stable trait--something the individual has more or less of.

High need for achievement motivation originates in the family or cultural group of the child. Children with a high need for achievement generally come from families where they have been encouraged to try regardless of the outcome.

Others see achievement motivation as being situational in that you can be highly motivated in some situations yet in other situations, especially if you have experienced difficulty or failure, you may be less inclined to strive for achievement. This addresses another dimension of the achievement theory called **resultant motivation.**

Resultant motivation: Whichever is the stronger tendency-the need to achieve or the need to avoid failure. **Examples:**

1. If the person's need for achievement > their need to avoid failure, then failure will serve to further motivate, indicating more effort is needed. I think a great example of this is when children learn to ride a bike. Their initial failures are not enough to stop their strivings for achievement.

2. If the person's need for achievement < their need to avoid failure, then failures will decrease motivation to put forth effort. I was in a self-defense course with much younger, stronger men. I would give it my all and after repeated injuries and torn ligaments, decided my need for a black belt was not as strong as my need to survive. I finally quit the class.

Application Four: Need for Achievement or Need to Avoid Failure

Read the following statements to determine if the individuals described there are high or low in resultant motivation.

1.   "I don't care how many lousy cups of coffee I make or how much money I spend on coffee beans. I'm going to stick with it until I figure out how to brew the perfect cup of coffee." _____

2.   "Everyone wants me stop to stop playing the same song on the guitar; but it took me so long to get it down. It was such a struggle and I don't know any other songs. I don't want to have to go through that again." _____

---

3.   "When I fell on my skiis, I couldn't get back up and I know everyone was laughing at me as I rolled around like a turtle on its back. I'll never try that again." _____

4.   "OK, so what if I threw my bowling ball into the other lane. I really want to stay on the team since all of my friends are on it. I know I'll get better eventually." _____

5.   "I am really struggling with this statistics course, but I don't want to give up because I'm going to need statistics to do research in my field." _____

6.   "Now that I've beaten Mario-Kart on my Nintendo, I'm going to sell it back to the video store at the mall and get some credits toward some more challenging games." _____

One of the reasons that motivating your students will be such an incredible challenge for you is that motivation is an extremely complex variable. So many factors appear to influence motivation. Listed below are several factors that influence individuals' motivational levels.

1. The need for self-determination: Choices that are self-imposed versus imposed by the external environment, are more motivating. When people feel that they are in control and are empowered as decision makers, the results of their actions are far more gratifying than if their actions were imposed by others. I know Cali tackles her room with greater enthusiasm and pride when *she* has decided that it needs cleaning versus when I tell her to get in there and do it. Richard de Charms has differentiated between students who are **"origins"** taking responsibility because they are intrinsically motivated versus students who are **"pawns"** who lack control and are motivated only through external influences. Teachers need to support student self-determination and independence. Ways to accomplish this are by helping them to set realistic goals, plan activities to reach the goals, assume personal responsibility for their actions, all resulting in increased self-esteem.

2. The need for relatedness: Relatedness is the need to establish close emotional bonds and the desire to be connected to the important people in our lives. When parents and teachers are responsive to children, the children show high intrinsic motivation. Relatedness has two components, involvement and autonomy support. **Involvement:** the degree to which teachers and parents are interested and knowledgeable about, and devote time to their children's activities and experiences. **Autonomy support:** is the degree to which teachers and parents encourage children to make their own choices. High involvement and autonomy support=greater competence, academic achievement, responsibility, and less aggression in children.

Attribution Theory

We would all like to understand the causes of our successes so that we can repeat what lead to the successes and we want to understand the causes of our failures so that we can avoid them in the future. The study of perceived causes of successes and failures is **attribution theory.**

Motivation: Issues and Explanations

Attribution Theory: Descriptions of how individuals' explanations, justifications, and excuses influence their motivation and behavior. **Example:** If I think I failed because I didn't study, I will probably be motivated to study in the future.

Weiner is one of the leading educational psychologists responsible for examining how attributions relate to school learning. He suggests that most of the causes to which students attribute their successes or failures can be categorized along three dimensions:
- **locus:** location of the cause internal or external to the person
- **stability:** whether the cause stays the same or can change
- **responsibility:** whether the person can control the cause

Weiner suggests that these dimensions are closely related to personal emotions and motivations.

Locus (internal/external)--If students feel that their successes are due to internal locus, i.e., "I was born with superior intellect" or "I put forth tremendous effort," then the students will experience increased pride and self-esteem. But if the student attributes failue to internal locus, i.e., "I was born lacking intellect" or "I put forth very little effort," then that student would feel either shame at their own ignorance or guilt from lack of effort. Failures attributed to external locus can be blamed on others or outside circumstances and therefore absolve the individual from personal blame.

Stability--If students attributes their successes or failures to stable causes, then they will expect the same outcomes in the future as they have experienced in the past. In other words, if students believe their failures result from stable causes, their motivation will be low because the outcomes will always be the same anyhow, i.e., "I always stink at math and I always will. There's no use even trying."

Responsibility--If we succeed at something that we control, then we feel pride. If we fail at something and feel it is within our control, we will feel guilt. If we fail, and feel it was beyond our control, we will feel anger and hostility at the person who caused our failure or at the situation.

Feeling in control, results in students putting forth more effort toward achieving goals. Educators must downplay native ability (a factor that is internal, generally believed to be stable, and also uncontrollable) and emphasize effort (a factor that is also internal, but unstable because it is subject to change, and it is also subject to control by the individual) as the key to achievement and success. Individuals who believe that they are responsible for their successes and failures have internal **locus of control.**

Locus of Control: "Where" people locate responsibility for successes or failures--inside or outside of themselves. These people believe they are responsible for their fate, possess good self-esteem, and like to work in situations in which skill and effort lead to success. People who have an external locus of control feel that other forces are in control of their lives, and prefer to work in situations where luck determines the outcome. Very often these individuals experience low self-esteem. When students possess an external locus of control they may also develop **learned helplessness.**

Learned Helplessness: The expectation, based on previous experiences with a lack of control, that one's efforts will lead to failure. Students who feel helpless will be unmotivated and reluctant to put forth effort.

Application Five: Attributions

Read the following statements to determine if the student perceives her or his failures or successes as internal/external locus, stable/unstable, controllable/uncontrollable. Check your responses in the answer key.

1. "I could have passed the test but I didn't study."
2. "I didn't expect to pass the math test and I didn't. I stink at math."
3. "I had the worst luck getting that teacher. She hates my brother and that's why I failed."
4. "I passed all of the gymnastic exercises in PE because my family is very athletic."
5. "I studied for three weeks leading up to the test and I got an 'A'."
6. "I can't seem to get the hang of archery but if I continue to practice, I know I'll master it."
7. "I have won many beauty contests because I was born beautiful."
8. "I rarely have to study because I am so naturally smart."

Adults tend to use two basic concepts of ability, **entity view of ability** and the **incremental view of ability.**

Entity View of Ability: Belief that ability is a fixed characteristic that cannot be changed. This is the worst case scenario. Students believe failures are (1) due to internal locus (native ability), (2) stable and not subject to change, and (3) uncontrollable. These students generally possess low **self-efficacy.**

Incremental View of Ability: Belief that ability is a set of skills that can be changed. This is the best case scenario. Students believe successes are (1) due to internal locus (effort), (2) unstable and subject to change, and (3) controllable. Students who subscribe to the incremental view believe that their successes and failures are their own responsibility and that they have the power to influence the outcome. These students generally possess high **self-efficacy.**

Self-Efficacy: Beliefs about personal competence in a particular situation. Our own past experiences are the most powerful determinants of self-efficacy. If we have high self-efficacy in a given area, we will set higher goals, be less afraid of failure, and persist longer when we encounter difficulties. If self-efficacy is low, we may avoid a task altogether or give up easily when problems arise. Also important to student self-efficacy and student achievement, is **teaching efficacy.**

Teaching Efficacy: A teacher's belief that he or she can reach even the most difficult students and help them learn. Teachers with a high sense of efficacy work harder and persist longer even when students are difficult to teach.

Covington and associates suggest that our need for achievement, beliefs about ability, self-efficacy, and self-worth combine to result in three types of motivational sets:

1. Mastery-Oriented Students: Students who focus on learning goals because they value achievement and see ability as improvable. They'll take risks, perform best in competitive situations, learn fast, have more self-confidence and energy, are more aroused and not threatened by feedback. They experience persistent, successful learning.

2. Failure-Avoiding Students: Students who avoid failure by sticking to what they know, by not taking risks, or by claiming not to care about their performance. They lack a strong sense of self-worth and their own competence separate from their performance. They have low self-efficacy. They may eventually become **failure-accepting students.**

3. Failure-Accepting Students: Students who believe their failures are due to low ability and there is little they can do about it. They may become depressed, apathetic, and helpless. Teachers may be able to help failure avoiding students from becoming failure accepting students by helping them to find new and more realistic goals. Instead of pitying or excusing these students, teachers need to teach them how to learn and then hold them accountable.

Motivation: Issues and Explanations

Figure 10.1

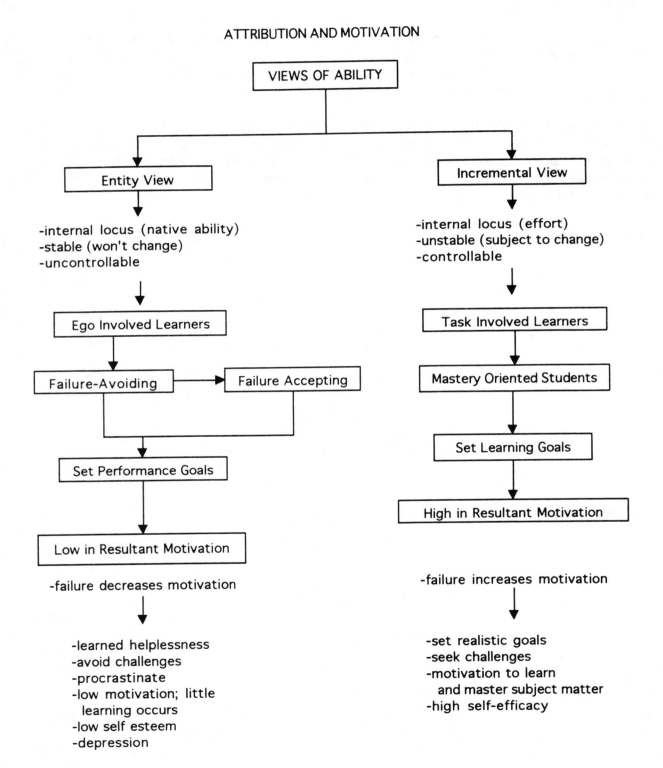

ATTRIBUTION AND MOTIVATION

VIEWS OF ABILITY

Entity View

-internal locus (native ability)
-stable (won't change)
-uncontrollable

Ego Involved Learners

Failure-Avoiding → Failure Accepting

Set Performance Goals

Low in Resultant Motivation

-failure decreases motivation

-learned helplessness
-avoid challenges
-procrastinate
-low motivation; little
  learning occurs
-low self esteem
-depression

Incremental View

-internal locus (effort)
-unstable (subject to change)
-controllable

Task Involved Learners

Mastery Oriented Students

Set Learning Goals

High in Resultant Motivation

-failure increases motivation

-set realistic goals
-seek challenges
-motivation to learn
  and master subject matter
-high self-efficacy

Anxiety and Coping in the Classroom

Whenever there are pressures to perform, severe consequences for failure, and competitive comparisons among students, **anxiety** may be increased.

Anxiety: General uneasiness, a feeling of tension. **Example:** Many of us may experience anxiety before a presentation or an exam. Anxiety can be both a cause and an effect of school failure. Anxiety can be both a trait and a state that is especially high in some situations.

Tobias offers a model of anxiety that explains how it interferes with learning at three points in the performance cycle.

- **attention:** when students are learning new material, their preoccupation with their anxiety may interfere with their ability to attend to the new material. They may miss much of the information.
- **learning:** they are more easily distracted when the material is unorganized and have trouble focusing on significant details. They may have poor study habits because they are not relaxed.
- **testing:** they may know more than they can demonstrate on a test because they lack critical test-taking skills or they may have learned the material but "freeze and forget" on tests.

Teachers can help anxious students by teaching them coping strategies.
1. Problem-focused strategies might include planning a study schedule, borrowing good notes, or finding a protected place to study.
2. Emotion-focused strategies are attempts to reduce the anxious feelings by using relaxation techniques.
3. Help anxious students to set realistic goals nurturing a sense of self-efficacy.
4. Anxious students need help working at a moderate pace and will also benefit from instruction that is structured and allows for repetition of parts of the lesson that are missed and forgotten.

Teachers must work at keeping the level of **arousal** right for the task at hand so the learning situation is optimal even for students with high anxiety.

Arousal: Physical and psychological reactions causing a person to be alert, attentive, and wide awake.

Practice Tests

Essay Questions

1. There is currently debate as to whether schools can successfully increase students' levels of self esteem. Many suggest that attempts to increase students' self esteem actually falls short of having any beneficial effects on their achievement levels. Discuss the pros and cons of self-esteem training.

2. In an exercise that I conduct with my students, I ask them to think about preschool children and their high levels of natural curiosity and need to explore and master their environments. We don't have to promise rewards to children to get them to e.g., take apart a clock, or drag all of the pots and pans out of the

kitchen cabinets. What do you think happens to their natural motivation to learn, once they enter elementary school? Why, as time goes on, do we have to rely on extrinsic means to get them to perform? What are your thoughts on this issue?

Multiple Choice:

1. Goals that tend to enhance motivation and persistence are
    a. specific, moderately difficult, and likely to be reached in the near future
    b. specific, extremely challenging, and long-range
    c. specific, relatively easy, and short term
    d. ambiguous, leaving room for interpretation, and teacher imposed

2. The Expectancy X Value model predicts that motivation will be
    a. high if expectancy is low and value is high
    b. high if expectancy is high and value is high
    c. zero if expectancy is high and value is low
    d zero only if expectancy is zero and value is zero

3. Research found that third and sixth grade students solved significantly fewer math problems when
    a. they were encouraged to try to do their best
    b. they were encouraged to understand how to do these puzzles
    c. they were encouraged to learn new things in math
    d. they were encouraged to show how smart you are in math

4. Results from a study where adults were told that they had accomplished either 75% of the standards set or they had fallen short of the standards by 25% indicated that
    a. negative feedback motivated adults toward higher standards
    b. the type of feedback made no difference to subsequent performance as long as they received some form of feedback
    c. positive feedback left the participants with a false sense of security
    d. positive feedback increased self-confidence, analytic thinking, and subsequent performance

5. Students with low resultant motivation tend to
    a. avoid tasks that present no challenge
    b. select tasks that will further comprehension and understanding
    c. engage in risk taking behaviors
    d. attempt tasks at which they have experienced previous success

6. The origins of high achievement motivation are assumed to be
    a. genetically determined
    b. found in cultures where performance is extrinsically rewarded
    c. found in families where parents push children toward success
    d. found in families where parents encourage independent problem solving without criticism for failures

7. The theory that examines the perceived causes of individuals' successes or failures is called
    a. attribution theory
    b. need for achievement theory
    c. performance goal theory
    d. the entity theory of motivation

8. Research shows that when teachers respond to students' mistakes with pity, praise for a "good try", or unsolicited help, students are more likely to
    a. show appreciation for their teachers and try harder
    b. model these empathic behaviors with one another
    c. attribute the causes of their failures to lack of ability
    d. cheat

9. Young children before the ages of 11 or 12 tend to believe that ability
    a. is largely what you're born with
    b. won't change no matter how hard you try
    c. is related to effort and trying hard makes you smart
    d. means that someone who succeeds without working at all must really be smart

10. Anxiety in the classroom
    a. is a general uneasiness, a sense of foreboding, a feeling of tension
    b. is both a cause and an effect of school failure
    c. both a trait and a state
    d. all of the above

Answer Key

Application One: Locus of Causality
1. extrinsic
2. trait & probably intrinsic
3. trait
4. extrinsic, state
5. extrinsic, state
6. intrinsic, extrnsic
7. intrinsic, extrinsic
8. extrinsic, state
9. extrinsic
10. intrinsic

Application Two: Psychological Theories of Motivation
1. Cognitive & Humanistic
2. Social Learning Theorist
3. Behavioral
4. Cognitive
5. Humanistic
6. Behavioral
7. Cognitive & Social Learning Theorist
8. Cognitive

Application Three: Maslow's Hierarchy of Needs
1. Love   2. Aesthetic   3. Safety   4. Physiological   5. Self-Actualization
6. Esteem   7. Intellectual

Application Four: Need for Achievement or Need to Avoid Failure
1. high   2. low   3. low   4. high   5. high   6. high

Application Five: Attributions
1. internal (effort)/unstable/controllable
2. internal (native ability)/stable/uncontrollable
3. external/unstable/uncontrollable
4. internal (native ability)/stable/uncontrollable
5. internal (effort)/unstable/controllable
6. internal (effort)/unstable/controllable
7. internal (native ability)/stable/uncontrollable
8. internal (native ability)/stable/uncontrollable

Essay Questions

1.   Many suggest that attempts to get students to feel good about themselves have fallen short of the mark becuase many of these so-called, commercialized programs overlook the conditions that may cause students to have low self-esteem in the first place. If students are depressed because no matter how hard they try to succeed in math, they fail, then no amount of stating that they feel good about themselves will change the fact that they are experiencing difficulties in mathematics. A better approach might be to help them experience success levels within this area and then talk about feeling good. Those in favor of enhancing student self-esteem suggest that schools have a moral responsibility to provide the types of situations and settings that will convey to students that they are worthy individuals regardless of areas of difficulty rather than tracking them or placing them in competitive situations destined for failure. Helping students to realize their self-worth is a good starting place for increasing their confidence toward other academic challenges.

2.   When children enter school, the direction of their natural learning and motivation changes drastically. Whereas prior to formal schooling, their learning was spontaneous, unstructured, and not segmented by subject area, now they are told what to learn, when to learn, how to learn and it is all teacher directed and subject specific. It is no longer spontaneous and natural, but now it is contrived, competitive, and very structured. Extrinsic rewards and punishments are used to motivate and from your chapter readings, you should know that students experience decreased intrinsic motivation when someone else imposes tasks and activities upon them rather then allowing them to assume responsibilty for their own learning. But playing the devil's advocate, if it were left up to students to devise their own curriculum, would English, Math, and History be part of it? What do you think?

Multiple Choice

1. a   2. b   3. d   4. d   5. d   6. d   7. a   8. c   9. c   10. d

Chapter Eleven

Motivation, Teaching, and Learning

"Since we are all likely to go astray, the reasonable thing is to learn from those who can teach."
Sophocles

As your text suggests, people will change jobs seven times over the course of a lifetime. These changes require that people be prepared to change skills and engage in continual learning. Even though Sophocles suggests that we should rely on the expert knowledge of teachers, one of the aims of today's educators is to produce independent, **self-regulated learners.**

Self-regulated learners: Students whose academic learning abilities and self-discipline make learning easier, so motivation is maintained. Three factors influence whether individuals will become self-regulated learners; **knowledge, motivation,** and **volition.**

1. **Knowledge** is considered in a broad context and a variety of forms:
• about themselves and how they learn best, preferred learning styles, strengths and weaknesses, interests and talents
• about the subject being studied
• understanding that different tasks require different approaches--can apply different strategies
• consider the contexts in which they will apply their knowledge--when and where so they can connect their present knowledge to future applications

2. **Motivation** drives the self-regulated learner:
• naturally motivated to learn
• even in circumstances where the learner is not intrinsically motivated, they are serious about obtaining benefit from the task and will look to extrinsic gains
• they know the reasons for their learning so their actions and choices are self-determined

3. **Volition:** Will power; self-discipline. Even with the qualities of knowledge and motivation, the learner must additionally possess self-discipline:
• knowing how to protect yourself from distractions
• knowing how to cope when will power and self-discipline falters
• knowing the times and locations of the most productive learning

Corno describes four environmental aspects that serve to cultivate student volition:
1. invest heavily in students' own interests--often this will provide intrinsic motivation
2. provide opportunities for improvements and revisions--when I want my students to see the connection between effort and success, I give their assignments back to them for revisions and I find that in time, after repeatedly re-doing their assignments, they take greater care and invest more effort the first time around so that they don't have to do their assignments repeatedly. For some students, opportunities to improve are

greatly appreciated because they benefit greatly from the feedback I provide and maybe need more than "one shot" at fully comprehending the best approach.

3. the value of peers as learning partners-- students can help each other to reflect and can provide learning support for each other by questioning each other and providing suggestions.

4. gradually shift from teacher direction to student independence.

The **TARGETT** approach to motivation and self-regulated learning examines seven areas where teachers' actions may influence student motivation. We will examine separately each one of the TARGETT areas:

- task
- autonomy
- recognition of accomplishments
- grouping practices
- evaluation procedures
- time scheduling in the classroom
- teacher expectations

Tasks for Learning

Academic Tasks: The work the student must accomplish, including the content covered and the mental operations required.

Academic tasks vary relative to subject content. Some tasks may be interesting whereas others are boring. I sometimes look longingly at my colleagues' *methods for teaching classes* where they are always engaged in fun experiments (often involving food) whereas my class is primarily theoretical. The challenge to me, is to inform about theory, while providing humorous, practical, real-life examples to keep my students interested. My tasks also need to be fun applications of theory to real-world settings. Curiousity and challenges can help to supplant motivation in situations where students are not intrinsically motivated by any personal interest in the subject matter. Doyle has suggested that the types of tasks that are engaged in by our students, also influence their motivational levels to perform.

Task Operations: Risk and Ambiguity- Doyle (1983)

Doyle posits that tasks fall into the following four categories:
- memory--students must recognize or reproduce information they have seen before
- routine/procedural--following prescribed steps or rules to achieve an outcome or problem solve
- comprehension--take information and combine several ideas, originate a procedure, debate the issues, etc.
- opinion--state a personal preference or belief

According to Doyle, motivation to perform these four tasks is also influenced by two other factors; **risk** and **ambiguity.** Students want to decrease both risk and ambiguity.

Risk: the possibility of failure at a task
Ambiguity: how straightforward or vague the assignment is

Different tasks have varying associated levels of risk and ambiguity as outlined in the chart below;

		High	Comprehension	Opinion
Ambiguity				
		Low	Difficult Memory or Difficult Routine	Simple Memory or Simple Routine

High   Low

Risk

Comprehension tasks possess the highest degree of risk and ambiguity. Comprehension tasks are generally complicated so they are risky and very often, they are not straightforward because teachers want students to be able to independently apply their skills, make decisions, and take initiative. This is threatening to students who feel more comfortable with their tasks specifically delineated. Because students may be apprehensive as to how to approach the task to reduce the possibility of failure, their motivation decreases. The result is then to negotiate the task with the teacher by requesting specific directions, number of pages, etc. If the teacher gives in, motivation (to complete the task) is temporarily increased but by giving in, the task has now become a routine task and the benefits to the students are not as great as they would have been had it been left as a comprehension task. Furthermore, they experienced no increase in motivation to learn, just increases in motivation to get the grade and motivation to negotiate future tasks. To reach an equitable compromise where students are motivated and teachers need not reduce the task quality, teachers should provide some structure but not heavily penalize students when they fail to meet their expectations. Likewise, teachers should give plenty of practice with comprehension type tasks so that students feel more comfortable with some degree of ambiguity.

Task Value

As you know, value of the activity or task influences motivation to perform. Tasks are said to have three kinds of value to students; **attainment value, interest or intrinsic value, or utility value.**

Attainment Value: The importance of doing well on a task; how success on a task meets personal needs (the needs to be competent, well-liked, etc.) **Example:** Very often, I do not feel like being a committee member, but I do it because there is a need within our division and I want to be perceived by my colleagues as someone who will competently work for the good of the college.

Intrinsic or Interest Value: The enjoyment a person gets from a task. **Example:** I love fishing. I don't even have to catch anything to enjoy myself. I just love to sit tranquilly in my boat and float along. It has interest value for me.

Utility Value: The contribution of a task to meeting one's goals. **Example:** Having come from a computer age when we typed information onto IBM punch cards, when it was time to learn personal computers I dreaded moving forward into unknown territory. Knowing that it would help me in the long run if I moved into the computer age, I grit my teeth and allowed the utility of my goal to motivate me to learn PCs.

Application One: Identifying Task Value

Read the following scenarios and decide whether the activity has attainment, intrinsic, or utility value for the individual. Some tasks may have a combination of attainment, intrinsic, and utility value. When you think about it, these would probably be the most worthwhile tasks. Check your responses in the answer key.

1. My mom, Louise Mowrer, is a great cook. Her meals are always delicious and well-balanced. She cooks as an expression of love and caring for her family. She is considered to be a wonderful wife and mother. The only problem is that she hates cooking. _____

2. My dad, Phil Mowrer, is a dynamic, well-informed speaker. He exhibits many leadership qualities. He served in high administrative positions within his corporation, chaired church council, so when he was asked to be the President of their campground, in spite of the time and work obligations, he agreed. _____

3. My backyard is sloped and nearly impossible to mow without rolling the lawn mower. I purchased a gas powered weed whacker as an alternative to mowing. My neighbor borrowed it and ran out of cutting line while doing his yard. He asked me if I had changed the line, (I hadn't) and asked me if I wanted to learn how. I really had no interest in it but knew that if I wanted to weed whack in the future, I had better learn how. _____

4. Cali Popiel was presented with the task of writing a poem in class. After receiving much positive feedback in response to her poetry it was submitted for publication and published in the local newspaper. Recognizing her efforts, her teacher hung the newspaper article in the classroom. _____

5. As an experienced middle-school instructor, Jeff was asked to respond to a classroom situation in the *Instructors' Resource Manual* of this text. He enjoyed responding, as motivation is a topic that interests him and it would also mean a publication for him. _____

6. Theresa Luke does beautiful stained glass artwork. She gives most of it away as gifts for friends and family. When I tell her she should sell it, she says that isn't why she does it. _____

7. John Smith joined the Nature Club at his school. He professed to having little intellectual expertise regarding aspects of nature, but expressed an appreciation for being outdoors surrounded by beauty and tranquility. _____

8. Becky Jones is very proficient in Algebra, so much so that her friends call her the professor and she is extremely embarassed about it. The funny thing is that she doesn't really enjoy Algebra but she knows she will need to do well in all of her mathematics courses if she someday will become an astronaut. _____

9. Paul Waters was a beautiful ice-skater and would gracefully glide across the ice. A very modest man, he didn't want a lot of fuss made over his accomplishments. _____

10. Greg Mowrer didn't want to be president of the senior class because he knew it would be a lot of time and effort that he would rather devote to his lawn service. He was making quite a bit of money to help out with future college expenses but his friends said that he would be of great service to the class if elected, so he agreed. _____

Going back to the utility value example, computers have a great value to our world. They contribute to our learning and more than likely, most of us will utilize computers in our professions. Therefore, learning how to operate a computer can also be considered an **authentic task.**

Authentic Task: Tasks that have some connection to real-life problems the students will face outside of the classroom. A form of authentic learning is called **problem-based learning.**

Problem-Based Learning: Methods that provide students with realistic problems that don't necessarily have "right" answers. Students meet an ill-structured problem before they receive any instruction. Probing issues with the teacher acting as facilitator, students monitor and organize their own problem solving.

Supporting Autonomy

The second area in the TARGETT model is autonomy. Self-determination is a key component of intrinsic motivation. Classroom environments that support student autonomy foster greater student interest, sense of competence, self-esteem, creativity, conceptual learning, and preference for challenge. In autonomy-oriented classrooms, students are more likely to believe that the work is important. They tend to internalize educational goals as their own. Controlling environments tend to improve performance only on rote recall tasks. According to the **cognitive evaluation theory** when events are highly controlling, students' intrinsic motivation will decrease.

Cognitive Evaluation Theory: Suggests that events affect motivation through the individual's perception of the events as controlling behavior or providing information.

If the event provides information that increases the student's sense of self-efficacy and competence, intrinsic motivation will increase. If the information provided makes the student feel less competent or is very controlling, motivation will decrease. Teachers must provide learning environments that encourage student independence and initiative. Teachers must acknowledge students' points of view and attempt to understand negative emotions. Teachers should provide explanations for rules, limits, and constraints and use non-controlling, positive feedback.

Recognizing Accomplishment

The third TARGETT area is recognition. Praise needs to be specific, and distributed equally and evenly among the students. At times students may misinterpret praise to mean, "I'm really surprised that someone of your low level ability is doing so well." Be genuine and sincere in your praise without going overboard. Specify the exact behaviors that are being acknowledged versus offering comments such as "super" or "good" or "nice work." This type of praise really offers no information. Students should be recognized for improvement, for tackling difficult tasks, and for creativity to name a few.

Grouping

Johnson and Johnson (1994) have examined how individuals strive to achieve their goals relative to the ways they relate to one another. They have labeled this interpersonal factor the **goal structure** of the task.

Goal Structure: The way students relate to others who are also working toward a particular goal. Three types of goal structures are **individualistic, competitive**, and **cooperative.**

Competitive Goal Structures occur when individuals striving to achieve their goals have a bearing on whether or not you will achieve your goals. **Example:** There can be only one winner of a foot-race. If someone else wins, you lose. When you and your classmates are graded on a curve, only the top 10% for example, will receive "A's." Do you see why it is competitive?

Individualistic Goal Structures occur when an individual's efforts to achieve his/her goal is not influenced by anyone else's attempt to achieve their goals. **Example:** Every child who reads 20 books this month, will receive a new book from the *I Love to Read Program*. Every students who receives a 90 on the test will get an "A," regardless of how many students get a 90.

Cooperative Goal Structures: arrangement in which students work in mixed-ability groups and are rewarded on the basis of the success of the group. **Example:** When a basketball team wins the NBA championship, every member on the team is rewarded. When teams of students score an average of 10 improvement points on the exam, they will all be rewarded with a field trip. One form of cooperative learning structures is called **STAD.**

Student Teams-Achievement Division (STAD): Cooperative learning with heterogenous groups and elements of competition and reward. Slavin and colleagues developed this approach in which every student takes a test or quiz, and that becomes their baseline score against which future improvement is determined. This baseline score or average of past performances, is called the **ILE.**

Individual Learning Expectation (ILE): Constantly recomputed average score in a subject.

Once the teacher has established ILEs for each student, she is able to form teams of 4-5-6 students of mixed abilities. Other variables to be considered are gender, ethnicity, extroversion/introversion, etc. Students work together in teams to study and prepare for twice-weekly quizzes, but they take the quizzes individually, as usual. Team members can earn improvement points that surpass their ILE's and are then contributed to a team average. Rewards are offered dependent upon how many group improvement points were obtained. All team members are interested in helping each other to do well so that the entire team benefits. Even the low achieving students who may have low self-esteem have the opportunity to contribute points to the group and feel good about their successes. All team members benefit from this goal structure, even those students who assume much of the instructional capacity because research shows that the best way to really learn a topic is to teach it to someone else. Try it. This approach has been shown to be beneficial in decreasing racial conflict and increases the performance levels of mainstreamed students. Another form of cooperative learning structure is called **TGT**.

Teams-Games-Tournaments (TGT): Similar to STAD, learning arrangement in which team members prepare cooperatively, then meet comparable individuals of competing teams in a tournament game to win points for their team. The tournaments replace exams for determining points. One problem is that the losing teams experience the negative influences of a loss. In the STAD approach all teams can obtain points and the equivalent rewards.

Application Two: Cooperative Learning Groups

Nowadays, you can use computer programs to create your student teams by plugging in the ILEs, gender, ethnicity and other variables. When you have multiple variables, this is the recommended procedure, however, if you are trying to comprise groups based on gender and ILE, your task is rather simple. Try this with the ILE scores below (we won't consider gender, but you would separate your roster into male and female lists and then apply the following procedure). Rank the students in terms of ILE from high to low. There are a number of ways to select teams, but you want to ensure that your teams are comprised of high, high-average, low-average, and low achieving students. To make this simple, I have included 16 students so you will want to select four students for each group. Put the numbers, 1, 2, 3, or 4 next to each student's name and that will determine which group they will be in. Check your response in the answer key.

Student Name	ILE	Team Number	Quiz #1 (improve. pts.)	Quiz #2 (imp. pts.)
Gretta	94			
Tom	92			
Jack	90			
Ronna	87			
Sasha	86			
Roberto	85			
Kai	85			
Tanya	83			
Kim	80			
Jim	79			
Steve	77			
Sue	73			
Carl	70			
Pam	68			
Shelly	65			
Mark	59			

```
TEAMS' ILEs

Team 1= .

Team 2 =

Team 3 =

Team 4 =
```

Later, you would enter their individual quiz scores and calculate improvement points by figuring the difference between the ILE and the quiz scores. Teams can be re-formed after several quizzes have been administered and rankings change.

Evaluation

The fifth TARGETT area is evaluation. The type of evaluation you select, whether it is based on individual mastery or competitive grading on a curve, will influence the types of goals students set, be they performance or learning goals. When students feel they are working for grades, and if the amount of good grades to be handed out is limited, students will be less likely to want to assist each other in their attempts to achieve high grades. As educators, it must be our aim to help students to value learning over grades. Unfortunately, research indicates that teachers project the importance of doing work as a means to get grades and further project classroom work as "something to be gotten through."

Time

The sixth TARGETT area is time. Students and teachers alike feel the pressure of too little time for learning and learning tasks, often frantically hoping to complete the designated curriculum for that year. Teachable moments should be indulged without constant concern for the schedule. Constant interruptions of class bells, subject changes, and not enough time for project completion, can defeat the motivation of students when they are not permitted to experience activities to fruition.

Teacher Expectations

The seventh TARGETT area is teacher expectations. Rosenthal and Jacobsen (1968) conducted a study in which they told teachers that several of their students would make larger than usual academic gains that year, and sure enough, they did. The researchers suggested that this was due to **self-fulfilling prophecy.**

Self-fulfilling Prophecy: A groundless expectation that comes true simply because it was expected. Because of its similarity to the story of King Pygmalion's transformed statue from Greek Mythology, this has come to be known as the **Pygmalion Effect.**

Pygmalion Effect: Exceptional progress by a student as a result of high teacher expectations for that student.

Teachers do form beliefs about their students and the extent to which their beliefs and expectations influence student behavior depend upon whether students are high or low achievers, whether teachers believe the information about their students, and other variables. There is debate as to whether self-fulfilling prophecy is fact or artifact. Another form of expectation is called **sustaining expectation effect.**

Motivation, Teaching, and Learning

Sustaining Expectation Effect: Student performance maintained at a certain level because teachers don't recognize improvements. **Example:** A student has a rough start in the beginning of the year due to relocation and the teacher forms the opinion that this student lacks academic ability and motivation. In spite of increased effort and improved achievement on behalf of the student, the teacher continues to maintain his belief about the performance level of the student, making it more difficult for the student to achieve.

There are many other sources of teacher expectation such as gender, IQ scores, medical or psychological reports, knowledge of ethnic background, physical characteristics, names, previous achievement, and socioeconomic class.

Students who are expected to achieve:
- tend to be asked more and harder questions
- tend to be given more chances and a longer time to respond
- tend to be interrupted less than students who are expected to do poorly.
- are given more cues and prompts by teachers
- are more encouraged in general by teachers
- are smiled at more often and shown greater warmth by teachers through non-verbal response
- have higher demands for better performance
- are praised more for good answers by teachers

Students who are not expected to achieve:
- are asked easier questions by teachers
- are allowed less time for answering
- are less likely to be given prompts
- are more likely to receive sympathetic acceptance or even praise for inadequate answers and criticized for the wrong answers
- receive less praise than high-achieving students for the same correct answer

Motivation, Teaching, and Learning

Figure 11.1

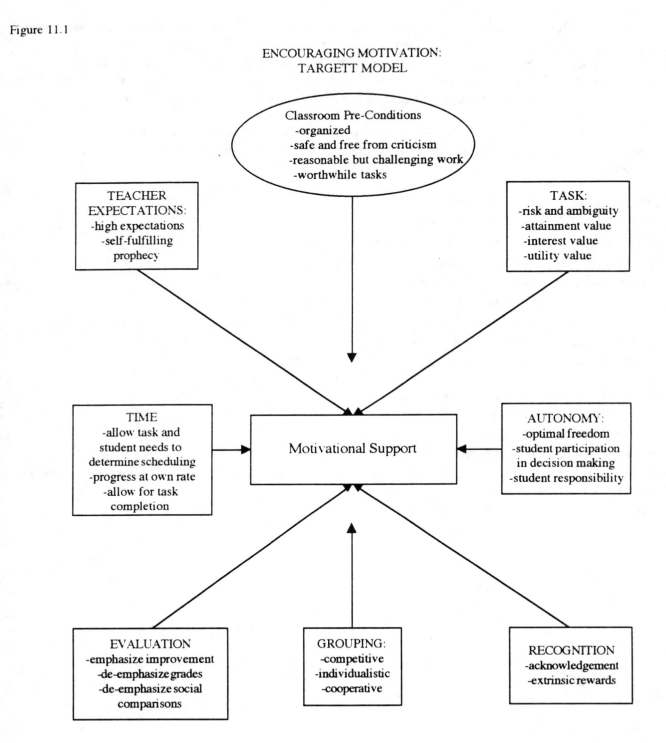

ENCOURAGING MOTIVATION:
TARGETT MODEL

Classroom Pre-Conditions
  -organized
  -safe and free from criticism
  -reasonable but challenging work
  -worthwhile tasks

TEACHER
EXPECTATIONS:
-high expectations
-self-fulfilling
  prophecy

TASK:
-risk and ambiguity
-attainment value
-interest value
-utility value

TIME
-allow task and
student needs to
determine scheduling
-progress at own rate
-allow for task
completion

Motivational Support

AUTONOMY:
-optimal freedom
-student participation
  in decision making
-student responsibility

EVALUATION
-emphasize improvement
-de-emphasize grades
-de-emphasize social
comparisons

GROUPING:
-competitive
-individualistic
-cooperative

RECOGNITION
-acknowledgement
-extrinsic rewards

Strategies to Encourage Motivation and Thoughtful Learning

Four basic classroom conditions should be met, to increase motivation:
1. The classroom must be relatively organized and free from constant interruptions and disruptions
2. The teacher must be a patient, supportive person who never embarrasses students for mistakes, *everyone in class should see mistakes as opportunities for learning.* There is no shame in initial failure. The shame is in quitting. I always remind my students that the learning that is worthwhile, does not come easily. I tell my students to reflect on learning to ride a bike. None of them got it the first time, but they stuck with it and inevitably their failures were transformed into successes.
3. The work must be challenging but reasonable.
4. The learning tasks must be authentic.

Once the above conditions are met, to **ensure genuine progress** you should do the following:
1. Begin work at the students' level and move in small steps.
2. Make sure learning goals are clear, specific, and possible to reach in the near future.
3. Stress self-comparison, not comparison with others
4. Communicate to students that academic ability is improvable and specific to the task at hand
5. Model good problem solving

To foster attainment value, we must connect the learning task with the needs of the student. To foster **intrinsic motivation**, we should follow some of the recommended guidelines.
- Tie class activities to students' interests and allow them options
- Arouse curiousity
- Make the learning task fun
- Make use of novelty and familiarity

When students lack intrinsic motivation teachers need to focus on **extrinsic motivation** and emphasizing the **instrumental value** or utility of tasks. Ways to accomplish this are outlined below.
- Explain the connections to your students when they fail to see the value of what they are learning to their futures
- Provide incentives and rewards for learning, taking care not to undermine intrinsic motivation
- Use ill-structured problems and authentic tasks in teaching, connecting them to real problems outside

Lastly, part of ensuring student success is to help them to stay on task. Listed below are some strategies for **helping students to stay focused**.
- Give students frequent opportunities to respond through questions and answers, short assignments, or demonstrations of skills.
- When possible, have students create a finished product because completion is a reward in itself.
- Avoid heavy emphasis on grades and competition
- Reduce task risk without oversimplifying the task
- Model motivation to learn for your students
- Teach the particular learning tactics that students will need to master the material being studied

Application Three: Case Studies in Motivation

Read the four case studies and imagine that these are students in your class. Try to determine the most effective general approaches toward increasing their motivational levels and then state specifically what methods you would use.

General Motivational Approach
1. Provide extrinsinc reinforcements
2. Incorporate student interests in lessons and activities
3. Provide challenging work
4. Acknowledge and praise success
5. Ensure a safe learning environment
6. Clearly express your expectations
7. Set up a cooperative learning task
8. Use individualized instruction
9. Help student to establish reasonable goals
10. Address student's need for affiliation and belonging
11. Ensure that the student experiences realistic success experiences

Case One
Jackie is one of those students who breaks your heart the minute you set eyes upon her. Her face is dirty, hair uncombed, her clothes are torn and wrinkled and she is shy, listless, and sucks her thumb with a vacant look to her eyes. She sits motionless at her desk in your second-grade class, hardly ever responding unless you speak directly to her. Her learning from her first two years of schooling is barely marginal and based on her performance thus far, you doubt that she will learn much this year either. How would you encourage Jackie to actively engage in the learning process?

General Motivational Approach (es) _____

Specific Strategies _____

_____

Case Two
Jesse is known throughout the region for his rebel ways and practice of challenging authority. His two older brothers also came through the school system and were known for being smart but disruptive in class. Jesse appears to be following in his brothers' footsteps and has established a reputation in class as being "ultra-bad" commanding the admiration of every student in class. Jesse thrives on the attention from his classmates and even though he seems to have great academic potential, he invests his energies in the wrong direction. How can you help Jesse to be motivated to use his intellect and leadership qualities in a more positive way?

General Motivational Approach(es) _____

Specific Strategies _____

_____   _____

Case Three

Jennifer is an extremely gifted, sociable girl who has been working independently on math assignments because she is more advanced than the rest of her classmates. At first she was pleased about the special priviledge of working by herself, but now that she has been working individually for the past month, she is showing less interest in doing mathematics and her performance is starting to decline. How could you help to re-establish Jennifer's motivation to complete her mathematics assignment?

General Motivational Approach(es) _____

Specific Strategies _____

_____

Application Four: Key Terms and Definitions

To check your comprehension, see if you can come up with terms to match the definitions below. Some of the terms may have two words but there will be no space in between the words. Check your responses in the answer key.

Clues

Down:

1. A groundless expectation that is confirmed because it has been expected
2. Will power; self-discipline
4. The way students relate to others who are also working toward a particular goal
5. Tasks that have some connection to real-life problems the students will face outside the classroom
7. Type of value that shows the importance of doing well on a task; how success on the task meets personal needs
8. Constantly recomputed average score in a subject; used in cooperative learning structures
9. Arrangement in which students work in mixed-ability groups and are rewarded on the basis of the success of the group
11. Type of cooperative learning with heterogenous groups and elements of competition and reward

Across:

3. Exceptional progress by a student as a result of high teacher expectations for that student
6. Student performance maintained at a certain level because teachers don't recognize improvements
10. Type of value that reflects the enjoyment a person gets from a task
12. Type of value that addresses the contribution of a task to meeting one's goals

Key Terms and Definitions

Practice Tests

Essay Questions

1. Summarize and discuss the research by Thorkildsen, Nolen, & Founier (1994), and Nicholls, Nelson, & Gleaves (1995) which examined students' beliefs about motivation and fairness.

2. Discuss the notion of self-fulfilling prophecy and the controversy as to whether or not teacher expectations influence student achievement.

Multiple Choice

1   The highest rating given by 200 junior high schools students cited _____ as the primary explanation for failure.
   a. lack of teacher concern
   b. lack of effort
   c. poor study strategies
   d. lack of interest in the topic

2.   According to Doyle when students encounter tasks that they find to be risky and ambiguous, they will
   a. cheat to succeed
   b. negotiate the task with the teacher
   c. demonstrate increased motivation to succeed at the task that they find more challenging
   d. none of the above

3.   The type of task requiring students to go beyond the information given by combining several ideas is called
   a. memory
   b. routine procedure
   c. comprehension
   d. opinion

4.   When students are required to engage in activities that have some connection to the real-life problems and situations that students will face outside of the classroom this is aptly named
   a. false learning
   b. inert knowledge
   c. authentic tasks
   d. problem based learning

Motivation, Teaching, and Learning

5. Jeremy joined the soccer team because he truly loves soccer even though he spends most of his time on the bench. Soccer has what kind of value for Jeremy?
   a. attainment
   b. interest
   c. utility
   d. authentic

6. Classroom environments that support student autonomy are associated with
   a. creativity
   b. self-esteem
   c. preference for challenge
   d. all of the above

7. A study of low-achieving first grade students found that in order to finish a task, students
   a. made up answers
   b. filled in the page with patterns
   c. copied from other students
   d. all of the above

8. Students who are young, conforming, dependent, or really like the teacher
   a. demonstrate the highest levels of intrinsic motivation
   b. are most likely to have their self-esteem affected by the teacher's views
   c. receive more positive attention and praise from their teachers
   d. respond better to incentives and rewards than older children

9. In a study conducted by Newby, first year elementary school teachers used about 10 different motivational strategies per hour and half of them were
   a. geared toward the students' own interests
   b. focused on the value of the learning tasks
   c. rewards and punishments
   d. game-simulated activities

10. The theory that suggests that events affect motivation through the individual's perception of the events as controlling behavior or providing information is known as
    a. problem-based learning
    b. cognitive evaluation theory
    c. perceptual control theory
    d. collaborative inquiry theory

Answer Key

Application One: Identifying Task Value

1. attainment value
2. attainment and intrinsic value
3. utility value
4. attainment value and intrinsic value
5. attainment, intrinsic, and utility value
6. intrinsic value
7. intrinsic value
8. utility value
9. intrinsic value
10. attainment and utility value

Application Two: Cooperative Learning Groups

Student Name	ILE	Team Number	Quiz #1 (improve. pts.)	Quiz #2 (imp. pts.)
Gretta	94	1		
Tom	92	4		
Jack	90	2		
Ronna	87	3		
Sasha	86	1		
Roberto	85	2		
Kai	85	4		
Tanya	83	3		
Kim	80	4		
Jim	79	1		
Steve	77	3		
Sue	73	2		
Carl	70	4		
Pam	68	2		
Shelly	65	3		
Mark	59	1		

TEAMS' ILEs

Team 1= 94, 86, 79, 59

Team 2 = 90, 85, 73, 68

Team 3 = 87, 83, 77, 65

Team 4 = 92, 85, 80, 70

Application Three: Case Studies in Motivation

Case One: General Approaches--2, 5, 7, 8, 9, 10, 11 Specific Strategies--Help Jackie with her appearance and conference with her to find out her interests. She appears to lack motivation so working with her interests may provide the necessary spark. She appears to come from a neglectful environment, so make sure that she is made to feel welcome and accepted. Placing her within a cooperative learning structure may help her to become acquainted with classmates and help her to socialize. Individualized instruction may give her the attention she needs and by giving her special attention and feedback there is a greater likelihood that she will be able to experience the success necessary to increase her self-esteem.

Case Two: General Approaches--1, 2, 4, 6, 7, 10, 11 Specific Strategies--Jesse may respond well to extrinsic rewards because his negative behaviors are already intrinsically satisfying. Work out an incentive plan for Jesse and appeal to his intellectual ability and need for affiliation by requesting *his* help in assisting the learning process of lower achieving students. Re-direct his positive energies and leadership qualities toward successful outcomes which if acknowledged, will replace the attention he receives for his negative behaviors. Allow him the freedom to pursue his interests and set his own goals if he can demonstrate appropriate behaviors for the classroom.

Case Three: General Approaches--2, 3, 4, 7, 9, 10 Specific Strategies--Jennifer, although intrinsically motivated by her initial success, is now feeling isolated and not as pleased with the novelty of her learning situation as she was in the beginning. Help her to establish goals with which she will be happy and reintroduce her to the group, perhaps in a cooperative learning structure where she can apply her skills as well as help others and meet her needs for social affiliation. Continue to provide praise and acknowledgement for her successes.

Application Four: Key Terms and Definitions
Key Terms and Definitions

Motivation, Teaching, and Learning

Essay Questions:

1. Thorkildsen et. al., interviewed 93 students grades 2 through 5. The interviewers described four approaches to motivation--encouraging focus on the task (thought to be fair by 98% of the students), praising excellent performance (only 30% believed public praise is fair), giving rewards for excellent performance (seen as fair by 50% of the students), and giving rewards for high effort (seen as fair by 85% of the students). Students from this study held different beliefs on motivation and surprisingly many emphasized task focus and effort over reward and praise. The Nicholls et. al., study interviewed 128 African-American students on their opinions regarding collaborative learning versus traditional instruction. Older students were more likely than younger students to see collaborative inquiry as fairer and more motivating. The older the students, the more strongly they agreed that schools should foster motivation and understanding, not just memory for tasks.

2. Rosenthal and Jacobsen's original experiment has been greatly criticized on the grounds that most of the self-fulfilling effects were confined to students in grades one and two and in actuality to just five students. Other researchers have not been able to replicate the results and it is also argued that if teachers have low expectations it does not necessarily mean that students will exhibit lower achievement. Others argue that when 400 classrooms in the Southwest were examined, it was reported that Hispanic-American students received consistently less praise and encouragement and fewer positive teacher responses and questions than Anglo-American students. In classes where teachers treat high-achieving students differently from low-achieving students, the teachers' evaluation of student ability appears to influence the students' achievement in the class. It is important to keep in mind that teachers convey attitudes, beliefs, and expectations and students easily pick up on cues in the classroom

Multiple Choice:
1. d   2. b   3. c   4. c   5. b   6. d   7. d   8. b   9. c   10. b

Chapter Twelve

Creating Learning Environments

"Education is the ability to listen to almost anything without losing your temper or your confidence."
Robert Frost

We would like to believe that by establishing a positive learning environment in the classroom from the very beginning of the school year, we will prevent any problems from occuring throughout the year. But problems will arise and appropriate responses by the teacher can stop small problems from exploding into large ones. The *Phi Delta Kappa* Gallup Poll has consistently identified lack of discipline as one of the primary problems facing schools. Every classroom has its own dynamic environment with teachers, students, and the academics in constant interaction. Doyle suggests that every classroom is influenced by six factors regardless of teacher or student characteristics:

- Multidimensionality: Classrooms are comprised of people, tasks, time pressures, goals, preferences, abilities, and the list goes on and on. All of these dimensions interact to make the classroom a very complex place.
- Simultaneity: Many things are happening at once. The teacher is explaining, students are writing, students are not writing, and the teacher must have 50 eyes to watch all that is transpiring.
- Immediacy: Classroom life is fast-paced. Teachers have literally hundreds of exchanges with students throughout the day.
- Unpredictable: Even when you are completely prepared, your students are engaged and responding, you can bet that someone will mow the lawn right outside of your window.
- Public: You will always be observed. Your students will judge how you equitably interact with students, handle situations, and acknowledge their efforts.
- Histories: All the events that transpire combine to form the "classroom history." Your responses to your students will evolve as history develops.

Gaining student cooperation is the key to smoothly operating classroom procedures. Gaining student cooperation can be a challenge that is contingent upon the ages of your students.

The Goals of Classroom Management

Using **classroom management** solely for the purpose of keeping students docile would be unethical; its true aim is to maintain a positive, productive learning environment.

Classroom Management: Techniques used to maintain a healthy learning environment, relatively free of behavior problems. Effective classroom management results in:

Creating Learning Environments

1. More time is allotted for actual learning--examination of time of actual instruction, reveals that much of the school day is spent on other activiities. An important goal is to expand **allocated time.**

Allocated Time: Time set aside for learning.

Generally, due to many classroom interruptions, allocated time never equals **engaged time** or **time on task.** Engaged time or time on task does not insure that actual learning is occuring. Students may be experiencing comprehension difficulty and frustration with absence of productive learning. Successful productive learning is called **academic learning time.**

Engaged Time: Time spent actively learning.

Time on Task: Time spent actively engaged in the learning task at hand.

Academic Learning Time: Time when students are actually succeeding at the learning task, working at the correct difficulty level.

2. Access to learning--One of the ways that students access the information that is available to them in the classroom is through **participation structures.**

Participation Structures: Rules defining how to participate in different activities.

Some students do not know appropriate rules for when to question, make contributions, for how long they should dominate the floor, etc. I'll bet you have encountered classmates at the college level who don't know when to quit talking. Teachers must teach students how to verbally participate and convey to them the classroom rules and expectations. Students who don't know how to verbally access information or have been rebuked for inappropriate attempts at participation, may refrain from future attempts and miss out on learning.

3. Management for Self-Management--Students need to gradually assume responsibility for controlling their own behaviors. So the third goal of classroom management is **self-management**. This requires extra effort on the part of the teacher but it is a worthwhile investment for both the student and the teacher in the long run.

Self-Management: Management of your own behavior and acceptance of responsibility for your own actions.

How to Become Good Classroom Managers

The following classroom management principles were developed from research that compared methods of teachers who had harmonious, high achieving classes with those of teachers whose classes were fraught with problems. The first step toward establishing effective management is the establishment of **procedures.**

Procedures: Prescribed steps for an activity. Weinstein et. al. suggests that procedures be established for the following areas:

1. *administrative routines*--taking attendance, pledge of allegiance, lunchroom orders
2. *student movement*--lining up, entering and leaving the room, hall passes
3. *housekeeping*--hanging up coats, stowing galoshes, putting books in a locker or cubby
4. *routines for accomplishing lessons*--collecting assignments, handing out materials
5. *interactions between teacher and student*--how to get the teacher's help when needed
6. *talk among students*--such as giving help or socializing

Rules

Unlike procedures, rules are often written down and posted. A few rules that cover specific do's and don'ts of the classroom are much better than an extensive list covering every possible action.

Rules: Statements specifying expected and forbidden behaviors.

Rules differ contingent upon the age of the student. Whatever the age, however, students need to be taught the behaviors that the rule includes and excludes. Different situations call for different rules, which may be confusing for elementary students. A good strategy would be to post rules clearly where everyone can see them, leaving no ambiguity. All rules should be explained and discussed to have their full effect. A good way to construct classroom rules is to have both a teacher's and students' Bill of Rights. Rather than posting a list of don'ts, the Bill of Rights states the rights of individuals that are to be respected and maintained by all in the classroom. This teaches democratic procedures as well as responsible decision-making and independence.

Application One: Whose Rules are They?

Read the following rules and determine the rule is appropriate for elementary or secondary school, or both.

1. _____ Do not hit, shove , or hurt others
2. _____ Respect other people's property
3. _____ Listen and stay seated while someone else is speaking
4. _____ Bring all needed materials to class
5. _____ Be in your seat and ready to work when the bell rings
6. _____ Be polite to everyone
7. _____ Obey all school rules

Consequences

As soon as rules and procedures have been selected, you must determine the consequences for infractions. Weinstein and Mignano (1997) found that teachers' negative consequences fell into seven different categories.

Application Two: Categories of Penalties

Listed below are seven categories of penalties. Based on what you know about consequences from previous chapters, next to each penalty decide whether it is negative reinforcement, presentation punishment, or removal punishment. Explain your choices. Check your responses in the answer key.

1. Expressions of disappointment by the teacher _____
   (if students like their teachers, this may cause them to stop and reflect)

2. Loss of privileges _____
   (this generally means a loss of free time, or recess)

3. Exclusion from the group _____
   (can mean separation from group, or time-out room, or isolation box)

4. Written reflections on the problem _____
   (students write essays on what they did and how it affected others, or letters of apology--these
    statements are kept within the student's file to be shown to parents or used by administrators)

5. Detentions _____
   (after school or during recess, these can be meetings to discuss the problem or at the high school level can
    precede suspension or expulsion)

6. Visits to the principal's office _____
   (rarely used unless a serious infraction such as fighting)

7. Contact with parents _____
   (if problems become a pattern, most teachers contact the family primarily as support measures for the
    student)

Planning Spaces for Learning

Classroom space can be segmented into two areas: interest areas and personal territories. Interest-area arrangements may be a science corner with manipulatives or a reading corner. To plan classroom space, you must first decide the nature of your projects and activities and how you plan to physically group your students.

Creating Learning Environments

Personal territories address the physical location of students within the classroom. Interested students generally position themselves near the front of the classroom and the instructor. Adams and Biddle (1970) found that the area of verbal interaction between the students and teachers occured in the center front of the classroom and in a line directly through the center of the room. This area is called the **action zone.**

Action Zone: Area of a classroom where the greatest amount of interaction takes place.

Students who sit in the back of the classroom are NOT within the action zone. Teachers should physically move through the classroom space to maintain eye contact and verbal interaction with all students. Another approach is to vary seating arrangements of your students for different objectives and activities.

Application Three: Identifying Classroom Arrangements

To check for comprehension fill in the blanks with the appropriate terms or phrases. Some terms may be used twice. Check your responses in the answer key.

fishbowl--clusters--horizontal rows--circle arrangements--clusters of four

A poor arrangement for large-group discussion _____ permit students to work more easily in pairs. _____ are also useful for independent seatwork and for teacher, student, or media presentations. The two best approaches for student interaction are _____ or _____. _____ are useful for discussion but still allow for independent seatwork. _____ permit students to talk, help one another, share materials, and work on group tasks. The _____ where students sit close together near the focus of attention should be used only for short time periods because it is not comfortable and can lead to discipline problems.

Effective Elementary Teachers gain students' cooperation within the first critical days and weeks by:
- starting with a well-organized first day--name tags, interesting activities and materials, addressing the students' most pressing concerns, and reasonable rules taught with explanation, examples, and practice.
- throughout the first few weeks--continue teaching rules and procedures, worked with the class as a whole on enjoyable activities, misbehavior was stopped quickly and firmly

Ineffective Elementary Teachers operated their rooms quite differently:
- rules were not workable--vague, complicated, and consequences were not clear or consistent
- procedures for accomplishing routine tasks varied from day-to-day and these were never taught or practiced
- students wandered aimlessly and relied on each other for direction teachers frequently left the room, became absorbed in paperwork or in helping one student classrooms were unorganized and inconsistent

Creating Learning Environments

Figure 12.1

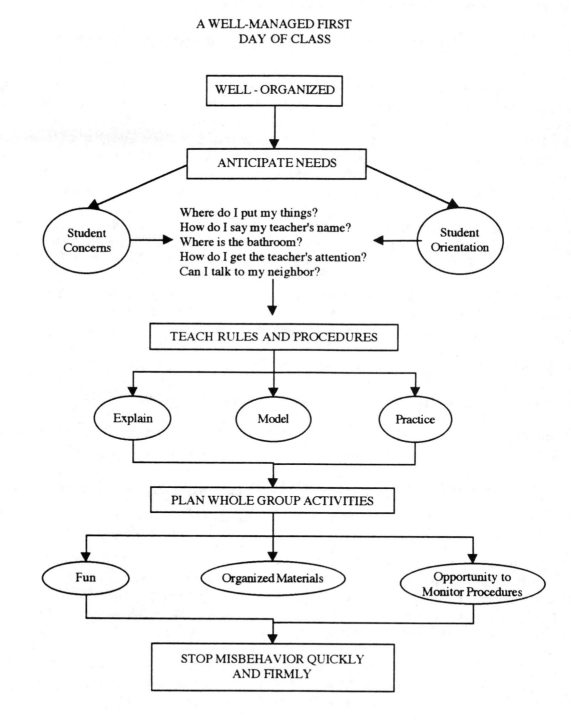

A WELL-MANAGED FIRST
DAY OF CLASS

WELL - ORGANIZED

ANTICIPATE NEEDS

Student Concerns

Where do I put my things?
How do I say my teacher's name?
Where is the bathroom?
How do I get the teacher's attention?
Can I talk to my neighbor?

Student Orientation

TEACH RULES AND PROCEDURES

Explain   Model   Practice

PLAN WHOLE GROUP ACTIVITIES

Fun   Organized Materials   Opportunity to Monitor Procedures

STOP MISBEHAVIOR QUICKLY
AND FIRMLY

Effective managers for secondary students demonstrated many of the same characteristics as effective elementary teachers. Student behavior was closely monitored and infractions dealt with quickly. Teachers closely monitored student progress so that students could not avoid working, yet effective teachers also demonstrated a sense of humor and joked with their students.

Maintaining a Good Learning Environment

As stated previously, an effective way of dealing with problems is to prevent their occurrence in the first place. Students who are engaged in activities are less likely to generate problems. Research informs us that elementary students working with a teacher were on task 97% of the time, while students working on their own were on task only 57% of the time. Of course teachers cannot be expected to work with students all of the time, but keeping students engaged is one way to prevent problems. Kounin (1970) compared effective classroom managers to ineffective managers and concluded that effective managers were skilled in four areas: **withitness, overlapping activities, group focusing,** and **movement management.**

Withitness: Awareness of everything happening in the classroom. **Example:** A teacher friend of mine positioned a large circular mirror in the front corner of the classroom so that when he was writing on the board, he could still watch what was happening in his classroom behind his back.

Withitness prevents **timing errors** (waiting too long to act) and **target errors** (blaming the wrong individual while the culprit escapes cupability). When more than one problem occurs at the same time, the withit teacher deals with the more serious problem first.

Overlapping: Supervising several activities at once.

Group Focus: The ability to keep as many students as possible involved in activities.

Movement Management: Ability to keep lessons and groups moving smoothly. The effective teacher avoids abrupt transitions as well as transitions that progress too slowly, losing students in the process.

Dealing with Discipline Problems and Special Programs for Classroom Management

Stopping misbehaviors may be accomplished subtly without calling the attention of everyone in the class to the situation. Frequent reprimands do not translate to mean the best behaved classes. Some effective ways are (1) to make eye contact or move in closer proximity to the offender, (2) remind students of the correct procedure if they are not following it correctly, (3) ask students to state the correct rule and then follow it, and (4) tell the student in a clear, assertive, and unhostile way to stop the misbehavior.

Many classroom management procedures are aimed at the global behavior of the class. Many of Cali's teachers would give points for good behaviors and when they accumulated enough points they would have a pizza party. This is an example of the **good behavior game.**

212

Creating Learning Environments

Good Behavior Game: Arrangement where a class is divided into teams and each team receives demerit points for breaking agreed-upon rules of good behavior. The team with the least marks at the end of the period receives a special reward. If both teams receive less marks than the previous period, both teams receive a reward.

Without dividing the class into teams, you could also use **group consequences.** Peer influences can be a positive form of support for establishing appropriate behaviors but cautions must be taken lest a single troubled student is held responsible for the majority of his or her team's penalties, potentially creating even further problems for that individual. Teachers should show students how to give each other constructive feedback and support.

Group Consequences: Rewards or punishments given to a class as a whole for adhering to or violating rules of conduct.

Another system in which students are reinforced for appropriate behaviors are **token reinforcement systems.** Here, all students are provided with the opportunity to earn tokens that provide the students with purchasing power.

Token Reinforcement System: System in which tokens earned for academic work and positive classroom behavior can be exchanged for some desired reward.

Once again, cautions must be exercised because extrinsic rewards are replacing intrinsic satisfaction. Once a system is working well, tokens should be distributed on an intermittent schedule and saved for longer periods of time before they are exchanged for rewards. Token reinforcement systems should be used in only three situations:

- to motivate students who are completely uninterested in their work and have not responded to other situations
- to encourage students who have consistently failed to make academic progress
- to deal with a class that is out of control

Some students benefit from token economy systems more than others. Students who are slow learners or mentally challenged, children who frequently fail, have few academic skills and behavior problems, all respond to token systems yet teachers must re-evaluate their curriculum, material, and teaching practices before resorting to token systems.

Another special program that fosters active goal setting, self-management, and independence is called a **contingency contract.** Contracts may be used for any subject area, any topic and at any age. They teach the very valuable lesson of time management and breaking a large long-term project into short-term do-able tasks. What helps to make this effective, is that students receive reinforcements throughout rather than waiting to be reinforced only upon project completion.

Contingency Contract: A contract between the teacher and an individual student specifying what the student must do to earn a particular privilege or reward.

Contingency Contract

I, _____ agree to complete each step of my book report by the following due dates.

Dates   *Activity*

March 1st	Select a book
March 14th	Finish reading the book
March 21st	Compile an outline of the book report
March 28th	Submit a rough draft for approval
April 4th	Submit completed book report

    I will hand I each activity card upon completion of the activity by the designated date and pick up my next card. The activity card will specify the reinforcement I will receive if the activity is completed on time.

_____   _____   _____

Teacher   Student   Date

The Need for Communication

Communication must be a two-way exchange between the student and the teacher including non-verbal messages. Very often the messages we send are misinterpreted. Often, people will respond to what they *think* was said and not what was intended by the speaker. To send and receive messages accurately practice the **paraphrase rule** in your class.

Paraphrase Rule: Policy whereby listeners must accurately summarize what a speaker has said before being allow to respond. **Example:** I teach Educational Psychology to large sections of students (80 and more). We are in a large lecture hall with very bad acoustics. We engage in a lot of dialogue and sometimes I have trouble hearing my students so everytime they respond, I try to paraphrase what they have said so that I know that I interpret them correctly and so that everyone else in the class can hear what was said. When I paraphrase, I also try to use their names so that they become acquainted with one another and inter-student communication is also improved.

Another way to foster good teacher student relationships is by diagnosing who owns the problem, the student or the teacher. If the student's behavior interferes with your capacity to reach your goals as a teacher, then it is your problem. If the behavior does not directly interfere with your teaching, then it is probably the student's problem. Once you decide who owns the problem, act! If the problem is yours, confront the student and seek a solution. If the problem belongs to the student, try to counsel the student by paraphrasing for clarification and employ **empathetic listening.**

Creating Learning Environments

Empathetic Listening: Hearing the intent and emotions behind what another says and reflecting them back by paraphrasing.

Avoid jumping in too quickly and permit the student the time to openly express his or her concerns. Attend to both the verbal and non-verbal messages. Try to differentiate between the intellectual and emotional content of the message. Make inferences regarding what the speaker is feeling. Students learn to trust teachers who will openly listen to them without value judgments.

Application Four: Teacher-Student Owned Problems

Decide whether the following classroom problems are student owned, teacher owned, or shared. Check your responses in the answer key.

1. "Mr. Jones, I don't think I can deliver my oral presentation to the class. I start to stutter from nerves."

2. "Janet, your tardiness is disrupting the class lesson once again and you have missed the explanation regarding how to do your problems."

3. "Girls, the notes you are passing clear across the classroom will have to wait until lunch. It is very distracting to everyone to have to pass your notes and I'm finding it difficult to concentrate."

4. "Mrs. Smith, Bobby is pulling my hair. Ow!"

5. "Francis, I will ask you one more time to sit down and if you refuse to cooperate, I will be forced to ask you to go to the office."

6. "This is a dumb assignment. Why do I have to memorize the periodic table anyway? I'll never use it."

Confrontation and Assertive Discipline

As stated previously, when the student is interfering with your teaching, you must confront the student. This is the time for an **"I" message.**

"I" Messages: Clear, nonaccusatory statement of how something is affecting you. **Example:** "When you are talking to the person next to you, I can't concentrate on what I'm trying to teach the class."

Canter and Canter (1992) suggest that another direct approach for dealing with teacher owned problems is **assertive discipline.** The Canters suggests that all too often, teachers are either passive (wishy-washy or questioning the student as to why they're misbehaving without informing them of the proper behaviors) or hostile ("You are NOT listening! You straighten up or else!"). Assertive responses indicate that you care about the student and their learning. Assertive responses are calm statements of expectations delivered with confidence and controlled emotions.

Assertive Discipline: Clear, firm, unhostile response style.

When people are in conflict they have two major concerns, (1) to satisfy their needs and meet their goals, and (2) to maintain an appropriate relationship with the other party in the conflict. Both of these concerns range in importance. Given the current state of increasing violence in our schools, more attention must be devoted by educators toward prevention, mentoring programs, conflict resolution, parent and community involvement programs, etc.

Peer Mediation: Johnson et.al. trained 227 second through fifth grade sudents 5 steps for conflict resolution.
- jointly define the conflict--separate the person from the problem and establish both parties' goals
- exchange positions and interests--each party presents a proposal and makes a case for it
- reverse perspectives--reverse roles and argue for the other party's perspective
- invent at least three agreements that allow mutual gain-- brainstorm and invent solutions
- reach an integrative agreement--make sure both sets of goals are met and if this appears to be impossible, flip a coin or call in a third party mediator

Peer mediation has been successful with older students and with serious problems such as gang violence. "The magic of the mediation process was communication." (Sanchez & Anderson, 1990).

Application Five: Key Terms and Definitions

To check your comprehension, see if you can come up with terms to match the definitions below. Some of the terms may have two words but there is no space in between the words. Check your responses in the answer key.

Clues

Down:
1. Statements specifying expected and forbidden behaviors
3. Form of discipline characterized by a clear, firm, unhostile response style
4. Prescribed steps for an activity
5. Area of the classroom where the greatest amount of interaction takes place
7. Type of reinforcement in which tokens earned can be exchanged for desired reward
8. Supervising several activities at once

Across:
2. When listeners accurately summarize what a speaker has said before being allowed to respond
6. A contract between the teacher and a student specifying what the student must do to earn rewards
9. Awareness of everything happening in the classroom
10. Time set aside for learning
11. Listening characterized by hearing the intent and emotions behind what another says
12. Time spent actively learning

Key Terms and Definitions

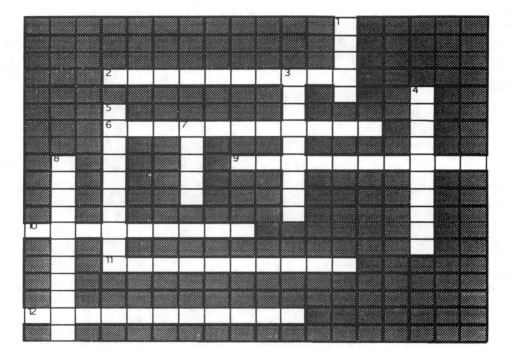

Practice Tests

Essay Questions

1. Suppose you are a secondary teacher and a very large, senior boy is openly defying you in front of the class. You have repeatedly told him to take his seat but he towers over you, smirking, and mimicking your words. How do you handle the situation?

2. A current classroom management approach that is hotly debated among educators, is the assertive discipline approach by Canter and Canter. Provide arguments both pro and con for the utilization of this approach in the classroom.

Multiple Choice

1. According to Doyle, the fast pace of classroom life is called
   a. simultaneity
   b. immediacy
   c. multidimensionality
   d. unpredictability

2. A very important goal of classroom management is to expand the sheer number of minutes available for learning. This is called
   a. allocated time
   b. engaged time
   c. time on task
   d. academic learning time

3. Ms. Brown was busy writing the class assignment on the board with her back turned toward the classroom. A spit wad hit the board by Ms. Brown. She had been watching the reflection of the class in her classroom door and said , "Jimmy, you've just earned yourself a detention. Now come clear this slop off of the board." Ms. Brown can be said to possess
   a. an uptight attitude
   b. skill at overlapping
   c. withitness
   d. movement management

4. Sometime students miss out on classroom learning because they are too intimidated or don't know how to go about asking questions. They have been laughed at before and they always seem to say the wrong thing. An area that should be addressed with these students is
   a. participation structures
   b. contingency contracts
   c. self-management techniques
   d. administrative routines

5. Class rules are designed to inform the class
   a. how materials are to be distributed in the classroom
   b. how grades will be determined
   c. the way activities are accomplished in the classroom
   d. the expected and forbidden actions in the class

6. It is a good idea to post a sign listing the rules for each activity prior to that activity because
   a. different activities require different rules
   b. it provides clear and consistent cues about participation structures
   c. they serve as reminders for the rules that have been previously explained and discussed
   d. all of the above

7. An effective way to ensure that your *entire classroom* becomes an "action zone" is to
   a. rely heavily on the use of horizontal rows
   b. call on students all around the classroom
   c. utilize a circle formation and circulate around the classroom
   d. conduct the majority of your instruction at special interest stations

8. A consequence of utilizing a *group consequences approach* for classroom management is that
   a. the whole group may suffer because of one individual
   b. hostility is usually generated between the two teams
   c. academic achievement improves greatly
   d. it produces few improvements in the behaviors listed in the good behavior rules

9. Which of the following is NOT an instance where a teacher would use a token reinforcement system?
   a. to reward successful students for academic achievement
   b. to encourage students who consistently fail
   c. to motivate students who are completely uninterested in their classwork
   d. to deal with a class that is out of control

10. The paraphrase rule encourages accurate communication because
    a. if students aren't paying attention, they have a second chance to hear the information
    b. many students will drop their negative attitudes when required to repeat what they first said
    c. many respond to what they think was said or meant, not necessarily to the speaker's intended message
    d. the teacher's tone of voice and facial expression may inhibit students from expressing what they really think

Answer Key

Application One: Whose Rules Are They?
1. elementary
2. elementary and secondary
3. elementary and secondary
4. secondary
5. secondary
6. elementary and secondary
7. elementary and secondary

Application Two: Categories of Penalties
1. presentation punishment
2. removal punishment
3. removal punishment but if it is a prolonged state of exclusion until the proper behavior is demonstrated then it is negative reinforcement
4. presentation punishment (unless they like to write, in which case it is positive reinforcement)
5. presentation punishment (because you are presented with an undesirable detention) This could also be removal punishment in that you are losing your free-time due to the detention

6. presentation punishment (unless you like to go the principal's office and the it is positive reinforcement. I taught at a school for high risk students. We couldn't understand why there was such an increase in knife usage because violators were taken to the principal's office. Then we found out that the principal was giving them cookies and a fatherly talk (He was an ex-priest). Needless to say, we dealt with knife episodes by ourselves from then on.
7. presentation punishment (although this is done in support of the student, most students would perceive this as presentation punishment)

Application Three: Identifying Classroom Arrangements

A poor arrangement for large-group discussion _____ (horizontal rows) permit students to work more easily in pairs. _____ (horizontal rows) are also useful for independent seatwork and for teacher, student, or media presentations.   The two best approaches for student interaction are _____ (clusters of four) or _____ (circle arrangements). _____ (circles) are useful for discussion but still allow for independent seatwork. _____ (clusters) permit students to talk, help one another, share materials, and work on group tasks. The _____ (fishbowl) where students sit close together near the focus of attention should be used only for short time periods because it is not comfortable and can lead to discipline problems.

Application Four: Teacher-Student Owned Problems
1. student
2. shared
3. teacher
4. student
5. teacher
6. student

Application Five: Key Terms and Definitions

Key Terms and Definitions

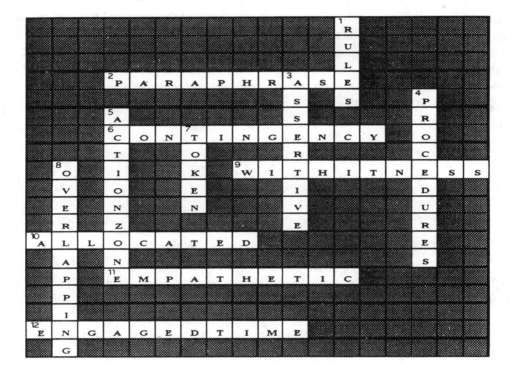

Essay Questions:

1. Rather than engage in a public power struggle in front of the class where you have the potentiality of losing and appearing out of control in front of your class, it is best not to repeatedly tell him to take his seat. After the first time that you tell him to sit down and he refuses, you should change your strategy. Tell him to wait out in the hall and you will join him for a private talk as soon as you get the rest of the class started on a project. If he refuses to comply, send another student to the office for assistance so that you do not leave your class unattended. Whenever possible, try to defuse this type of situation as quickly as possible, but remember to stay calm and always stay in control, especially since the rest of the class is witnessing your ability to manage the problem.

2. Opponents of assertive discipline argue that it is a demeaning approach that utilizes threat tactics and public humiliation as a means for controlling students' behaviors. It is suggested that after a student's name is recorded on the board many times, the parents are informed and if the child's problem stems from a dysfunctional family, then what purposes have actually been served. It is argued that assertive discipline does nothing to enhance student self-esteem, self-worth, or responsibility and does not teach students the reasons behind moral behaviors, only that they should behave in a certain way because it is the rule. Proponents of the approach report that 78 to 97 percent of 8,700 teachers saw improvements in student behavior as a result of using the approach. Canter suggests that it is through making choices and learning to accept the consequences, that students learn to develop self-worth and responsibility. Others have suggested that it is the improper implementation of the approach that has given assertive discipline a bad name in some camps

Multiple Choice:
1. b   2. a   3. c   4. a   5. d   6. d   7. c   8. a   9. a   10. c

<u>Chapter Thirteen</u>

Teaching for Learning

"A teacher affects eternity."
Henry Brooke Adams

The seed of classroom instruction and learning is teacher planning. This has become an area of great interest to educational researchers. Their findings reveal:

- Planning influences what students will learn--planning transforms time and materials into activities, assignments, and tasks for students
- Teachers must plan on several levels and all levels must be coordinated with one another--by the term, year, month, week, day
- Plans reduce uncertainty in teaching--yet they should be flexible and not rigid scripts
- To plan creatively and flexibly, teachers need wide-ranging knowledge about:
    1. students--their interests and abilities
    2. subjects being taught
    3. alternative ways to teach and assess understanding
    4. working with groups
    5. expectations and limitations of school and community
    6. how to apply and adapt materials and texts
    7. how to combine all of the above into meaningful activities
- There is no one model for effective planning--it is a creative problem-solving process

Flexible and Creative Plans Using Taxonomies

Many years ago, a group of experts lead by Benjamin Bloom examined educational objectives and divided them into three domains: affective, cognitive, and psychomotor. These objectives comprised a **taxonomy.**

Taxonomy: Classification system. **Example:** Bloom's taxonomy for the **cognitive domain** can be seen on the next page.

Cognitive Domain: In Bloom's taxonomy, memory and reasoning objectives.

Bloom's Taxonomy for the Cognitive Domain		
Objectives	**Description of Process**	**Examples of Processes**
1. Knowledge	remembering, recognizing without necessarily understanding, using or changing it	How many ounces in a pound....................... What is the possessive rule............................. Define algorithm..
2. Comprehension	understanding the material without necessarily relating it to anything else	Why convert unlike fractions....................... Define a mammal... Explain photosynthesis...................................
3. Application	using a general concept to solve a particular problem	Using volume, figure amount of sandbox sand.. Construct a geometric figure that..................... Conjugate these verbs......................................
4. Analysis	breaking something down into its parts	Analyze the properties of H2O....................... The Roman empire fell because....................... Causal factors of gang violence are................
5. Synthesis	creating something new by combing different ideas	Combine household items for your art project... Reggae is a blend of .... Biology plus philosophy equal Piaget's theory..
6. Evaluation	judging the value of materials or methods as they might be	Are basals or whole language better................... How can we cheaply reduce pollution .... Which form of classroom management.............

Educators have commonly thought that these objectives are hierarchical, each skill building on the preceding ones, but this is not always so. Knowledge and comprehension are often thought of as *lower level* objectives and the other objectives fall into the *higher level* category. These objectives are useful in planning assessments. Knowledge-level objectives, for example can be measured by true-false, short answer, or multiple choice tests. For measuring synthesis however, reports, projects, and portfolios may be more appropriate.

Affective Domain: Emotional objectives. **Example:** Listed below are basic objectives from the emotional domain.
1. Receiving: Being aware of or attending to something in the environment.
2. Responding: Showing some new behavior as a result of experience.
3. Valuing: Showing some definite involvement or commitment.
4. Organization: Integrating a new value into your general set of values, giving it some ranking among your general priorities.

5. Characterization by value: Acting consistently with the new value.

These objectives are very general and if you were to write affective objectives you would have to specifically state what your students are doing when (for example), *receiving*: the kindergarten students will demonstrate awareness of sharing versus selfish behaviors.

Psychomotor Domain: Physical ability objectives. **Example:** The students will demonstrate proficiency in writing the circular letters from the alphabet, in cursive.

These taxonomies range from the simplest perceptions and reflex actions to skilled creative movements. To assess student performance, you would ask them to demonstrate the skill and then using a rating scale, assess levels of proficiency.

Application One: Assessment Statements for Bloom's Cognitive Objectives

Read the following examples that might be used to assess student performance. Determine which objective of Bloom's Cognitive taxonomy is being addressed. Check your responses in the answer key.

_____ 1. Compare and contrast enrichment versus acceleration in terms of readiness, academic benefits, and social and emotional adjustment for precocious youth.

_____ 2. Explain what is meant by the melting pot philosophy.

_____ 3. What is the associative rule of multiplication?

_____ 4. Solve the geometric proofs by utilizing the appropriate theorems.

_____ 5. Read the following passage and diagram the sentences found there.

_____ 6. Generate a theory of adolescent purchasing practices from observations of mall behaviors, questionnaires, and personal interviews.

Planning From a Constructivist Perspective

Traditionally, the sole responsibility for planning has been the teachers', but that is changing with the **constructivist approach.** Here, the students and the teacher work together to plan activities, content, and approaches that will ultimately achieve the teacher's global goals.

Perrone suggests that the students and teachers try to identify ideas, themes, and issues that will provide understanding of the subject matter. Perrone suggests the use of a topic map as a way of thinking about how the theme can generate learning and understanding and as a guide, help students and teachers to identify activities, materials, projects and performances that will support the development of the students' understanding and abilities. The focus is not so much on students' products as on the *process* of learning and thinking behind the products.

Today, themes and integration across subject areas, guide the planning and designing of units. In a previous chapter, I mentioned a project at the university that examined the reclamation of Paradise Creek, polluted by fertilizer and insecticide run-off from the wheat fields. Students and teachers worked to design a project that would integrate knowledge of ecology, natural, life and chemical sciences, computer skills, and writing to name a few.

Constructivist Approach: View that emphasizes the active role of the learner in building understanding and making sense of information.

With the constructivist approach, assessment differs from the traditional paper-and-pencil approach and may include such *authentic assessments* as portfolios, exhibitions, demonstrations, and performances.

Teaching: Whole Group and Directive

How does one turn objectives into action and active learning in the classroom? First, let's explore the most basic way to transmit knowledge in the classroom; **lecturing.**

Lecturing: Organized explanation of a topic by a teacher.

There are a variety of ways to lecture in the classroom. More lecturing will occur at higher educational levels than in elementary school. Lectures are particularly efficient for transmitting large amounts of organized knowledge in a short amount of time. Lectures are good for:
- introducing new topics
- giving background information
- motivating students to learn more on their own
- helping students to listen accurately and critically
- allowing teachers to make on the spot assessments of students comprehension and address confusion
- lower-level cognitive and affective objectives

Scripted Cooperation: is one way of incorporating active learning into lectures by asking students (during the presentation or lecture) to work in pairs with one student serving as the summarizer while the other student critiques the summary. This gives students the chance to check their understanding, organize their thinking, and translate ideas into their own words.

Consistent with Ausubel's expository method from the previous chapter, phases of lecturing should include (1) *preparation* for learning: state objectives, rationale, advanced organizers, (2) *present* the material from simpler to complex understandings using visual aids, and (3) *review learning* and connect to students' knowledge and experiences.

The lecture method has disadvantages in that some students listen for only for a few minutes and then they tune you out. Furthermore, all of the cognitive work has been done for the students requiring nothing more than a passive mode of learning. Also the pace of learning is set by the instructor but students comprehend and learn at different paces.

Teaching for Learning

Recitation: Format of teacher questioning, student response, and teacher feedback. A typical recitation pattern consists of the following:
- *structure:* setting the framework
- *solicitation:* asking questions
- *reaction:* praising, correcting, and expanding

Regarding solicitation or asking questions, educators ask both high-and low-level questions and research indicates that both are effective. Simple questions that allow for a high percentage of correct responses, are better for younger and lower-ability students. Harder questions at both higher and lower levels, with more critical feedback, are better for high-ability students. Questions should also be both **divergent** and **convergent.**

Convergent Questions: Questions that have a single correct answer. **Example:** In what year did Columbus discover America?

Divergent Questions: Questions that have no single correct answer. **Example:** In what ways can we work toward eliminating air pollution?

Application Two: Questions and Answers

Read the following statements regarding question and answer practices in the classroom. Indicate whether the statements are TRUE or FALSE as shown by research. Change the false statements to make them true. Check your responses in the answer key.

1. In order to promote learning, students need to be given time to reflect upon questions.
_____

2. Some researchers have shown that high school teachers ask an average of 395 questions per day.
_____

3. Researchers have shown that teachers wait an average of only one second for students to answer.
_____

4. Students are generally more confident in their answers when teachers wait a full minute before calling a student to answer
_____

5. When teachers wait 3 to 5 seconds before calling on a student to answer, students tend to give longer answers. _____

6. When your questions are met with blank stares, provide your students with the answer and move on.
_____

---

7. When teachers wait 3 to 5 seconds before calling on a student to answer, students' comments involving analysis, synthesis, inference, and speculation tend to increase.

---

8. Extending wait time enhances learning even at the university level.

---

9. It is best to call on volunteers to get a good idea about how well students understand the material.

---

10. When teachers wait 3 to 5 seconds before calling on a student to answer, students are more likely to participate, ask questions, and volunteer appropriate answers.

---

11. The most common teacher reaction to student response (75% of the time) is "OK" or "Uh-huh."

---

12. If the student's answer is correct but hesitant, give the student feedback *why* the answer is correct.

---

13. If the student's answer is wrong, but the student has made an honest attempt, praise the attempt and ask someone else to respond.

---

14. If the student's wrong response is silly or careless, it is better to correct the response and go on.

A clearly overused classroom technique is **seatwork.** One study found that American elementary students spend 51% of mathematics time in school working alone, while Japanese students spend 26% and Taiwanese students spend only 9 %. Seatwork should follow a lesson, provide students with supervised practice, and not become the primary mode of instruction. Whereas research has indicated that there exists a strong positive correlation between the amount of homework assigned and student grades, all too often, too much busywork is assigned that does not meet objectives nor effectively contribute to learning.

Seatwork: Independent classroom work.

To benefit from seatwork and or homework, students must stay involved, be held accountable for completing work correctly, be offered feedback and guidance and in the case of homework, the scaffolding should come from the parents.

Teaching: Small Group and Student-Centered

Implementation of the constructivist approach to teaching requires that the teacher capitalize on the student's natural ways of thinking about the subject matter and also begin with the student's current level of understanding. Other student centered approaches are: **group discussion, humanistic education,** and **technology.**

Group Discussions: Conversations in which the teacher does not have the dominant role; students pose and answer their own questions. There are many advantages to group discussions:
- students are directly involved and have the chance to participate
- students learn to express themselves clearly, to justify opinions, to tolerate different views
- provides students with the opportunity to ask for clarification, examine their own thinking, follow personal interests, and assume responsibility for taking leadership roles
- students are helped to evaluate ideas and synthesize personal viewpoints
- discussions are useful when students are trying to understand difficult concepts

Disadvantages to group discussions are:
- unpredictable and may digress into exchanges of ignorance
- some members of the group may have difficulty participating
- teachers must ensure group members possess background knowledge on which to base the discussion large groups may be unwieldy and some people may dominate the conversation

Humanistic Education

Consistent with the constructivist approach and student-centered teaching many psychologists and educators suggest that each individual constructs his or her own reality and that education should stress the importance of feelings, open communication, and the value of every student. This is the **humanistic view.**

Humanistic View: An approach to motivation that emphasizes personal freedom, choice, self-determination, and striving for personal growth.

Computer Technology

One of the most recent innovations to student-centered teaching strategies are computers and instructional technology. There are three main roles of computers in schools:
- *learning environments*: to help students learn content and problem solving skills
- *tools*: to help students and teachers with such tasks as word processing, computing, locating and managing information, doing graphics or programming computers
- *tutees*: the student teaches the computer what to do through programming using BASIC, LOGO, Pascal or some other language

An invaluable use of computer technology for education, places students in a problem solving scenario similar to what they would encounter in real life called **computer simulations** and **microworlds.**

Computer Simulations: Simplified versions of situations that the student would encounter in real life. **Example:** *SimCity* is one such program that allows students to plan and build cities from the ground up, complete with power, transportation, water systems, governmental issues, residences, etc.

Microworlds: Small but complete parts of the environments that encourage discovery through exploration. Working in the environments, students construct knowledge as they explore and experiment.

Computer assisted instruction has been shown to be moderately more effective than conventional methods. When used effectively, computers can provide back-up or extended instruction and allow students to get help privately. Not only can computers be used individually but also by small-groups and large-groups in cooperative learning exercises. An alternative to computer technology is video technology. Video-based learning environments provide students with complex and life-like problem solving environments. One problem based approach is called **anchored instruction.**

Anchored Instruction: The anchor is an interesting situation that provides a focus--a reason for setting goals, planning, and using mathematical tools to solve problems. The intended outcome is to develop knowledge that is useful and flexible, not inert.

Successful Teaching: Focus on the Teacher

Although research in this area is incomplete, evidence suggests that three characteristics of effective teachers are knowledge, clarity, and warmth.

1. Knowledge: Teacher's knowledge of facts and concepts is not directly related to student learning, however, teachers who know more may make clearer presentations and recognize student difficulties more readily. Therefore, it is believed that knowledge is necessary but not sufficient for effective teaching because being more knowledgeable helps teachers be clearer and more organized.

2. Organization and Clarity: Teachers who provide clear presentations and explanations tend to have students who learn more and who rate their teachers more positively. For greater clarity:
* try to anticipate students' problems with the material
* have definitions ready for new terms and prepare examples for concepts; think of analogies
* organize the lesson in a logical sequence and include checkpoints to ensure comprehension
* plan a clear introduction to the lesson; what the students will learn and how they'll approach it
* during the lesson, make clear connections between facts using **explanatory links**
* stick with your plan, use familiar words, don't digress, and signal transitions to new topics

Explanatory Links: Words such as *because, therefore, consequentially,* used to connect facts and concepts. Explanatory links tie ideas together and make them easier to learn. **Example:** Because the sun lines up with satellite dishes during the month of March, we experience disturbance to our television picture.

3. Warmth and Enthusiasm: Research has found that ratings of teacher enthusiasm for their subject are correlated with student achievement gains. Warmth, friendliness, and understanding are the teacher traits most strongly related to student attitudes.

Much of the research that examined effective instruction from the 1970s and 1980s pointed toward a teaching model of **direct instruction** (discussed in chapter nine) that embraces Rosenshine and Steven's (1986) six *Teaching Functions*. Key components to effective instruction emphasizes teaching lessons that help students to perceive links among main ideas, well-organized presentations, clear explanations, guided practice, and reviews. If done well, direct instruction can be a resource that helps students to construct understanding.

Successful Understanding: Focus on the Student

Some researchers have examined *what the students are doing* and found that many different teaching approaches and activities can be effective if the activities create environments in which students think deeply. Studies conducted in New Zealand reported three clusters of factors that must come together for learning to be strong and enduring.
1. The student must have the personal, social, and technical *resources* to learn
2. The student must have many *opportunities* to learn.
3. The student must take *advantage of these resources and opportunities.*

If students pay attention, become involved in activities and express an understanding, they can connect the newly learned representations to related information in semantic memory. If these representations are integrated and connected, then the ideas become established in long term memory.

Effective learning must focus on what teachers think, say, and do and what their students think, say, and do. Regardless of whether you are using traditional teacher-centered direct instruction or the open constructivist method or a combination of both, teachers must match instructional methods to learning goals.

Application Three: Key Terms and Definitions

To check your comprehension, see if you can come up with terms to match the definitions below. Some of the terms may have two words but there is no space in between the words. Check your responses in the answer key.

Clues

Down:
2. The domain from Bloom's taxonomy dealing with memory and reasoning objectives
3. Organized explanation of a topic by a teacher
5. A motivational approach that emphasizes personal freedom, choice, self-determination, and striving for personal growth
7. Questions that have no single correct answer

Across:
1. Format of teacher questioning, student response, and teacher feedback
4. Independent classroom work
6. An instructional approach tailored to individual students' needs, interests, abilities, and work pace.
8. Schools in which students are grouped by activity rather than by age
9. Classification system
10. The domain from Bloom's taxonomy dealing with emotional objectives
11. Questions that have a single correct answer

Key Terms and Definitions

232

Figure 13.1

APA's LEARNER-CENTERED PSYCHOLOGICAL PRINCIPLES

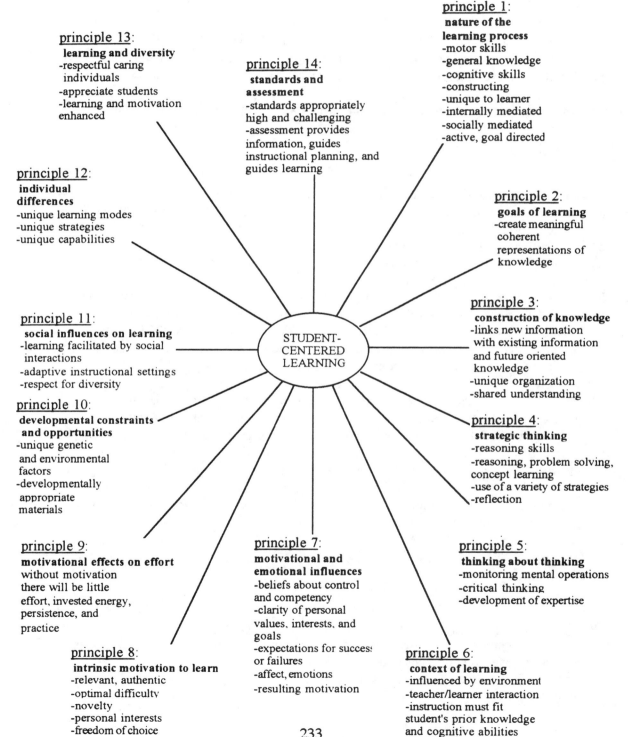

principle 13:
learning and diversity
-respectful caring
individuals
-appreciate students
-learning and motivation
enhanced

principle 14:
standards and assessment
-standards appropriately
high and challenging
-assessment provides
information, guides
instructional planning, and
guides learning

principle 1:
nature of the learning process
-motor skills
-general knowledge
-cognitive skills
-constructing
-unique to learner
-internally mediated
-socially mediated
-active, goal directed

principle 12:
individual differences
-unique learning modes
-unique strategies
-unique capabilities

principle 2:
goals of learning
-create meaningful
coherent
representations of
knowledge

principle 11:
social influences on learning
-learning facilitated by social
interactions
-adaptive instructional settings
-respect for diversity

principle 3:
construction of knowledge
-links new information
with existing information
and future oriented
knowledge
-unique organization
-shared understanding

STUDENT-CENTERED LEARNING

principle 10:
developmental constraints and opportunities
-unique genetic
and environmental
factors
-developmentally
appropriate
materials

principle 4:
strategic thinking
-reasoning skills
-reasoning, problem solving,
concept learning
-use of a variety of strategies
-reflection

principle 9:
motivational effects on effort
without motivation
there will be little
effort, invested energy,
persistence, and
practice

principle 7:
motivational and emotional influences
-beliefs about control
and competency
-clarity of personal
values, interests, and
goals
-expectations for success
or failures
-affect, emotions
-resulting motivation

principle 5:
thinking about thinking
-monitoring mental operations
-critical thinking
-development of expertise

principle 8:
intrinsic motivation to learn
-relevant, authentic
-optimal difficulty
-novelty
-personal interests
-freedom of choice

principle 6:
context of learning
-influenced by environment
-teacher/learner interaction
-instruction must fit
student's prior knowledge
and cognitive abilities

233

Practice Tests

Essay Questions

1. Educators debate the best practices for reaching students who are to be considered "at-risk" or in jeopardy of academic failure. What are some of the teaching practices that are shown by research to be effective and why are these methods criticized by other educators and psychologists?

2. Discuss ways that teacher planning can influence how and what the students learn in the classroom?

Multiple Choice

1. Regarding instructional planning, which of the following is most important?
   a. teachers should "overplan" and fill every minute so there is no "dead-air" in instruction
   b. teachers should stick to their plans no matter what, because they guide instruction
   c. unit planning with a specific goal in mind
   d. that teachers select a model of planning, stay with it, and refine it over time

2. Which of the following statements reflects the *organization level* of the affective domain?
   a. I think I'll attend the Ultimate Kick-Boxing Tournament when it comes to town
   b. I think I might like to attend the introductory Tai Kenpo class to see if I like it
   c. I'm enrolling in Tai Kenpo and arranging my schedule so that I can attend class every Monday
   d. I' m going to enter the kick-boxing tournament now that I have my black belt

3. The best way to evaluate a student's performance in the psychomotor domain is to
   a. grade on effort and perseverance since this domain addresses inherited abilities
   b. observe and rate the student's proficiency in producing a product or performing a skill
   c. select a panel of unbiased judges as in professional competitions
   d. allow the students to rate their own performances

4. According to your text, an appropriate instructional method for communicating a large amount of material to many students in a short amount of time is
   a. lecture
   b. recitation
   c. questioning
   d. seatwork

5. Which of the following is consistent with the constructivist approach
   a. teachers and students together make decisions about content, activities, and approaches
   b. teacher has overarching goals that guide planning
   c. the focus is on students' processes of learning and thinking
   d. all of the above

6. A key component to effective seatwork within the classroom is
   a. careful monitoring to ensure that students are not copying each others' work
   b. having students work independently so that you can spend the majority of your time with the one or two students who require extra help
   c. ensuring that students know what to do if they need help
   d. requiring that students spend no more than 10 minutes on task or they will lose interest

7. In which of the following situations would lecture be more appropriate than the constructivist approach?
   a. fostering a complete understanding of the theory of relativity
   b. learning which primary colors combine to create secondary colors
   c. learning the average amount of chocolate chips in a bag of store-bought cookies
   d. understanding the relative position of plants, crickets, and snakes within the food chain

8. Which of the following is one of the shortcomings of direct instruction?
   a. a direct instruction lesson cannot be a resource that students use to construct understanding
   b. direct instruction cannot ensure that students understand
   c. direct instruction cannot help students perceive connections among ideas
   d. direct instruction prevents teachers from addressing misconceptions

9. Group discussions are most appropriate when
   a. students are attempting to evaluate ideas and synthesize personal viewpoints
   b. students are discussing common sense issues with little chance of misconceptions
   c. when teachers wish to pose questions and probe for information
   d. when some members have difficulty participating and need encouragement

10. Which of the following is NOT a component of the recitation format?
    a. teacher questioning
    b. student response
    c. teacher reaction such as praising, correcting, and expanding
    d. individualized seatwork

Answer Key

Application One: Assessment Statements for Bloom's Cognitive Objectives
1. evaluation
2. comprehension
3. knowledge
4. application
5. analysis
6. synthesis

Application Two: Questions and Answers
1. true
2. true
3. true

Teaching for Learning

4. false--teachers should have a 3 to 5 second wait time
5. true
6. false--rephrase the question or ask if anyone can explain the confusion
7. true
8. false--extending wait time does not affect learning in university classes
9. false--calling only on volunteers may create misconceptions about how well students understand the material
10. true
11. false--"OK" or "uh-huh" occurs about 50% of the time
12. true
13. false--you should probe for more information, give clues, simplify the question, review the previous steps, or reteach the material
14. true

Application Three:
Key Terms and Definitions

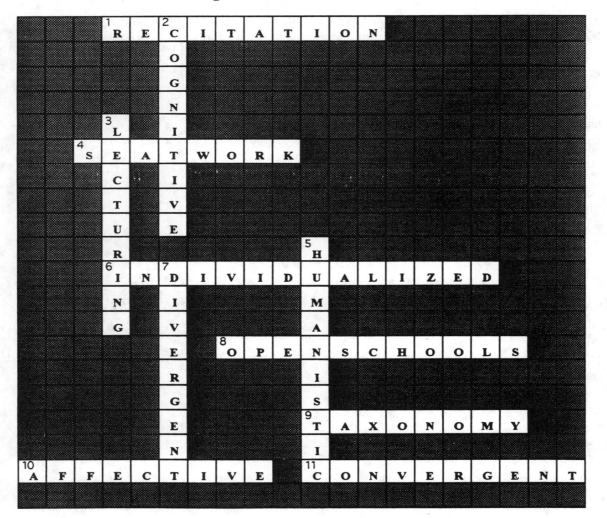

Essay Questions:

1. Research on effective teachers of low achievers has identified strategies consistent with direct instruction as beneficial to "at-risk" students. These basic approaches, i.e., break instruction into small steps, cover material thoroughly and at a moderate pace, give practice, feedback, praise, use whole group, avoid independent work, and emphasize short, frequent paper-and-pencil exercises, NOT games, discovery learning, or interest centers, which are less helpful for learning. Other effective approaches are to keep the level of difficulty consonant with guaranteeing success, ask convergent questions (only one answer), and avoid open-ended questions. The opponents of direct instruction object to these practices on the premise that they address only the lower level objectives from Bloom's taxonomy and that at-risk students are underestimated, unchallenged, and deprived of a meaningful motivating context for learning or for employing the skills that they have been taught. Opponents suggest that better approaches would be to provide scaffolding, embed basic skills within more challenging, authentic tasks, model powerful thinking strategies, and encourage multiple approaches to academic tasks. Furthermore, keep the level of the tasks high enough that the purpose of the task is apparent and makes sense to the student.

2. Planning takes the time that a teacher has available to him or her and transforms it into amount of classroom instruction, activities, assignments, and tasks for the day. Some teachers, especially at the elementary level, may have preferences or strengths for one subject area over another. I know of one teacher who feels weak in the artistic realm and as a result, her students spend little time in artistic endeavors yet great amounts of time in history-related activities, her personal favorite. These students will be much stronger in history than in art. The knowledge levels of educators plays a crucial role in determining planning also. The plans of beginning teachers sometimes don't work because they lack knowledge about the students or the subject. They may not know students' interests and abilities, how long it will take students to complete activities, or how to respond when asked for an explanation when they aren't real strong in a subject area. Effective planning is something that comes with experience.

Multiple Choice:
1. c   2. c   3. b   4. a   5. d   6. c   7. a   8. b   9. a   10. d

Chapter Fourteen

Standardized Testing

"All things are to be examined and called into question There are no limits set to thought."
Edith Hamilton

To know whether we have successfully attained our teaching goals and whether our students have successfully achieved their learning goals, we must make judgments about the quality of learning that has occurred. These judgments are called **evaluations.**

Evaluation: Decision making about student performance and about appropriate teaching strategies. **Example:** Do my first grade reading students benefit more from basals or a whole language approach?

When we take an evaluation and express it as a number for reference purposes, we call it a **measurement.**

Measurement: An evaluation expressed in quantitative (number) terms. **Example:** On her statistics exam, Sheila scored an 88 which was in the 95th percentile for her class.

Measurements mean nothing without a reference point against which to compare. Your weight on the scale means nothing without comparing it to height/weight charts for someone your age and body build, or you could compare it to yesterday's weight, or to the weight you would like to attain (or lose). So measurements mean nothing without comparing them to something else and in education we commonly make two kinds of comparisons; **norm-referenced** and **criterion-referenced.**

Norm-Referenced Testing: Testing in which scores are compared with the average performance of others. **Example:** Juanita scored in the top 5% of her swimming class. Jamie's reading score is average for his honors class but superior to national scores for someone his age.

In norm-referenced testing, we can find a student's relative standing by comparing her or his performance to the average performance of a **norm group.**

Norm Group: A group whose average score serves as a standard for evaluating any student's score on a test. **Example:** When you take a college entrance exam, your score is compared to other students across the nation who are also hoping to enter college. Regardless of the actual scores, the top students will have the best chance to pick the colleges of their choice.

There are three types of norm groups in education: class, district, or national. Listed below are some advantages to norm-referenced tests.

1. Norm-referenced tests are good for covering a wide range of general objectives.

Standardized Testing

2. Norm-referenced tests are useful for measuring the overall achievement of students who have come to understand complex material by different routes.
3. Norm-referenced tests are useful for selecting the top candidates when only a few can be admitted to the program.

Norm-referenced measurements also have their limitations.

1. Knowing students' percentiles or ranks does not tell us what they know or can do. Knowing that Juanita is the top swimmer in her class does not tell us how well she can swim.
2. Norm-referenced tests are not appropriate for measuring affective and psychomotor objectives.
3. Norm-referenced tests foster competition and comparison of scores and may be damaging to the self-esteem of low achievers.

The second type of comparison of test scores is called **criterion-referenced testing.**

Criterion-Referenced Testing: Testing in which scores are compared to a set performance standard. Criterion referenced tests measure the mastery of very specific objectives. **Example:** We don't care that Juanita is the top swimmer in her class (norm-referenced). We want to know whether she has mastered the criterion of being able to swim 10 laps and tread water for fifteen minutes. Jamie may have to meet the criterion of getting 90 out of 100 reading questions correct if he wants to maintain his "A" in reading.

Some of the advantages of criterion-referenced testing are listed below.

1. Teachers know exactly what a student can and cannot do, by how well they have mastered the objectives.
2. When teaching basic skills, it is more important to know that a child has mastered the basics versus knowing where that child stands relative to other students.
3. Some standards for performance must be set at 100%, eg. driving ability, how to operate a skill-saw, knowledge of the alphabet.

Criterion-referenced tests also have their limitations.

1. Many subjects cannot be broken down into a specific set of objectives.
2. Standards may be arbitrary; is one point difference that important in setting standards?
3. It may important to know how others are doing nationally if your criteria are too low and the performances that you are measuring as "As" might only be "Cs" nationally.

Application One: Criterion or Norm-Referenced?

Read the following evaluation situations and determine whether it is criterion or norm-referenced. Check your responses in the answer key.

1. Peggy's reading comprehension score far exceeds the national average for her age group. _____

2. Jack got 9 out of 10 throws in the basketball hoop. _____

3. George can jump 15 feet in the long jump. _____

4. Ms. Duplessey's morning French class has a higher average achievement score than the afternoon class. _____

5. Rebecca's painting won the blue ribbon at the county fair. _____

6. Franklin can type 45 words per minute. _____

7. Our baseball team won the league championship. _____

8. Tim got 560 verbal and 600 math on his SATs. _____

9. Jerome got a 90 on his chemistry test. _____

10. Hamako can recite every line of the Gettysburg Address with no errors. _____

What Do Test Scores Mean?

Everyday, more than one million **standardized tests** are administered in schools throughout this country. Most are norm-referenced.

Standardized Tests: Tests given, usually nationwide, under uniform conditions and scored according to uniform procedures.

All students all over the country are supposedly tested according to the same conditions. But before your students are administered the test, the test will be piloted on a **norming sample.**

Norming Sample: Large sample of students serving as a comparison group for scoring standardized tests.

Whether your students have scores from standardized tests or classroom made tests, there are a variety of ways that their scores can be represented. The first of these is called a **frequency distribution.**

Standardized Testing

Frequency Distribution: Record showing how many scores fall into set groups. **Example:** See the following example of a frequency distribution.

Application Two: Constructing a Frequency Distribution

Examine the distribution of students' scores in your classroom. Construct a frequency distribution showing how many students got each score. The first few scores have been done for you. Of course, in real life, your classes may be much larger. Check your responses in the answer key.

Distribution of Grades			Frequency Distribution	
Students	Math Scores		Math Scores	Frequencies
Adam Brock	83		100	0
Pam Castle	84		99	0
Tim Crow	98		98	2
Bob Drew	90		97	
Sue Grahm	98		96	
Jim Gregory	78		95	
Ken Harris	85		94	
Karen Howe	82		93	
John Jackson	86		92	
Pat Johnson	79		91	
Kwan Lee	89		90	
Brad Lipton	85		89	
Sam Moore	85		88	
Kip Mumby	86		87	
Jan Neils	82		86	
Carrie Paul	87		85	
Jan Ramie	84		84	
Lynn Reed	79		83	
Kim Rice	81		82	
Sara Sands	83		81	
Tara Trask	80		80	
Jill Vale	93		79	
Tom White	84		78	

Standardized Testing

The information from a frequency distribution can also be represented pictorially or in the form of a **histogram.**

Histogram: Bar graph of a frequency distribution.

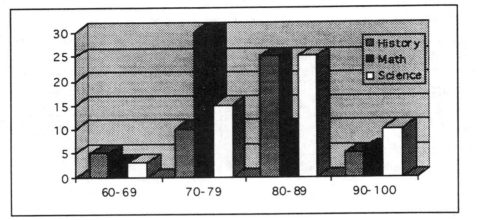

Measures of Central Tendency

When we want to describe the typical or average scores of our students, we may talk about **measures of central tendency.**

Central Tendency: Typical score for a group of scores. There are three measures of central tendency; the **mean, median,** and **mode.**

Mean: Arithmetical average **Example:** You add all of the scores together and divide by the number of scores. The formula for finding the mean is as follows:

$\sum$=the sum of
N=the number of scores
X=a student's score

Therefore, to find the mean (written as $\overline{X}$) use this formula: $\overline{X} = \dfrac{\sum X}{N}$

Median: Middle score in a group of ranked scores. **Example:** In the following ranked array of scores, the median is the middle score or "75." 70. 72, 72, 73, 75, 77, 79, 81, 81

Mode: Most frequently occurring score. **Example:** In the following array, the mode is "81."
75, 75, 78, 79, 80, 81, 81, 81, 81, 82, 82, 83, 84, 86

Standardized Testing

Sometimes, more than one score occurs with the same frequency as another score and both scores occur more than any other score. This signifies a **bimodal distribution.**

Bimodal Distribution: Frequency distribution with two modes. **Example:** In the following distribution, the two modes are "83" and "88." 79. 80, 82, 83, 83, 83, 84, 86, 88, 88, 88   Both 83 and 88 occur three times.

The measure of central tendency gives us just that; a central measure, an average measure, a middle measure, a typical measure. It gives us the best representation of that distribution of scores. If we want to know the typical performance of the students in our classes, we look to the measure of central tendency. But it doesn't tell us how the scores range or spread out from the mean. For example; the mean of the following distribution of scores (78, 82, 82, 82, 82, 84) is 82. But the mean of the following distribution of scores (40, 78, 90, 92, 94, 96) is also 82 and look at how different the scores are in each distribution. If we were to draw conclusions based only on the means, we really wouldn't have the whole picture. That is why it is also important that we examine the **standard deviation.**

Standard Deviation: Measure of how widely the scores vary from the mean. Scores that spread out further from the mean have greater **variability.**

Variability: Degree of difference or deviation from the mean. **Example:** The means from the two previous distributions are 82. The second distribution has scores that spread out further from the mean so we say that it has greater variability.

The Standard Deviation
The formula for calculating the standard deviation follows:

1. Calculate the mean of your scores (written as $\bar{\chi}$).

2. Subtract the mean from each score to find how far each score deviates from the mean. $(\chi - \bar{\chi})$

3. Square each difference to get rid of the negative signs. $(\chi - \bar{\chi})^2$

4. Add all of the squared differences. $\sum(\chi - \bar{\chi})^2$

5. Divide this total by the number of scores. $\dfrac{\sum(\chi - \bar{\chi})^2}{N}$

6. Find the square root and you will have the standard deviation. $\sqrt{\dfrac{\sum(\chi - \bar{\chi})^2}{N}}$

Standardized Testing

Knowing the mean and the standard deviation of a set of scores can tell us quite a bit of information. If the mean of a set of history test scores is 70 and the standard deviation is 4, and if you got a 78, then you know that you scored two standard deviations above the mean or in the 97.5% for your class. Refer to the normal distribution curve in your text to figure out the percentiles. But if the mean of a set of math test scores is 70 and the standard deviation is 8, and if you got a 78 on your math test, then in math you scored only one standard deviation above the mean, placing you at the 84% within your class. Your performance in math is good but you are even stronger in history relative to your classmates (this is assuming the performance levels in both classes are equivalent).

Standard deviations are very useful for helping us to understand test scores. Knowing the standard deviation tells us much more than just knowing the **range** of scores.

Range: Distance between the highest and the lowest score in a group.

Standard deviations are particularly helpful when the distribution of scores conforms to the **normal distribution** or the bell-shaped curve.

Normal Distribution: The most commonly occurring distribution, in which scores are distributed evenly around the mean. See your text for an example of a normal distribution. The normal distribution has certain properties:

- the mean, median, and mode are all the same score
- 68% of the scores are located within ± 1 standard deviation from the mean
- approximately 16% of the scores fall beyond one standard deviation on both ends of the distribution comprising the remaining 32% of the scores

Types of Scores

One kind of score reported from standardized tests is called a **percentile rank** score.

Percentile Rank: Percentage of those in the norming sample who scored at or below an individual's score. **Example:** If the mean from the norming sample is 500 (as it is with the SAT college entrance exam) and you got a score of 500, then you would be at the 50th percentile.

Another type of score tells us whether our students are performing at levels equivalent with other students their own age or **grade-equivalent.**

Grade-Equivalent Score: Measure of grade level based on comparison with norming samples from each grade. **Example:** If all of the sixth graders take a reading test and the average score is 44, and you score a 44, then on that reading test, you scored as well as the average sixth grader.

Often, we would like to make comparisons between scores achieved by students in different districts and on different tests and maybe even in different subject areas. But how are we to do this when tests and test conditions were not identical across test situations? It would be like comparing apples to oranges. Therefore, we have to transform or standardize our test scores by putting them in a common scale. **Example:** An analogy I give to my students deals with adding unlike fractions. If we want to add 1/4 to 1/3

Standardized Testing

then we have to put them in a common scale or give them a common denominator. In this case we would turn them both into twelfths and 1/4 would become 3/12 and 1/3 would become 4/12 and then we could add them resulting in 7/12. **Standard scores** do essentially the same thing with test scores. Common standard scores are **z scores** and **T scores**.

Standard Scores: Scores based on the standard deviation.

z Score: Standard score indicating the number of standard deviations a person's score is either above or below the mean. **Example:** If the mean on the test is 70 and the standard deviation is 4, and you scored a 78, then you are two standard deviations above the mean and you would have a z score of 2. If on another test, you also scored a 78, and the mean on that test was 70 but the standard deviation was 16, then you scored one-half of a standard deviation above the mean and your z score would be .5. If the mean was 70, and the standard deviation was 8 and you got a 62, well then you scored one standard deviation below the mean giving you a z score of -1. z scores can be positive (if you score above the mean) and negative (if you score below the mean) and they can also be decimals. The formula for a **z score** follows.

$$z = \frac{X - \bar{X}}{SD}$$

1. Take each student's score and from it, subtract the mean for that set of scores.
2. Divide the difference obtained in step 1 by the standard deviation for that group of scores.
3. Remember that z scores can be positive or negative, whole numbers or decimals.

Since it is often inconvenient to use decimals and/or negative numbers, we can perform one more score transformation called **T scores.**

T Scores: Standard score with a mean of 50 and a standard deviation of 10. A T score of 50 means an individual got an average score. Multipling the z score by 10 gets rid of the decimal and adding 50 to it, makes it a positive number. The formula for transforming z scores into T scores is written below.

$$T = 10(z) + 50$$

Standardized Testing

Figure 14.1

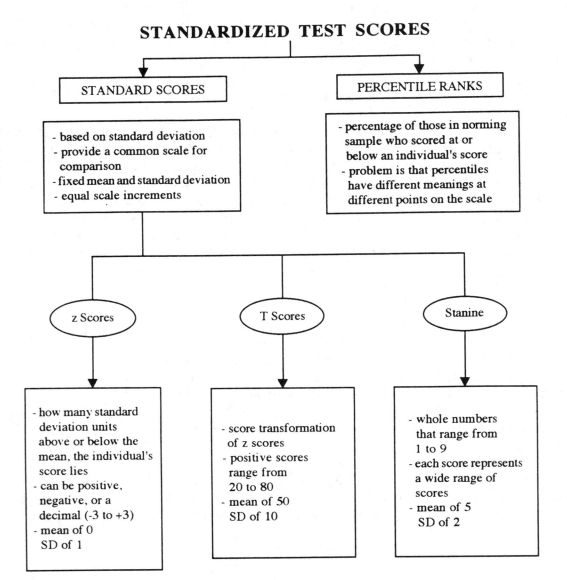

STANDARDIZED TEST SCORES

STANDARD SCORES

- based on standard deviation
- provide a common scale for comparison
- fixed mean and standard deviation
- equal scale increments

PERCENTILE RANKS

- percentage of those in norming sample who scored at or below an individual's score
- problem is that percentiles have different meanings at different points on the scale

z Scores

- how many standard deviation units above or below the mean, the individual's score lies
- can be positive, negative, or a decimal (-3 to +3)
- mean of 0 SD of 1

T Scores

- score transformation of z scores
- positive scores range from 20 to 80
- mean of 50 SD of 10

Stanine

- whole numbers that range from 1 to 9
- each score represents a wide range of scores
- mean of 5 SD of 2

Application Three: Calculating Standard Scores

Take the following students' scores from their exams and using the means and standard deviations from each test, calculate the z score and T score for each student.

Student	Math mean=80 SD=5	History mean=50 SD=10	English mean=34 SD=8
Todd	X=85	X=55	X=50
Stephanie	X=90	X=40	X=30
Carlos	X=80	X=60	X=42
Terri	X=70	X=65	X=38
Todd	z=	z=	z=
Stephanie	z=	z=	z=
Carlos	z=	z=	z=
Terri	z=	z=	z=
Todd	T=	T=	T=
Stephanie	T=	T=	T=
Carlos	T=	T=	T=
Terri	T=	T=	T=

One other widely used standard score method is called **stanine scores**. Developed and most widely used by the military, stanines comes from the name, standard nine.

Stanine Scores: Whole number scores from 1 to 9, each representing a wide range of raw scores. The mean is 5 and the standard deviation is 2.

Interpreting Test Scores

One of the most difficult challenges that educators face is understanding exactly what is meant by our students' scores. We must remember that test scores do not tell the whole story and that a score is just one sample of behavior. We must also consider the quality of our tests for assessing achievement and therefore we must consider two other factors regarding our tests; **reliability** and **validity.**

Reliability: Consistency of test results. **Example:** If you were to take a test one day and then, assuming you forgot no information nor checked answers with anyone, if you took it again, we would expect that your performance would be relatively consistent. There are three types of reliability:

1. Test-Retest Reliability--When you give the exact same test at two separate times and obtain consistent results.

Standardized Testing

2. Alternate Forms Reliability--Different but equivalent forms of a test that cover the same content area, eg. your ACT, SAT college boards. You get a different form each time you take it.

3. Split-Half Reliability--This yields a measure of internal consistency because you compare half of the test items with the other half (odd versus even numbered items).

Although we try to develop the most reliable tests possible, no test is without its flaws. Sometimes test conditions are imperfect, or maybe you don't feel well, or maybe you devoted most of your study time to the questions that aren't on the test. If we were able to test you repeatedly and then average your scores over time, we would probably get the best idea of what you really know and this is called the **true score.**

True Score: Hypothetical average of all of an individual's scores if repeated testing under ideal conditions were possible.

However, since you are tested only once, we tend to think of your scores as being part true score and part error score, eg., you didn't feel well so your test score doesn't really reflect what you know. Test developers and statisticians take this error component into consideration when they calculate the **standard error of measurement.**

Standard Error of Measurement: Hypothetical estimate of variation in scores if testing were repeated. A reliable test has a small standard error of measurement.

When interpreting test scores, teachers also must take into consideration this margin of error. Teachers should never formulate opinions about student ability by the exact score a student obtains. Many test companies will report students scores within a band of likely scores called **confidence intervals.**

Confidence Intervals: Range of scores within which an individual's true score is likely to fall.

The next factor that must be considered once we have established that our test is reliable is whether or not the test measures what it is supposed to measure and nothing else. This is called **validity.**

Validity: Degree to which a test measures what it is intended to measure. **Example:** We know that when we use a thermometer, it will measure temperature and nothing else. It is a valid instrument. There are three types of validity related evidence that we may try to gather with the first having the greatest impact for the classroom teacher.

1. Content-Related Validity Evidence--This is where we must ask ourselves if our test items reflect the content that was addressed in class and in the texts.

2. Criterion-Related Validity Evidence--This is an indicator of how well we can predict performance on a criterion on the basis of a prior measure. There is good criterion validity between the PSAT and the SAT.

3. Construct-Related Validity Evidence--This addresses some psychological construct or characteristic such as IQ or motivation. This evidence is gathered over years to determine patterns within the contruct being measured.

Content validity is an important issue when interpreting the scores from teacher made tests. I know of a teacher who would deduct points from students' science tests when they had inaccurate dates at the top of their papers. Given this situation, you have to question what their science scores mean. It is not a valid representation of science achievement.

Types of Standardized Tests

The most common standardized tests administered to students are **achievement tests.**

Achievement Tests: Standardized tests measuring how much students have learned in a given content area.

These tests can be given to groups or to individuals and in any subject area. As teachers you will encounter a wide variety of norm-referenced achievement tests. To aid teachers with information from the test results, test publishers will usually provide teachers with individual profiles for each student showing scores on subtests. These scores may be presented in a variety of ways such as raw scores, stanine scores, grade-equivalent scores, national percentile scores, scale scores, and the range in which the student's score is likely to fall. If a student is experiencing difficulty within subject areas or is evidencing learning disabilities, then professionals (school psychologists, counselors) may rely on the use of **diagnostic tests.**

Diagnostic Tests: Individually administered tests to identify special learning problems. Elementary school teachers are more likely than secondary school teachers to receive information from diagnostic tests. Diagnostic tests may be used to:
1. assess the ability to hear differences among sounds
2. remember spoken words or sentences
3. recall a sequence of symbols
4. separate figures from their background
5. express relationships
6. coordinate eye and hand movements
7. describe objects orally and blend sounds to form words
8. recognize details in a picture
9. coordinate movements and other abilities needed to learn, remember, and communicate learning

Both aptitude and achievement tests measure developed abilities. Achievement tests may assess abilities developed over a short amount of time such as a week long unit on spelling or they measure abilities developed over time such as an IQ test. **Aptitude tests** serve yet another pupose.

Aptitude Tests: Tests meant to predict future performance. **Example:** The Scholastic Aptitude Test (SAT) is meant to predict how well students will do in college.

Issues in Standardized Testing

Our country currently faces a state of test escalation due to such factors as accountability, minimum competency, and international competition. Because of the emphasis placed on test scores, many refer to this as **high-stakes testing.** Many are suggesting the establishment of a national exam while others suggest that we should decrease the use of standardized tests in schools because the consequences may lead to "teaching to the test" or decision making that may adversely effect minority group students.

High Stakes Testing: Standardized tests whose results have powerful influences when used by school administrators, other officials, or employers to make decisions.

A topic that is hotly debated involves testing of preschool children to determine whether they will be allowed to enter kindergarten. These measures are called **readiness tests.**

Readiness Testing: Testing procedures meant to determine if an individual is ready to proceed to the next level of education or training. Opponents of readiness testing believe:

- group administered paper-and-pencil tests are inappropriate for preschool children and should not be used as the basis for decisions about school entry
- using readiness tests narrows the preschool curriculum, making it more academic and less developmentally appropriate
- the evidence shows that delaying entry into first grade or retaining students in kindergarten is not effective in that students who are retained do no better than similar students who are not held back

In spite of these criticisms, almost every state uses some form of readiness testing to determine if students are ready for kindergarten or first grade. A recommended more appropriate procedure would be to have adults make cognitive, social/emotional, and physical observations that would be ongoing assessments rather than requiring children to answer questions directly on paper.

Comparisons with students from other countries reveal that American students demonstrate lower academic achievement. This has resulted in discussion regarding standards for allowing students to move on to the next level or to graduate as determined by a **minimum competency test.** Many argue that this form of testing further reduces academic freedom among teachers and the tests ultimately control the curriculum.

Minimum Competency Testing: Standardized tests meant to determine if students meet minimum requirements to graduate or to proceed in school.

Advantages in Taking Tests-Fair and Unfair

We know that IQ tests are biased in favor of students from middle-class socioeconomic status but research on test bias reveals that most standardized school tests predict school achievement equally well across all groups of students. Whereas, standardized aptitude and achievement tests are not biased against minorities in predicting school performance other factors may put minority students at a disadvantage.

- language of the test and tester is often different from the language of the students

- questions are often more geared to the dominant culture
- answers that support middle-class values are often awarded more points
- being verbal and talking a lot is rewarded on individually administered tests
- some minority-group children may not value doing well on tests

Concern about cultural bias has lead some psychologists to develop **culture-fair** or **culture-free tests.**

Culture-Fair/Culture Free Test: A test without cultural bias. **Example:** Many of these tests rely more on performance than on verbal content. Unfortunately, the performances of students from lower-socioeconomic backgrounds and minority groups are no better on these tests than on the standard Wechsler and Binet Intelligence Scales.

Courses designed to prepare students for college entrance exams yield positive results when students practiced on a parallel form of the test for brief periods, when they familiarized themselves with the procedures of standardized tests, and when they received instruction in general metacognitive skills discussed in previous chapters.

New Directions in Standardized Testing

Critics of intelligence testing suggest that these tests fail to capture the child's potential for future learning. An alternative assessment approach has as its goal to reveal potential for learning and subsequent interventions to assist the individual in achieving his/her potential. One measure for accomplishing this is Feuerstein's **Learning Propensity Assessment Device.**

Learning Propensity Assessment Device: Innovative method for testing the student's ability to benefit from teaching, consistent with Vygotsky's theory of cognitive development. Often the examiner will teach the child how to solve problems and then assess the amount of instructional benefits to the child, consistent with Vygotsky's scaffolding and zone of proximal development.

Critics of traditional tests suggest that the test content is artifical, consisting of basic skills and facts and in no way resembles what students will be required to perform once out of the academic setting. A more viable method of assessment would be to assess student performance on real-life tasks. This approach is characteristic of **authentic assessment.**

Authentic Assessment: Measurement of important abilities using procedures that simulate the application of these abilities to real-life problems. A side comment; If we are to use authentic application as an instructional strategy, it makes sense to assess this type of learning with the same format.

Goals for the future of standardized testing include improvements more consonant with the demands of the twenty first century. Tests will have less of a focus on multiple choice-recognition types of responses and will emphasize the very types of problem-solving skills that we are attempting to foster through our teaching. Newer tests will feature more **constructed response formats.**

Standardized Testing

Constructed Response Formats: Assessment procedures that require the student to create an answer instead of selecting an answer from a set of choices.

With the introduction of new formats for assessment comes new problems and new decisions to be made. Will assessments be objective and without bias? Will one evaluator's decisions about a student's portfolio be consistent with another's? Will these new forms of evaluation be reliable and valid? Will they be capable of being standardized? Psychologists and classroom practitioners will need to consider these issues lest we encounter the same problems associated with traditional forms of assessment.

Application Four: Which Test Should be Used?

The following statements describes behaviors or aptitudes or potential weaknesses that could be identified through standardized testing and teacher-made tests. Select the type test that you think is being administered in each situation. Check your responses in the answer key.

1. Jeremy frequently stumbles when reading aloud. Sometimes he reverses letters, reading "was" for "saw" completely skipping over long words with many syllables. _____

2. Mr. Hill's social science class has been exploring the historical, geographical, political, and cultural aspects of Peru. He wants his students to express in essay form what they know about the impact of the conquerors on native civilizations and the changes this created within Peru. _____

3. Tyrone wants to go to college and knows that he must first take college entrance exams. _____

4. Seline is in fifth grade and along with her class will take a test to assess reading, language, math, spelling, science, and social studies. _____

5. Jackie's kindergarten teacher has reservations about whether Jackie should be promoted to first grade. She knows the arguments against retention yet suspects that Jackie, who is very young for her grade, is not developmentally ready in many areas and may benefit from remediation if not retention. _____

6. One of the tribal schools in rural Alaska has come under fire because its students have an alarming rate of alcoholism, absenteeism, and juvenile delinquency. College entrance exams have revealed that all of the students who were administered the exams, scored more than one standard deviation below the national average. Now there is discussion as to whether these students should even graduate. _____

7. Pablo just arrived in this country from Mexico. His English is limited and he seems to be having difficulty in all subject areas. His physical coordination is not good. He appears to lack motivational interest and rarely participates. _____

Application Five: Identifying Statistical Terms and Definitions

To check your knowledge, see if you can come up with terms to match the definitions below. Some of the terms may have two words but there is no space between the words. Check your responses in the answer key.

Clues

Down:

1. Most frequently occuring score
2. Consistency of test results
3. Middle score in a group of scores
4. An evaluation expressed in quantitative (number) terms
5. Degree of difference or deviation from the mean
7. Decision making about student performance and about appropriate teaching strategies
8. A group whose average score serves as a standard for evaluating any student's score on a test

Across:

3. Arithmetical average
6. Measures of how widely scores vary from the mean
9. Degree to which a test measures what it is intended to measure
10. Bar graph of a frequency distribution

Statistical Terms

Practice Test

Essay Questions

1. A large portion of a student's educational experience is devoted to standardized testing. Many suggest that standardized testing should be eliminated altogether. Discuss the pros and cons of standardized testing.

2. Discuss some of the notions regarding teacher competency tests. Provide reflective viewpoints as to why teacher competency tests should and should not be utilized.

Multiple Choice

1. Scores that are based on the standard deviation of a distribution of scores is (are) called
   a. T Scores
   b. z Scores
   c. Standard Scores
   d. all of the above

2. Norm-referenced tests are most appropriate for
   a. measuring affective and psychomotor objectives
   b. informing students about what students can do and what they know
   c. measuring mastery of basic skills
   d. assessing the range of abilities in a large group

3. Extreme scores in a distribution cause mean inflation or deflation. To yield an accurate representation of typical test scores a better measure would be the
   a. median
   b. mode
   c. range
   d. standard deviation

4. The kind of reliability evidence that is obtained by having individuals take two different test forms that assess the same content or subject matter is called
   a. split-half reliability
   b. alternate forms reliability
   c. test-retest reliability
   d. internal consistency

5. Which of the following is true regarding grade equivalent scores?
    a. they are obtained from a multi-age norming sample
    b. different forms of tests are used at different grade levels
    c. a seventh grader with a grade equivalent score of 10 should probably be promoted to a higher grade level
    d. grade quivalent score units mean the same thing at every grade level

6. When the score bands overlap when interpreting student performance on an achievement test, this indicates that
    a. the scores are within the average range compared to the national norming sample
    b. achievement levels in these two areas are very differnt
    c. achievement levels in these two areas are very similar
    d. we can be 95% confident that the scores actually fall within this range

7. Which of the following is true regarding a normal distribution?
    a. the mean, median and mode are all the same score
    b. the majority of scores lie within one standard deviation above and below the mean
    c. plotted scores form a bell-shaped curve
    d. all of the above

8. When teachers attempt to address the relatedness between testing and teaching they are trying to ensure that their teacher-made tests have
    a. content validity
    b. criterion-related validity
    c. construct validity
    d. external validity

9. On an IQ test with a mean of 100 and a standard deviation of 15, Selma obtained a score of 114 and Andy got a score of 105. What conclusions can be drawn about their performances?
    a. Selma is much smarter than Andy
    b. Selma and Andy's performances are essentially identical because they are both within one standard deviation above the mean
    c. Andy scored higher than approximately 61% of the students who took the test and Selma scored higher than approximately 83% of the students who took the test
    d. Both Andy and Selma possess average intelligence

10. The hypothetical estimate of variation in scores if testing were repeated is called
    a. the standard deviation
    b. the true score
    c. the standard error of measurement
    d. the range

Answer Key

Application One: Criterion or Norm-Referenced
1. norm
2. criterion
3. criterion
4. norm
5. norm
6. criterion
7. norm
8. norm
9. criterion
10. criterion

Application Two: Constructing a Frequency Distribution

Distribution of Grades		Frequency Distribution	
Students	Math Scores	Math Scores	Frequencies
Adam Brock	83	100	0
Pam Castle	84	99	0
Tim Crow	98	98	2
Bob Drew	90	97	0
Sue Grahm	98	96	0
Jim Gregory	78	95	0
Ken Harris	85	94	0
Karen Howe	82	93	1
John Jackson	86	92	0
Pat Johnson	79	91	0
Kwan Lee	89	90	1
Brad Lipton	85	89	1
Sam Moore	85	88	0
Kip Mumby	86	87	1
Jan Neils	82	86	2
Carrie Paul	87	85	3
Jan Ramie	84	84	3
Lynn Reed	79	83	2
Kim Rice	81	82	2
Sara Sands	83	81	1
Tara Trask	80	80	1
Jill Vale	93	79	2
Tom White	84	78	1

Application Three: Calculating Standard Scores

Student	Math mean=80 SD=5	History mean=50 SD=10	English mean=34 SD=8
Todd	X=85	X=55	X=50
Stephanie	X=90	X=40	X=30
Carlos	X=80	X=60	X=42
Terri	X=70	X=65	X=38
Todd	z= +1	z= +.5	z= +2
Stephanie	z= +2	z= -1	z= -1
Carlos	z= 0	z= +1	z= +1
Terri	z= -2	z= +1.5	z= +.5
Todd	T= 60	T= 55	T= 70
Stephanie	T= 70	T= 40	T= 40
Carlos	T= 50	T= 60	T= 60
Terri	T= 30	T= 65	T= 55

Application Four: Which Test Should be Used?
1. Diagnostic tests
2. Achievement Tests
3. Aptitude Tests
4. Achievement Tests
5. Readiness Tests
6. Minimum Competency Tests
7. This student requires an entire battery of tests. He should be given a culture fair IQ test to determine if his difficulties are language based. Achievement tests and Learning Propensity Assessment Devices would also be appropriate. Should these tests reveal low scores, a diagnostic test would be in order.

Application Five: Identifying Statistical Terms and Definitions

Statistical Terms

```
                     1
                     M
                     O
                     D                          2
                     E                          R
            3        |              4           |
            M  E  A  N              M           E
      5                             |           |
      V        E                    E           L
   6                              7                        8
   S  T  A  N  D  A  R  D  D  E   V  I  A  T  I  O          N
      R        I                 V     S     A             O
      I        A                 A     R     B             R
      A        N                 L     E     I             M
      B                          U     M     L             G
      I                          A     E     I             R
   9                             |     |     |             |
   V  A  L  I  D  I  T  Y        T     E     T             O
      I                          I     N     Y             U
  10
   H  I  S  T  O  G  R  A  M      O     T                  P
      Y                          N
```

Essay Questions:

1. Critics of standardized testing state that these tests measure disjointed facts and skills that have no use or meaning in the real world. Test questions often do not match the curriculum and therefore cannot measure how well students have learned the curriculum. Because tests are best at measuring lower-level objectives, these tend to drive the curriculum. Teachers are pressured to produce high test scores and jobs, raises and the price of real estate is all influenced by test scores. Students become labeled as low-achievers on the basis of their test scores and teachers are adversely influenced by test pressure, alienation from the process, and the reduction to their teaching time. Advocates for standardized testing procedures state that standardized tests sample what is typically taught and cannot be expected to match every school's curriculum, but still provide valuable information. To use a test properly, advocates suggest that tests should not be used as the only basis for decision making. Don't use the test unless there is a good reason for testing. Know what the test measures, know your students and don't use test results to compare students or to foster competition.

2. It is not unreasonable to expect that teachers are qualified competent individuals, knowledgeable in their subject areas as well as possessing educational pedagogy. By requiring teacher competency tests, teachers' knowledge is standardized regardless from which school or program they received their teacher certification.

Standardized Testing

The National Teacher Examination (NTE) identifies weaknesses in general skills and knowledge early on in the teacher education program. Exit portions of the test assess knowledge upon leaving the program. Critics of these tests posit that good test scores do not predict good teaching. Professors and students alike decry the redundancy of the test in light of the fact that it assesses much of the knowledge that was already measured in their college classes. The general consensus among students is that if you are willing to pay to take the test repeatedly, then everyone passes, nobody fails. If this in fact is the case, then the discriminatory power of the test for assessing qualified versus unqualified teachers is an issue of concern.

Multiple Choice:
1. d   2. d   3. a   4. b   5. b   6. c   7. d   8. a   9. c   10. c

Chapter Fifteen

Classroom Assessment and Grading

"The tests of life are not meant to break you, but to make you."
Norman Vincent Peale

Even though you may not have much of a voice in determining your district's or school's grading policy, you will ultimately decide how that policy is used and what measures you will use to assess your students' achievement. Two functions of assessment are **formative** and **summative.**

Formative Assessment: Ungraded testing used before or during instruction to aid in planning and diagnosis. **Example:** You may give your students a **pretest** in science to determine if review is required. You may also give your students a formative test in the form of a **diagnostic test** to monitor the learning process; to see if are they comprehending the material or if there are any trouble spots.

Pretest: Formative test for assessing students' knowledge, readiness, and abilities. **Example:** Mrs. Jones, (the teacher your fifth-grade students had last year), did not complete all of the fourth grade math curriculum and by giving a pretest you discover that you have to back up and teach fractions before you can begin teaching fifth grade mathematics.

Diagnostic Test: Formative test to determine students' areas of weakness, not to be confused with the standardized diagnostic test of learning disabilities. **Example:** You give your third graders a diagnostic reading test and discover that some of your "fastest" readers are not comprehending what they have read and together you work out strategies that will help them to slow down and become more reflective about their reading.

Pretests and diagnostic tests are not graded so they make good practice tests for students who suffer from test anxiety. Another type of formative assessment that frequently checks student performance is called **Curriculum-Based Assessment (CBA).**

Curriculum-Based Assessment (CBA): Evaluation method using frequent tests of specific skills and knowledge. CBA is a variety of approaches for observing student performance and making decisions about appropriate instruction. This method has been used primarily with students with learning problems but is effective for all students because instruction is adapted to meet the pace and needs of students as determined by the assessment probes.

Summative Assessment: Testing that follows instruction and assesses achievement. It provides a *summary* of accomplishments and levels of achievement. **Example:** At the end of the history unit, Mr. Grant gives his class a summative exam to see if they have learned a sufficient amount of material to warrant moving on to the next unit.

The only difference between summative and formative assessment is how the results are used. The same test can be used for summative or formative assessment, the purpose determines the type of assessment.

Planning for Testing

Before designing your tests, it is a good idea to use a behavior-content matrix. This is a test specification plan that will help you to generate items to match your learning objectives. More important objectives should have more items. Your test plan will increase the validity of your test by ensuring that you ask a reasonable number of questions to cover each topic. Dempster (1991) suggests that for testing to yield the most benefits:

- testing should occur frequently to encourage retention of material
- teach material, give students a test soon after, then retest on the material later
- cumulative questions are the key to effective learning and retention and increase the application of previously learned skills

Unfortunately, school curriculums are so full that there is little time for frequent testing. Dempster suggests that we teach fewer topics in greater depth to allow for more practice, review, testing, and feedback.

Objective Testing

One of the commonly used forms of classroom and standardized tests are called **objective tests**. As the name implies, these tests are objective and will be scored without bias as the answers are not open to interpretation. Gronlund suggests that the guiding principle in determining which types of test questions to use should be those items that best assess how accurately students have met the learning objectives.

Objective Tests: Multiple-choice, matching, true-false, short-answer, and fill-in tests; scoring these tests requires no interpretation as in essay exams.

Multiple choice questions are useful for asking factual questions but can also test higher level objectives as well. Items will assess more than recognition and recall if the student is required to apply or analyze concepts, but these items are much more difficult to write. Multiple choice questions are comprised of a **stem** and alternatives (the choices which include the correct response, and **distractors**). The difficult part of writing a multiple choice question is coming up with distractors that aren't obviously incorrect.

Distractors: Wrong answers offered as choices in a multiple-choice item..
Stem: The question part of the multiple choice question.

Whenever possible, phrase the stem in positive terms (unless you capitalize, italicize, underline or bold the word **_NOT_**), make it clear and simple, presenting only a single problem, and include as much wording as possible in the stem so that it doesn't have to be repeated in the alternatives.

Alternatives should fit the grammmatical form of the stem, so that no answers are obviously wrong, avoid the use of words such as *always, never, all,* or *only* because test-wise students detect these as obvious distractors, and don't have two alternatives that mean the same thing since this signals to students that both must be wrong. Avoid using the exact wording from the text as students will recognize the answers without knowing what they mean. Avoid overuse of *all of the above* and *none of the above* as these may be helpful to students who are guessing. Don't include any obvious patterns such as letter position or length because this may bias your test in favor of students who are test-wise.

Essay Testing

Essay exams are appropriate for assessing the written responses of students, for administering a test when you have more time for scoring than for test construction, and for assessing the types of objectives found in the higher levels of Bloom's taxonomy. By requiring students to generate answers, we can be sure that they have met some learning objectives. Essay tests take much more time answer than objective tests and therefore should be limited to the assessment of complex learning outcomes. Because they require more time, it may be best to break up your testing over several days. If you have an extensive amount of material to cover, objective tests may be a better route or you could combine essay with objective. The more items you include on a test, the lower the standard error of measurement and the more accurate the assessment. Whatever the choice, students need ample time to respond and time pressures may cause anxiety and lower performance in some students.

A major problem with essay exams is the evaluation of student responses. Starch and Elliot (1912) discovered that when 200 English teachers evaluated responses to the same essay questions, their scores ranged from 64 to 98. Several qualities of essays may influence scoring; (1) neatly written, verbose, jargon-filled essays with few construction or grammatical errrors were given the best grades, and (2) teachers may reward quantity versus quality. Gronlund suggests several strategies for effective grading of essay exams:

- construct a model answer and then you can assign points to its various parts
- give points for the organization of the answer and internal consistency
- then assign gades and sort the papers into piles by grade
- finally, skim the papers in each pile to ensure consistency
- when grading tests with several essay questions, grade all responses to one question before moving on to the next and after you finish scoring question number one, shuffle the papers so no student has all of their questions scored first, last, or in the middle.
- asking students to put their names on the backs of their exams to ensure anonymity
- a final check would be to have another teacher familiar with your goals grade your exams without knowing what grades you have assigned. This is especially helpful if you are a novice teacher.

Review Table 15.3 in your text for a summary of important components of both essay and objective testing.

Application One: Characteristics of Objective and Subjective Tests

The following statements are characteristic of either objective tests or essay tests. Reflect on each statement to determine which form of test applies. Check your responses in the answer key.

1. When you have an extensive amount of content area to cover, this test can sample much more. _____

2. Best for assessing ability to organize, integrate, and express ideas. _____

3. When your time for test construction is shorter than your time for scoring. _____

4. Characterized by quick, reliable, unbiased scoring procedures. _____

5. Most commonly used form of test by test experts and classroom practitioners. _____

6. Good for measuring outcomes at the knowledge, comprehension, and application levels of learning. ____

7. Easy to prepare, tough to score. _____

8. Encourages students to remember, interpret, and use the ideas of others. _____

9. Quality of the test is determined by the scorer. _____

10. More reliable when your number of students is small. _____

Innovations in Assessment

Some of the same criticisms of standardized tests (recall of facts versus problem solving, control of the curriculum, etc.) are also aimed at classroom tests. Some suggest that viable alternatives to traditional testing are **Authentic tests.**

Authentic Tests: Assessment procedures that test skills and abilities as they would be applied in real-life situations.

Wiggins (1989) suggests that if our instructional goals are for students to think critically and do research then we should have them think critically and do research and then assess their performances. Authentic assessment requires students to perform, accept criticism and feedback, and then to improve the performance.

Performance in Context: Portfolios and Exhibitions

An offshoot of authentic assessment are several new approaches with the goals of *performance in context*. Within this framework, students are required to engage in problem-solving activities. Knowledge of

263

facts are still required but they are applied in a procedural context to solve a real-life problem. Two new approaches are **portfolios** and **exhibitions.**

Portfolio: A collection of the student's work in an area, showing growth, self-reflection, and achievement. **Example:** written work, artistic pieces, graphs, diagrams, photographs, videotapes, lab reports, computer programs or anything that represents the subject being taught and assessed.

Components of portfolio assessment include work in progress, revisions, student self-analyses, and reflections on what the student has learned. Teach students how to create and use portfolios.

Exhibitions: A performance test or demonstration of learning that is public and usually takes an extended time to prepare. **Example:** Our graduate students have the option of presenting their theses research in the form of a poster presentation. Their research is evaluated by a committee, as is their poster, their presentation, and their abilty to orally convey the idea behind their research and how professionally they address questions.

With exhibitions, communication and understanding is essential as is extensive amounts of time dedicated to preparation. Many suggest that "exhibitions of mastery" replace tests for graduation or course completion requirements.

Evaluating Portfolios and Performance

Students' performances are NOT assessed relative to each other but are compared to set standards, in other words, they are criterion and not norm-referenced. Checklists, rating scales, and **scoring rubrics** are useful for assessing performances.

Scoring Rubrics: A general description of different levels of performance, equivalent to different scores or grades.
Students should be involved in the development of scales and scoring rubrics so they know in advance what is expected, and are challenged to perform to standards of quality. When they're given practice in designing and applying score rubrics, their work and performances improve. Performance assessment requires careful judgment by teachers and clear feedback to students as to what needs improvement.
As discussed in the previous chapter, of particular concern with these assessment methods is reliabilty, validity, and equity. As seen previously, ratings of portfolios and essays are not consistent across raters. The more expert the evaluator, however, the more reliable the scores. Regarding validity, some research suggests that students who are rated as master writers on portfolios are judged less capable on traditional methods but as to which method is more accurate, only further research will tell. Equity or fairness in grading is a concern, as with evaluation of essays, but having a network of support from teachers, peers, families, and others will help to round portfolios and exhibitions into shape with an extensive amount of feedback versus one teacher's evaluation.

Classroom Assessment and Grading

Figure 15.1

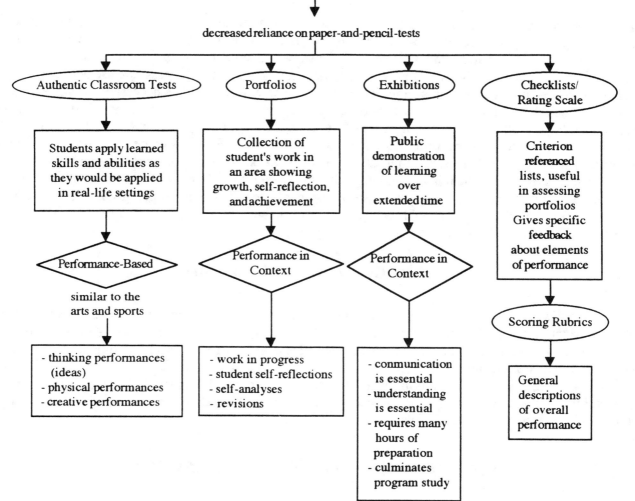

ALTERNATIVES FOR ASSESSMENT

decreased reliance on paper-and-pencil-tests

Authentic Classroom Tests

Students apply learned skills and abilities as they would be applied in real-life settings

Performance-Based

similar to the arts and sports

- thinking performances (ideas)
- physical performances
- creative performances

Portfolios

Collection of student's work in an area showing growth, self-reflection, and achievement

Performance in Context

- work in progress
- student self-reflections
- self-analyses
- revisions

Exhibitions

Public demonstration of learning over extended time

Performance in Context

- communication is essential
- understanding is essential
- requires many hours of preparation
- culminates program study

Checklists/ Rating Scale

Criterion referenced lists, useful in assessing portfolios Gives specific feedback about elements of performance

Scoring Rubrics

General descriptions of overall performance

Effects of Grading and Grades on Students

Research suggests that high standards, competitive class atmosphere, and low grades increases absenteeism and dropout rates, especially with disadvantaged students. Are we then to lower our standards and not give "Fs" when warranted? Failure has been shown to have both negative and positive consequences as some studies reveal that a 100% failure rate and a 100% success rate are both bad for learning to cope with failure, an important lesson in life. Sometimes failure is necessary for students to understand the relationship between hard work and success. Once again, remember how it was when you learned to ride your bike. Educators must replace easy success with challenge yet ensure that tasks are "do-able," but help students to learn from their mistakes when they fail. Failing a grade level, however, can be devastating and results from research suggest that it is best to promote and provide summer remediation.

Students often need help in determining why their mistakes are wrong. Teacher feedback plays an important role in correcting faulty strategies so that students don't make the same mistakes again. Written comments are effective but they should be kept brief for younger students and should recognize good work and improvements as well as provide corrective feedback .

Grades and Motivation

If grades are based on memorization, student study time will be spent on just that. If you test only at the knowledge level of Bloom's taxonomy you are motivating students to get the grade rather than engage in any sort of meaningful learning. If the grade reflects meaningful learning, working for a grade and working to learn become the same thing.

Low grades, however, do not motivate students. Rather than failing students, give them incompletes and the opportunity to revise and improve their work. Maintain high standards and provide needed help and they will see the relationship between effort and success.

Grading and Reporting: Nuts and Bolts

To determine final grades, decisions must be made as to what the grades reflect. Should students' performances be weighed against standards of mastery as in **criterion-referenced grading** or should they reflect what that student knows in comparison to classmates as with **norm-referenced grading.** We will explore each of these separately.

Criterion-Referenced Grading: Assessment of each student's mastery of course objectives. Here the grade represents a list of accomplishments.

Criterion-referenced grading has the advantage of spelling out the criteria in advance so that every student can achieve an "A" if he or she meets the criteria. Student performance can be compared to clearly defined instructional goals. Some school districts use reporting systems where report cards list objectives along with judgments about the student's attainment of each.

Classroom Assessment and Grading

Norm-Referenced Grading: Assessment of students' achievement in relation to one another. Here, the ability of students within the class will play a large role in determining individual grades. One form of norm-reference grading is called **grading on the curve.**

Grading on the Curve: Norm-referenced grading that compares students' performance to an average level. In this system, the middle of the curve is average and probably reflects "C" level performance.

If grading on the curve were done strictly in accordance with the normal bell-shaped curve and standard deviations, 68% of the grades would be Cs, approximately 13% would be Bs and 13% would be Ds, and 3% would be As and 3% would be Fs. Some teachers also use 10% As and Fs, 20% Bs and Ds, and 40% Cs. Both of these are strict methods and discourage students who work hard but perform below the average. Many variations of grading on the curve exist with varying levels of precision. The simplest approach is to rank order students' scores from highest to lowest and then to bracket the middle two-thirds of the scores with an average grade of C (or B if you believe B to be the average performance in your class). Since this is approximately 66%, that leaves 34%. The next 14% on either side of the Cs could be given Bs and Ds with the remaining 3% on either side for As and Fs. Given the range of scores and the fact that one point may make the difference between grades, a better approach may be to use what is called *naturally occurring gaps*. An example of this method follows.

A		B		C		D		F
96 92 91 90		85 81 79 76 73		69 68 67 67 64		61 60 60 59 57 54		48 45 43

Here, the teacher has used the naturally occurring gaps to establish grade boundaries.

Application Two: Naturally Occurring Gaps

You have just scored your students' science exams and obtained the following distribution. Assign grades based upon the naturally occurring gaps.

100 97 96 93 93 91 87 85 85 84 84 83 81 78 77 75 72 72 71 71 70 69 65 64 62 62 58 56 54 49 40

Classroom Assessment and Grading

Application Three: Decisions about Grading Standards

Read the following statements. Some are characteristic of criterion-referenced grading whereas some are indicative of norm-referenced grading, and still others will require that you make a decision as to whether norm-or criterion-referenced is more appropriate. Regardless of which system you select as teachers, you should make the decision prior to administering your classroom test and stick with your decision. For each statement, decide whether it is norm or criterion and check your responses in the answer key.

1. You have just given a test in your advanced math class and you are surprised that the majority of the grades were As and Bs.._____

2. You are offering an honors English seminar but have room for only 10 students. You will be making your selection on the basis of their midterm English exams. _____

3. You are teaching addition to your second grade class and you want to ensure that they have mastered the basics before moving on to the next unit. _____

4. Mrs. Franklin wants to know why you gave her daughter Susie a C on her science test when her score was an 88. You explain that 88 was an average performance for the class. _____

5. Your grading system ensures that your lowest achiever will receive an F regardless of the actual score point value. _____

6. The students in your class are eager to help one another learn because higher grades means a springtime camping trip. _____

7. You have plotted the scores from your students' first exam and since they conform to a normal distribution, you have decided to use this grading system from now on. _____

8. You want to average each of your students' social studies exams for the entire semester but they have different means and standard deviations so you plan to calculate T scores for each student. _____

9. Your principal has called you into his office very concerned about the unequal distribution of grades on your students' report cards (very few Ds and Fs) and suggests you switch to this grading system. _____

10. You want all of your Driver's Education students to master the objectives of safe driving and get an A in your course. _____

Preparing Report Cards

If you are using criterion-referenced grading with an objective list, you would not want to average mastery of independent objectives with other objectives. You would not want to average a test score of *addition of fractions* with a test score *of mutiplication of two digit numbers*. See Figure 15.6 for an example of a criterion-referenced report card for elementary grades. Likewise, if you are using norm-referenced grading, you cannot merge all of your tests, quizzes, etc. if they have different means and standard deviations. To understand this, examine the example below.

	Test 1 Class Mean=40 Standard Deviation=5	Test 2 Class Mean=60 Standard Deviation=20	Total Raw Score
Tammy	45	60	105
Tom	40	80	120

If we just look at their raw scores, it looks as though Tom outperformed Tammy. But these tests were different in terms of means and standard deviations, item number and difficulty. It would be wrong to try to average them as though they were the same tests. Therefore, we must put them into a common scale or a standard score. When you use the formulas for z scores and T scores from the previous chapter, you will see that Tom and Tammy's performances are equivalent.

$$Z= \frac{\text{Student's Score - Mean}}{\text{SD}} \qquad\qquad T= 10 \ (z) + 50$$

	Test 1 Class Mean=40 Standard Deviation=5		Test 2 Class Mean=60 Standard Deviation=20		Total T Scores
Tammy	z=1	T=60	z=0	T=50	110
Tom	z=0	T=50	z=1	T=60	110

Each student scored on the mean on one test and one standard deviation above the mean on another test. Teachers don't usually calculate T scores for assigning grades, but it is one appropriate way to do it and it addresses the problems associated with combining and averaging raw scores to establish grades.

Classroom Assessment and Grading

T scores can be combined and averaged and then compared to a percentile chart to assign letter grades. For example, a T score of 50 is at the mean or 50th percentile. That is average so you could give that student a C if you feel that the average performance in your class is reflected by a C.

A popular system for assigning grades is called the point system. Each assignment is given a certain number of points depending on its importance. A test worth 50% of the grade might be assigned 50 points. A homework assignment might be worth 10. At the end of the semester, the teacher could add up all of the points, for each student, rank the students, and using a norm-referenced grading system, assign grades by imposing a curve.

Another system for assigning grades is consistent with criterion-referenced grading in that grades are determined by percentage of mastery. It is called **percentage grading.**

Percentage Grading: System of converting class performances to percentage scores and assigning grades based on predetermined cut-off points. Two examples of the most typical percentages and cut-off scores follow.

90-100%=A; 80-89%=B; 70-79%=C; 60-69%=D; below 60%=F

94-100%=A; 85-93%=B; 76-83%=C; 70-75%=D; below 70%=F

As you can see, criterion-referenced percentage grading can be as arbitrary as norm-referenced grading in the assignment of grades. Futhermore, it suggests that we place a high premium on test construction to assume that if a student scores an 88 on the test, then that student has mastered 88% of the subject matter. Also, is one point difference so significant as to place one student at the B level and another student gets an A? No grading system is without its flaws which is why alternative methods for grading continue to be employed.

Contract System: System in which each student works for a particular grade according to agreed-upon standards. The contract lists what must be done at each grade level to receive that grade.

The contract system helps to reduce student anxiety about grades, however, the emphasis may be placed on accomplishing the tasks in a quantity rather than a quality mode. Teachers must be very specific about the standards that will distinguish acceptable from unacceptable work. If clearly developed rubrics specify what performances are expected for each assignment, then this may circumvent the problem of some students turning in inadequate additional work just to receive the next higher grade. A good way to prevent this is by including a **revise option.**

Revise Option: In a contract system, the chance to revise and improve work. This system helps to ensure quality control.

A theme that can be applied regardless of which grading system you utilize is grading on improvement and effort. We should all consider whether grades should be based upon the final level of performance and learning or on an average of performances throughout. Another consideration addresses the high achieving students who have little room for improvement based upon their intial high levels of achievement. A good improvement grading method for both low and high achievers would be to assign grades based upon their **individual learning expectation (ILE).**

Classroom Assessment and Grading

Individual Learning Expectation (ILE): Personal average score. **Example:** Remember this term from cooperative learning. Points are given for improvement over your own personal average or for perfect performance. Teachers can use this when figuring a final grade or giving other classroom rewards.

A system that requires that teachers accurately judge true ability and effort of all students (but is extremely subjective and can be very biased) is a **dual marking system.**

Dual Marking System: System of assigning two grades, one reflecting achievement, the other effort and ability. **Example:** A grade of B could have the following qualifications:

B1: Outstanding effort, better achievement than expected, good attitude
B2: Average effort, satisfactory in terms of ability
B3: Lower achievement than ability would indicate, poor attitude

Of course a grade of D1 could be quite detrimental to the self-esteem of a student, whereas a grade of B2 tells a bright student that you expect more from them. Whatever system you employ, it is important that grades be assigned without personal prejudice or bias. Many factors influence teacher assignment of grades from teacher expectations, to student effort, to classroom behaviors, to **halo effects.**

Halo Effect: The tendency for a general impression of a person to influence our perception of any aspect of that person. **Example:** Stephanie is popular, well-groomed, personable and helpful. Even though her performance is essentially equivalent to Poindexter's, who is pompous, argumentative, and superior, you give her a higher grade.

In order to ensure fairness of grading in your classroom;
- explain your grading policies early on to your students
- set reasonable standards
- base your grades on as much objective evidence as possible
- be sure students understand test directions
- correct, return, and discuss test questions as soon as possible
- as a rule, do not change a grade unless a clerical or calculation error
- guard against bias in grading
- keep pupils informed of their standing in the class
- give students the benefit of the doubt--no measurement techniques are without error

Application Four: Tests of Tests

To test your knowledge of tests, see if you can match the correct type of test with its corresponding definition. Select the word from the left column that best matches the phrase on the right. Put the number of the matching word in the blank in front of the letters next to the large letters in the matrix below. If your answers are correct, all numbers across, down, and diagonally will total the same number. Check your responses in the answer key.

1. Authentic Tests   _____ a. A collection of the students's work in an area, showing growth, self-reflection, and achievement

2. Portfolio   _____ b. A general description of different levels of performance, equivalent to different scores or grades

3. Exhibition   _____ c. System in which each student works for a particular grade according to agreed-upon standards

4. Contract System   _____ d. Norm-referenced grading that compares students' performance to an average level

5. Dual Marking System   _____ e. System of assigning two grades, one reflecting achievement, the other effort, attitude, and actual ability

6. Percentage Grading   _____ f. A performance test or demonstration of learning that is public and usually takes an extended time to prepare

7. Grading on the Curve   _____ g. System of converting class performances to percentage scores and assigning grades based on predetermined cutoff points

8. Diagnostic Test   _____ h. Assessment procedures that test skills and abilities as they would be applied in real-life situations

9. Scoring Rubric   _____ i. Formative test to determine students' areas of weakness

A	**B**	**C**
D	**E**	**F**
G	**H**	**I**

What is the correct number _____?

Beyond Grading: Communication

As educators, you will be the key figure in many of your students' lives. Elementary teachers in particular spend as much time with their students as the students' own parents. This will provide you with the opportunity to get to know your students as individuals with concerns, needs, and expectations. As educators, you will be expected to hold conferences with the parents of your students and the focus of many of these conferences may be the grades they have earned.

The Buckley Amendment (also called the Family Educational Rights and Privacy Act of 1974 and the Educational Amendments Act of 1974) guarantees the right of access of test results and any student records, to the student and parents of the student. If the records contain information that is thought to be incorrect, parents have the right to challenge the entries and have the infomation removed, if they win the challenge. This places a premium on accurate, valid, reliable tests and records. Scores and grades should be based upon firm, solid evidence. Comments and anecdotes should be accurate and unbiased.

Your parent/teacher interactions must be conducted as professionally as possible. You should assume a leadership role, but remain willing to listen and work toward the resolution of the problem. Maintain a friendly atmosphere and when dealing with parents who are angry and upset, try to hear the concerns of the participants rather than focus on the emotional tone of their words. Remember that both you and the parents have something in common, interest in the welfare of their child and promoting intellectual growth and self-actualization of that student. Listed below are some guidelines for a successful parent/teacher conference.

- plan ahead: formulate your goals for the conference
- begin with a positive statement about the student
- listen actively, empathize with the parents, accept their feelings
- establish a working partnership to assist the student
- plan follow-up contacts
- end with a positive statement about the student

Application Five: Key Terms and Definitions

To check your knowledge, see if you can come up with terms to match the following definitions. Some of the terms may have two words but there is no space between the words. Check your responses in the answer key.

Clues:

Down:

2. In a contract system, the chance to improve work
3. The question part of a multiple-choice item
4. Type of assessment method using daily probes of specific-skill mastery
5. Type of testing using multiple-choice, matching, true-false, short answer, and fill-in
7. Wrong answers offered as choices in a multiple-choice item

Across:

1. Type of assessment using frequent tests of specific skills and knowledge
6. Type of formative test to determine students' areas of weakness
8. The tendency for a general impression of a person to influence our perception of any aspect of that person
9. Type of assessment that follows instruction and tests achievement
10. Formative test for assessing students' knowledge, readiness, and abilities
11. Type of assessment that is ungraded testing used befor or during instruction to aid in planning and diagnosis

Key Terms and Definitions

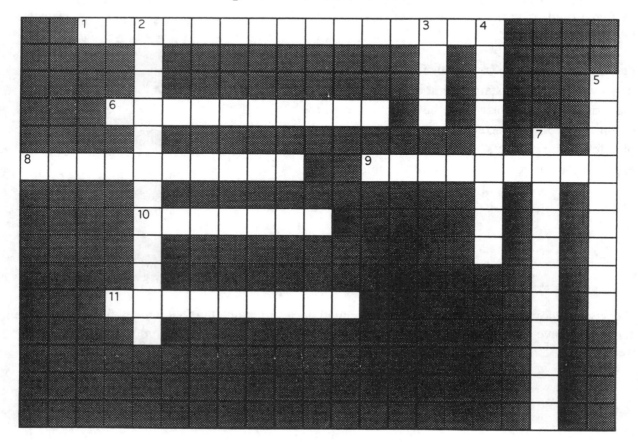

Practice Test
Essay Questions

1. From your *Point/Counterpoint* portion of the text, summarize Grant Wiggin's arguments against using traditional tests as standards of student performance.

2. Many educators incorrectly employ methods of norm-referenced grading. I know of instances where educators, upon seeing the low distribution of students' scores, will impose a curve shifting all grades upwards to the temporary satisfaction of students who are more concerned with maintaining a high grade point average than learning the material. Discuss some of the other disadvantages associated with norm-referenced grading systems.

Multiple Choice

1. When evaluating objective test items, the difficulty index
   a. is a summary of the global difficulty level of the test
   b. tells you how well each test item discriminates between those who did well and those who didn't
   c. is the proportion of people who answered the item correctly
   d. should be around .30 for norm-referenced tests

2. Starch and Elliot's research involving essays revealed that
   a. essays are actually incapable of measuring Blooms's *synthesis* objectives
   b. teachers are very subjective in their evaluations
   c. subjectivity was confined to specific subject areas
   d. students whose essays were verbose received the highest grade

3. Which of the following is **NOT** related to increased absenteeism and dropout rates?
   a. high standards
   b. competitive class atmosphere
   c. large percentage of lower grades
   d. authoritarian teachers

4. The primary difference between summative and formative assessments is
   a. the purpose for which they are administered
   b. formative assessments are graded and summative assessments are not
   c. formative assessments must be administered by licensed practitioners
   d. the time of year in which they are administered

5. The current thinking regarding retention or holding a child back a grade is
   a. if they appear socially and emotionally mature, it may be advantageous
   b. the opportunity to cover the same material again is beneficial
   c. promote and provide summer remediation
   d. that it decreases the likelihood that they will later drop out of school

6. Teachers don't always give the type of feedback that informs students why their answers are incorrect. In a study by Bloom and Bourdon, only _____ percent of the teachers noticed a consistent type of error in a student's arithmetic computation and informed the student.
   a. 4
   b. 8
   c. 16
   d. 32

7. With a point system of grading, if you convert each score to a percentage, average the percentages, rank the percentages and then look for natural gaps to assign grades you are using
   a. norm-referenced grading
   b. criterion-referenced grading
   c. authentic assessment
   d. dual marking systems

8. Behavior-Content Matrices are useful for
   a. assessing the validity of your teacher-made tests
   b. determining how many items you will need per topic
   c. observing and recording test-taking behaviors
   d. establishing the reliability of your teacher-made tests

9. The Buckley Amendment
   a. provides legal guidelines for conducting parent/teacher conferences
   b. establishes guidelines for financial assistance for students diagnosed with learning disabilities
   c. ensures that minority groups are administered culture-fair tests
   d. permits parents to review or challenge material in their child's school records

10. Which of the following is **NOT** an example of criterion-referenced grading?
   a. portfolios
   b. percentage grading
   c. grading on the curve
   d. exhibitions

Answer Key

Application One: Characteristics of Objective and Subjective Tests
1. objective
2. essay
3. essay
4. objective
5. objective
6. objective
7. essay
8. objective

9. essay
10. essay

Application Two: Naturally Occurring Gaps

A	B	C	D	F

100 97 96 93 93 91* 87 85 85 84 84 83 81 *78 77 75 72 72 71 71 70 69* 65 64 62 62 58 56 54*49 40

Application Three: Decisions about Grading Standards

1. criterion
2. norm
3. criterion
4. norm
5. norm
6. criterion
7. norm
8. norm
9. norm
10. criterion

Application Four: Tests of Tests

a. 2   b. 9   c. 4   d. 7   e. 5   f. 3   g. 6   h. 1   i. 8   The number is 15

Application Five: Key Terms and Definitions

Key Terms and Definitions

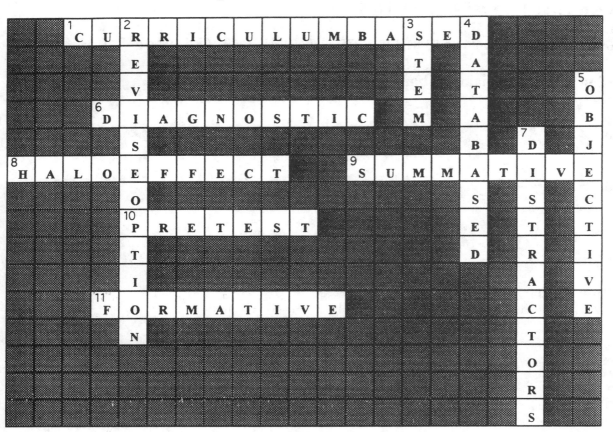

Essay Questions:

1. Wiggins suggests that we need high academic standards but that the standards should not be higher scores on multiple choice tests. He states that no where else in the real-world do we evaluate corporations, sports teams, symphonies, or vineyards on the basis of easy to test, common indicators. He further posits that understanding cannot be measured by tests that require students to apply learned skills out of context and that the only way that we will know if students truly comprehend is if we require them to apply their "knowledge wisely, fluently, flexibly and aptly in particular and diverse contexts."

2. When teachers impose grading curves for the sole purpose of masking poor student performance they are cheating the students in the long run. When a score of 54 on a scale of 100 becomes a C, the student is pacified but really possesses no comprehension of the material. Grading on the curve also implies a notion of limited good. Students are aware that only so many As will be administered which fosters student competition and resentment. Students would prefer that their classmates score poorly rather than succeed, bettering their own chances at a good grade. In actuality, there are not a limited number of As that teachers can give out. It should be the objective of every teacher to have their students be successful and master the material rather than guarantee certain failure before instruction has even begun. It is no wonder that some students suffer from a lack of motivation when they feel doomed to failure by the teacher's grading system.

Classroom Assessment and Grading

The classroom environment should be one that fosters achievement, success, and high self-esteem, not competition, learned helplessness, and lack of motivation. Given the right environment, all students can learn as long as the environment includes the right methods of grading employed for the right reasons.

Multiple Choice:
1. c   2. b   3. d   4. a   5. c   6. b   7. a   8. b   9. d   10. c

RESEARCH IN EDUCATIONAL PSYCHOLOGY
APPENDIX TO EDUCATIONAL PSYCHOLOGY, SEVENTH EDITION
BY ANITA E. WOOLFOLK

In order to achieve a better understanding of educational psychology, you must know how information in the field is created and how to judge the information you encounter. In this appendix we will explore the value and limitations of research, the major road to knowledge in educational psychology. Then we will examine a specific problem to determine how research might answer questions posed by teachers. Finally, we will describe how to judge a research study by evaluating a real experiment.

Asking and Answering Questions

To get a better understanding of a few of the basic methods for asking and answering questions in educational psychology, we will examine a question that may interest you: Do students' expectations about the competence of a new teacher influence the way the students behave toward the teacher? More specifically, do students pay more attention to a teacher they expect to be good? Suppose, for our purposes here, that an educational psychologist decided to look for an answer to this question. What methods might be used to gather information?

Forming a Research Question

The first step might be to frame a clear and specific question. In this case, we might begin with something like this: Do students' beliefs about a teacher's competence affect the amount of attention they pay to the teacher? Notice how specific the wording is. We will have problems if the question is too vague, as in: Do students' beliefs about a teacher affect the way they behave in class? There is too much territory to cover in answering the question. We need to be specific about what *kinds* of beliefs—beliefs about the teacher's *competence,* not age, intelligence, or marital status. And we need to be specific about what kind of behavior—attention to the teacher, not enthusiam for the subject or anxiety about a new year.

Choosing Variables and Selecting Measurement Techniques

At this point we are ready to identify the variables to be studied. A **variable** is any characteristic of a person or environment that can change under different conditions or that can differ from one person to the next. In our hypothetical study, we have decided to examine two variables—student beliefs about the teacher's competence and student attention to the teacher.

The next thing we must do is decide how we will define what we mean by *beliefs* and *attention.* This question leads to the issue of measurement, because our definitions will be useful only if they give us something we can measure.

To study any variable systematically, there must be a way to measure changes or compare different levels of the variable. To simplify matters, let us concentrate at this point on just one of the variables: student attention. We will need to find a way to measure the degree of attention shown by the students. The method chosen will depend in part on the design of the study and on the limitations imposed by the situation. Here we will look at four basic approaches to measurement: (1) self-report, (2) direct observation, (3) testing, and (4) teacher or peer ratings.

Using the **self-report** method, we could ask the students questions about how attentive they thought they were being. Answers could be given in writing or face to face, in an interview with the students.

If we decided instead to use **direct observation,** we could send researchers into the classroom to watch the students and assess their attention. These investigators might simply rate the students (on a scale of one to five, perhaps, from very attentive to very inattentive), or they could use a stopwatch to count the number of seconds each student watched the teacher. Observers could also work from a videotape of the class, replaying the tape several times so that each student could be observed and his or her level of attention rechecked. These are only a few of the systems that could be designed using observers to measure attention.

A **test** would be a little more difficult to construct in this case. Many variables are measured with tests, especially those involving learning or achievement. But since attention is a process rather than a product, it is difficult to design a test to measure it. One approach, however, would be to use a "vigilance task." We could see if the students were paying attention by having the teacher give an unpredictable signal, such as saying "Stand up," during the lesson. The measure of attention in this case would be the number of people who stood up immediately (Woolfolk & Woolfolk, 1974).

Finally, we might decide to use **teacher ratings** or **peer ratings.** We could measure attention by asking the teacher or the students to rate the attention of every student in the class.

Clearly, each of these approaches has advantages and disadvantages. Using self-reports or ratings of teachers or peers means relying on the judgments of the participants themselves. Using observers or tests can be disruptive to the class, at least initially. Videotaping is difficult and expensive. Let us assume, however, that we have chosen direct observation from videotapes. We will train the observers to time student attention with a stopwatch to determine how many seconds each student looks at the teacher during a 10-minute lesson. Note that our system of measurement has given us our definition of *attention:* the number of seconds each student looks at the teacher during a 10-minute lesson. This seems to offer a reasonably good definition. If the measurement system did not offer a good definition, we would need to find another way of measuring.

To define and measure our first variable—students' beliefs about the teacher's competence—we could also choose from a number of methods. Let us assume, at least for the time being, that we have selected a rating system. Students' answers to the question "How competent do you think this teacher is?" should give us a good idea of student opinion.

One other definition may be in order here, although in this particular study it seems rather obvious. Since we will be studying student beliefs and student attentiveness, the subjects in our investigation will be students. As you probably know, **subjects** is the term for the people (or animals) whose behavior is being measured. We would want to specify the grade, sex, and type of student to be studied. For our hypothetical study, we will select male and female sixth graders in a predominantly middle-class school.

Stating a Hypothesis and Choosing an Approach

At this point we have our research question, the variables to be studied, the definition of these variables, the system for measuring them, and the subjects to be studied. We are now ready to add two new details: a **hypothesis** or guess about the relationship between the two variables, and a decision about what kind of approach we will use in our study. To some extent, the hypothesis will dictate the approach.

At the most general level, there are two approaches to answering research questions. The first is to describe the events and relationships in a particular situation as they take place in real life. The second approach is to change one aspect of a situation and note the effects of the change. These two approaches are generally called descriptive and experimental.

A Descriptive Approach. One hypothesis we might establish in our study of student beliefs and attention is that students pay more attention to a teacher they believe to be competent. To test this hypothesis, we could go into several sixth-grade classrooms and ask students to rate their teachers on competence. Ideally, we would conduct the study in a middle school where sixth graders usually have more than one teacher each day. We could then observe the students and measure their level of attention to each teacher. At this point we could get some idea about whether the two variables—believing that a teacher is competent and paying attention to that teacher—go together.

Let's assume, for the sake of the argument, that the two variables do go together. What we have now is a **correlation.** If two variables tend to occur together, they are correlated. We have just assumed such a correlation between beliefs and attention. Other variables that are often correlated are height and weight, income and education, and colder temperatures and falling leaves. A taller person, for example, is likely to weigh more than a shorter person. A richer person is likely to have completed more years of education than a poorer person. And, for the sake of the argument, we are now assuming that a student who believes a teacher to be competent is more likely to pay attention to that teacher.

But what does this correlation give us? If educational psychologists know that two variables are correlated, they can then make predictions about one of the variables based on knowledge of the other variable. For example, because the IQ scores of parents and children are correlated, educators can predict a child's IQ based on that of the mother or father. The prediction may not be correct every time, because the correlation between parents' IQs and children's IQs is not perfect. But the prediction is likely to be correct or nearly correct much more than a prediction based on no information at all. Several studies have found a correlation between a teacher's enthusiasm and student learning. If we have information about a teacher's enthusiasm, we can make a prediction about the achievement level of the students in his or her class.

This last example brings us to a very important point about correlation and prediction, mentioned briefly in chapter 1. Knowing that two variables tend to occur together does not tell us that one variable is actually causing the other. Although enthusiastic teachers may tend to have students who achieve more than the students of unenthusiastic teachers, we cannot say that teacher enthusiasm leads to or causes student achievement. We know only that teacher enthusiasm and student achievement tend to occur together. Perhaps teaching students who are achieving more makes a teacher more enthusiastic. Perhaps a third factor—the interesting materials a teacher has chosen to work with, for example—causes both the teacher enthusiasm and student achievement.

Although being able to predict levels of one variable from information about levels of another is useful, teachers are often interested in finding out what factors actually will cause a desired change in behavior. For this, they would need a different kind of research—research based on experimental manipulation.

An Experimental Approach. Returning to our original question about student beliefs and attention, suppose we made a different hypothesis. Rather than just hypothesizing that student attention and beliefs about teacher competence go together, we could hypothesize that one of the factors actually causing students to pay attention is the belief that a teacher is competent. In this case, the hypothesis states a causal relationship. To test this hypothesis, we must change one of the variables to see if this change actually causes changes in the other variable. In our study, this assumed cause, known as the **independent variable,** is the belief that the teacher is competent. The purpose of our experiment will be to see if changes in this variable really cause changes in the other variable—the **dependent variable** of student attention to the teacher.

Assume that we create three comparable groups of students by randomly assigning the students to the groups. Since the selection and assignment of students to groups is totally **random**—by chance, based on no particular plan—the three groups should be very similar.

We then tell one group of students that the teacher they are about to meet is a "very good" teacher; we tell the second group that the teacher they will have is "not a very good" teacher; and we tell the third group nothing about the teacher they are going to have. This final group serves as the **control group.** It will give us information about what happens when there is no experimental manipulation. At some point in the experiment we would ask the students what they believed about the teacher to make sure they had accepted the description they were given.

Next, the teacher, actually the same person in all three cases, teaches the same lesson to each group. Of course the teacher should not be told about the experimental manipulation. We videotape the students in each group as they listen to the teacher. Later, raters viewing the tapes measure the number of seconds each student in the three groups has looked at the teacher. (You may have noticed that although the definition and measurement of the attention variable remain the same as they were in the descriptive study, the definition and measurement of the belief variable have changed. As you can see, such a change is necessary to turn the study into an experiment.)

What kind of results can we expect? If we find that students who believed the teacher was competent paid attention most of the time, students who believed the teacher was not very good paid very little attention, and students who were given no information paid a moderate amount of attention, have we proved our hypothesis? No! In psychology and in educational psychology it is assumed that hypotheses are never really proven by one study, because each study tests the hypothesis in only one specific situation. Hypotheses are "supported" but never proven by the positive results of a single study. Have we supported the hypothesis that student beliefs affect student attention? The answer to this question depends on how well we designed and carried out the study.

Since this is just a hypothetical study, we can assume, once again for the sake of argument, that we did everything just right. If you read the following list of requirements for a "true experiment," set forth by Van Mondrans, Black, Keysor, Olsen, Shelley, and Williams (1977), you will see that we were indeed on the right track:

> The "true experiment" is usually defined as one in which the investigator can (a) manipulate at least one independent variable; (b) randomly select and assign subjects to experimental treatments; and (c) compare the treatment group(s) with one or more control groups on at least one dependent variable. (p. 51)

With a real experiment, however, we would need to know more about exactly how every step of the investigation was conducted. And we would also want to know whether other researchers could come up with the same results if they did the same experiment.

Is the Research Valid?

Being able to evaluate research studies has a dual payoff. The kind of thinking needed is in and of itself valuable. It is the same kind of thinking required to evaluate any complex idea, plan, argument, or project. In all these cases, you need to search for errors, oversights, inconsistencies, or alternative explanations. The analytical ability necessary to evaluate research is useful in any occupation, from law to business to motorcycle maintenance. The second payoff is more specifically valuable for teachers. As an educator, you will have to evaluate research done in your school district or reported in professional journals to determine if the findings are relevant to your own situation.

To be valid, the results of an experiment must pass several tests. Changes in the dependent variable must be due solely to the manipulation of the independent variable. In the following pages, we will look at eight questions that can be asked in an evaluation of a research experiment.

1. *Were the groups to be studied reasonably equal before the experiment began?* If the subjects vary greatly from group to group, any changes found at the end of the experiment may be the results of the original differences in the groups and not of changes in the independent variable. Random assignment of subjects to groups usually takes care of this problem. If instead of randomly selecting the subjects in our own study we had used three different sixth-grade classes, our results would be questionable. Maybe one class already had more generally attentive students. Had they been given the teacher labeled "very good" in the experiment, their high degree of attention would have been relatively meaningless. With random selection from a number of sixth-grade classes, however, each group is likely to have gotten an equal share of the generally attentive and generally inattentive students.

2. *Were all the variables except the independent variable controlled so that the only real difference in the treatment of each group was the change in the independent variable?* We have just seen that the subjects in each group must be equivalent. This principle is equally true of everything else in the experiment. If different procedures were used with each group, it would be difficult to determine which of the differences caused the results. In our study, for example, if we had used different teachers or different lessons in each group, we would have run into this problem in evaluating the results. The students' attention to the teacher could have been based on many things other than the initial statement given by the experimenter about the teacher's competence (the independent variable).

3. *Were the measurement procedures applied consistently to each group?* Unreliable results may at times be caused by an inconsistent measurement system. In our study, if we had used a different videotape rater for each group, we could not have trusted our results. Perhaps one rater would give credit for student attention when students had their faces pointed toward the teacher even if their bodies were turned away. Perhaps another rater would give credit only if the students' entire bodies were directed toward the teacher. Ideally, one rater should make all the measurements. If more are used, there must be some test of the raters' ability to agree on the results. One way to check this would be to see if they agreed when measuring the same students' behaviors.

4. *Are the results of the study due to the experimental procedures rather than to the novelty of the situation?* It is always possible that subjects will respond in some special way to any change, at least temporarily. This possibility was pointed out dramatically by studies conducted at the Western Electric Plant in Hawthorne, Illinois. Investigators were trying to determine which changes in the plant environment would lead to greater worker productivity. As it turned out, everything they tried, every change in the working conditions, seemed to lead to greater productivity, at least for a while (Roethlisberger & Dickson, 1939). In other words, the workers were reacting not to the actual changes but to something new happening. Because the experiment took place in Hawthorne, Illinois, such results are now said to be examples of the **Hawthorne effect.** Our control group helped us avoid this problem. Although the independent variable of a "good" or "bad" teacher label was not applied to the control group, these students were given the special treatment of being in an experiment. If their attention ratings had been particularly high, we might have suspected the Hawthorne effect for all three groups.

5. *Has the investigator who designed the study biased the results in any way?* There are numerous obvious and subtle ways in which an investigator can influence the participants in an experiment. The investigator may have no intention of doing so but may still communicate to the subjects what he or she expects them to do in a given situation (Rosenthal, 1976). In our study, for example, if the investigator had told the teacher involved what the purpose of the experiment was, the teacher might have expected less attention from one of the groups and unintentionally done something to increase or decrease the attention actually given. If the investigator had told the videotape raters the purpose of the experiment, the same thing might have happened. Without meaning to, they might have looked harder for attention in one of the groups. In order to eliminate these problems, both teacher and raters would have to be unaware of the independent variable that was being studied.

6. *Is it reasonably certain that the results did not occur simply by chance?* To answer this question, researchers use statistics. The general agreement is that differences among the groups can be considered "significant" if these differences could have occurred by chance only 5 times out of 100. In reading a research report, you might see the results stated in the following manner: "The difference between the groups was significant ($p < .05$)." Unless you are planning to do your own scientific research, the most important part of this is probably the word *significant*. The mathematical statement means that the probability (p) of such a difference occurring by chance factors alone is less than ($<$) 5 in 100 (.05).

7. *Will the findings in this particular study be likely to fit other, similar situations?* This is really a question of generalization. How similar to the research situation does a new situation have to be to get the same results? Consider our own experiment. Would we get similar results (a) with much older or younger students? (b) with students who are more or less intelligent? (c) with students who already know the teacher? (d) with different teachers or different lessons? (e) with the removal of videotape cameras? (f) with a lesson that lasts more than 10 minutes?

We cannot answer these questions until the study has been repeated with many different subjects in many different situations. This brings us to the question of **replication.**

8. *Has the study been replicated?* A study has been replicated if it has been repeated and the same results are found. Replication may involve exactly the same study conditions, or it may involve changes in conditions that will give us a better idea of the extent to which the findings can be applied to other situations. If results have been replicated in well-designed studies, the findings form the basis for principles and laws.

Since our own study was only hypothetical, we cannot get a replication of it. But we can look at a similar study done by Feldman and Prohaska (1979). Analyzing this study should be useful to you in two ways. First, it will provide a model for considering other research articles you will find in textbooks and in professional journals. Second, the results of the study itself will probably be of interest because they suggest ways in which student expectations may cause teachers to be more or less effective.

A Sample Study: The Effect of Student Expectations

Feldman and Prohaska's 1979 study concerns student expectations about a teacher's competence and the effect of these expectations on the students' and the teacher's behavior. (Remember that we are looking only at student behavior in our hypothetical study.) You may want to read the study in *Journal of Educational Psychology* (vol. 71, no. 4, 1979). At the beginning of the article you will find specific information: the names of the authors, the university where they work, the name of the article, the name of the journal, and the basic facts about the study. The basic facts describing the design and results of the study are usually included in a brief summary called an **abstract,** found at the beginning of such an article.

Essential Data

The subjects in Feldman and Prohaska's first experiment were undergraduate female volunteers from an introductory psychology class. Each subject was randomly assigned to a positive-expectation group or a negative-expectation group, but was not told which group she was in.

Each subject arrived separately at the experimental center and was told she would have to wait a few minutes before she could see the teacher. While she waited, she met another student who had supposedly just been working with the teacher and was now completing a questionnaire evaluating the teacher. Actually, this student, a male, was a **confederate** of the experimenter—an assistant pretending to be one of the subjects. The confederate played one of two roles, depending on whether he was meeting a subject from the positive-expectation group or the negative-expectation group. (The subjects, of course, did not know what group they were in.) When the confederate met a subject from the positive group, he told her the teacher had been really good, effective, and friendly. He then gave her a completed questionnaire (which also said good things about the teacher) and asked her to turn it in for him, since he had to leave. When the confederate met a subject from the negative group, he said very uncomplimentary things about the teacher and gave the subject a questionnaire with very negative comments on it.

The subject then went into a room and met the teacher, who was the same person for both groups. The teacher did not know the subject had been given any expectations at all. While she was teaching two minilessons, she and the subject were secretly videotaped. After the two lessons, the subject took a short quiz on the material and filled out a questionnaire just like the one she had seen the confederate completing. The same procedure was repeated for each subject.

Finally, the videotapes of all the subjects were shown to trained coders who were unaware of the actual experimental conditions. These coders measured three things: (1) percentage of time each subject looked at the teacher, (2) each subject's forward body lean toward the teacher, and (3) each subject's general body orientation toward the teacher. Taken together, these student behaviors could be called *paying attention.* When the coders rated the same subject's videotape, their ratings of the three behaviors were highly correlated. Thus we can assume that the coders agreed about how to use the measurement technique.

Results showed that the subjects who expected the teacher to be "bad" rated the lesson as significantly more difficult, less interesting, and less effective than the subjects who expected the teacher to be "good." They also found the teacher to be less competent, less intelligent, less likable, and less enthusiastic than the other subjects did. Furthermore, the subjects who expected the teacher to be "bad" learned significantly less as measured by the short quiz. They also leaned forward less often and looked at the teacher less frequently than the subjects who expected the teacher to be good.

How would you evaluate this study? The full report (Feldman & Prohaska, 1979) gives many more details, but based on our summary alone, what can you tell about the validity of the findings?

Judging Validity

If you look back at the eight questions for evaluating a research study, it appears that numbers 1, 3, 5, and 6 have been met. (Do you agree?) We cannot yet be certain about question 2—equal treatment of the subjects—because in this first experiment we have no detailed information about the way the teacher behaved toward the subjects. We know only that the teacher was instructed to give the same lesson, in the same way, to each subject. But what if the differences in the subjects' behavior toward the teacher—the differences that were found in the study—caused the teacher to give the lesson in different ways to different students? Perhaps after the first minute or so, subjects were reacting to real differences in the way the teacher delivered the lesson.

Feldman and Prohaska looked at this very real possibility in their second experiment. They found that students' nonverbal behavior (leaning forward or looking at the teacher) actually could affect how well the teacher taught the lesson. Although this may, to some extent, lessen the validity of their first experiment, it is a worthy finding in and of itself.

You may have noticed that we have not yet discussed conditions 4, 7, and 8. Feldman and Prohaska did not include a control group. The fact that the two experimental groups reacted in significantly different ways, however, shows that they were not simply reacting to the novelty of the situation. If both groups had been particularly eager or bored, we might have had good reason to expect the Hawthorne effect.

We can't know anything about conditions 7 and 8, or course, until further research has been conducted. We can say, however, that two respected educational psychologists have reported findings that seem to support our initial hypothesis. In some cases, at least, student expectations about a teacher's competence do have an effect, not only on the students' behavior but also on the teacher's behavior.

The last two questions are equally difficult to answer. It is almost always possible to offer alternative explanations for the findings of any study. In a well-controlled study, an attempt is made to eliminate as many of these alternative explanations as possible. The question of educational versus statistical significance is also one on which reasonable people might easily differ. How large a difference between the test scores of the two groups is large enough to warrant a change in educational practice? This question must be answered in part by the individual teacher. Do the potential gains offered by the findings seem worthwhile enough to make whatever change is called for?

Closer to Home: Action Research

Thus far we have considered how to evaluate and apply research conducted by other people. But in teaching today there is another type of research--action research. **Action research** is conducted by teachers to examine their own practice and the impact of their teaching on students.

> Teachers throughout the world are developing professionally by becoming teacher-researchers, a wonderful new breed of artists-in-residence. Using our own classrooms as laboratories and our students as collaborators, we are changing the way we work with students as we look at our classrooms systematically thorough research. (Hubbard and Power, 1993, p. xiii)

The idea of action research--of teachers systematically studying and improving their own practice--is not new. It is based, in part, on Kurt Lewin's theory of social science research. Lewin (1948) believed that social science should focus on real situations, not laboratory situations. Stephen Corey (1953) applied Lewin's idea of action research to education. By planning and implementing changes, carefully noting effects, evaluating outcomes, and then revising based on results, teachers can understand and improve their teaching. Corey noted, "The value of action research...is determined primarily by the extent to which findings lead to improvement in the practices of the people engaged in the research" (p. 9).

There are many approaches to action research (Calhoun, 1993; McCutcheon & Jung, 1990; McKniff, 1993; McKernan, 1991; Richardson, 1996), but most include five phases that define a cycle of planning, action, and reflection:

• Reflecting on current practice to identify a problem or goal

• Planning a response (what will be done, what data will be collected, what observations made or records kept)

• Acting--implementing the plan

• Evaluating the evidence to determine the effects of the actions

• Reflection--revising plans based on the evaluation and continuing the cycle

This cycle is similar to the systematic approach to behavior change described in Chapter 6, Thomas Gordon's no-lose problem solving method explained in Chapter 12, and to many other approaches to planning. This cycle can be applied to a simple problem related to one student or to a school-wide project to revise the curriculum. The critical feature is that actions are planned and evaluated in light of carefully gathered and meaningful evidence. Very often action research in schools is collaborative--teachers working with each other, with university professors, with students, or even with parents to study and improve teaching and learning.

New References— Appendix

Calhoun, E. F. (1993). Action research: Three approaches. <u>Educational Leadership,</u> <u>51</u>(2), 55-60.

Corey, S. M. (1993). <u>Action research to improve school practices</u>. New York: Teachers College Press.

Hubbard, R. S., & Power, B. M. (1993). <u>The art of classroom inquiry: A handbook for</u> <u>teacher-researchers</u>. Portsmouth, NH: Heinemann.

Lewin, K. (1948). <u>Resolving social conflict.</u> New York: Harper and Brothers.

McCutcheon, G., & Jung, B. (1990). Alternative perspectives on action research. <u>Theory Into Practice, 29</u>(3), 144-151.

McKernan, J. (1991). <u>Curriculum action research: A handbook of methods and</u> <u>resources for the reflective practitioner</u>. London: Kogan Page Limited.

McNiff, J. (1993). <u>Teaching as learning: An action research approach</u>. London: Routledge.

Richardson, V. (1996). The case for formal research and practical inquiry in teacher education. In F. B. Murray (Ed.), <u>The teacher educator's handbook: Building a</u> <u>knowledge base for the preparation of teachers</u> (pp. 715-737). San Francisco: Jossey-Bass.

Key Terms — Appendix

Action Research
Abstract
Correlation
Confederate
Control Group
Dependent Variable
Direct Observation
Hawthorne Effect
Hypothesis
Independent Variable
Peer Rating
Random
Replication
Self-Report
Teacher Rating
Test

NOTES

NOTES

NOTES